Lost and Found

Harvard East Asian Monographs 364

Lost and Found

Recovering Regional Identity in Imperial Japan

Hiraku Shimoda

Published by the Harvard University Asia Center
Distributed by Harvard University Press
Cambridge (Massachusetts) and London 2014

Printed in the United States of America

The Harvard University Asia Center publishes a monograph series and, in coordination with the Fairbank Center for Chinese Studies, the Korea Institute, the Reischauer Institute of Japanese Studies, and other facilities and institutes, administers research projects designed to further scholarly understanding of China, Japan, Vietnam, Korea, and other Asian countries. The Center also sponsors projects addressing multidisciplinary and regional issues in Asia.

Library of Congress Cataloging-in-Publication Data

Shimoda, Hiraku, 1972–
Lost and found : recovering regional identity in imperial Japan / Hiraku Shimoda.
pages cm. — (Harvard East Asian monographs ; 364)
Includes bibliographical references and index.
ISBN 978-0-674-49201-1 (hardcover : alk. paper) 1. Aizu-han (Japan)—History.
2. Regionalism—Japan—Aizu-han—History. I. Harvard University. Asia Center, issuing body. II. Title.
DS894.39.F839A58686 2014
952'.117—dc23

2013032485

Index by June Sawyers

Printed on acid-free paper

Last figure below indicates year of this printing

24 23 22 21 20 19 18 17 16 15 14

Contents

Acknowledgments

Like any long journey, mine was made possible by the help of many. At Harvard, where I began this project, I was blessed with outstanding mentors, cohorts, and institutional support, especially from the Department of East Asian Languages and Civilizations and the Reischauer Institute of Japanese Studies. My gratitude goes first of all to Harold Bolitho, my late adviser without whom the life I now relish would never have been. I regret that I did not work quickly enough for him to see this work in print. Andy Gordon has had an immeasurable influence on how I think about not only Japanese history but our craft in general, and his vision continues to inform my own in ways that I sometimes do not even realize. Dani Botsman was kind enough to read this work at an early stage and offer valuable criticism. I can only wish I had the wherewithal to meet his lofty standards. John Dower, then at the Massachusetts Institute of Technology, provided me opportunities, encouragement, and good cheer at every turn. A Whiting Fellowship in the Humanities supported me at a critical stage.

In Tokyo, Kokugakuin University granted me affiliation with the International Exchange Center and the Institute of Japanese Culture and Classics, where Takashio Hiroshi and Shibata Shin'ichi were particularly helpful. I also benefited tremendously from my time at the Historiographical Institute at the University of Tokyo. Yokoyama Yoshinori was a gracious host who facilitated my stay in various ways, and the Japan Foundation kindly underwrote my time there. Ochanomizu University and Tōyō University hosted me as I worked to complete this manuscript.

In Aizu Wakamatsu, I was touched by the hospitality of several dedicated local historians, including Nakamura Toshi, Majima Isao, Mihashi Masao, and Nakaoka Susumu. The staff at the Aizu Wakamatsu City Library and the Fukushima Prefectural Library were always willing to go the extra mile for me. No work on regional history in Japan is possible without the pioneering efforts and support of such local scholars.

I spent five wonderful years in the History Department at Vassar College, where I was surrounded by model teacher-scholars. A part of them will always remain with me, far apart though we may now be. I thank the Jane Rosenthal Heimerdinger '25 Fund at Vassar for its support. Waseda University's Faculty of Law also provided generous funding toward publication, including the Waseda University Grant for Special Research Projects 2012A-812.

Thanks are due to my family: my grandmother, who always supported me from afar; my parents, who let me follow my bliss; and to my wife and our two boys.

Abbreviations

AGK Akizuki Kazue, ed. *Aizuhan gohattogaki kaidokusho.* (Aizu Wakamatsu: Rekishi shunjū, 1995).

AKJ Toyoda Takeshi, ed., *Aizu kasei jikki* (Tokyo: Yoshikawa kōbunkan, 1975–89).

AMK Iinuma Sekiya, ed., *Aizu Matsudaira kafu* (Tokyo: Iinuma Sekiya, 1938).

AWS Aizu Wakamatsushi shuppan iinkai, ed., *Aizu Wakamatsushi* (Aizu Wakamatsu: Aizu Wakamatsu-shi, 1965).

MG Aizu Wakamatsu-shi, ed., *Aizuhan daihachi hanshu Matsudaira Katataka "Masaosama gonenpu"* (Aizu Wakamatsu: Aizu Wakamatsu-shi, 2001).

MKS Irokawa Daikichi et al., eds., *Meiji kenpakusho shūsei* (Tokyo: Chikuma shobō, 1990).

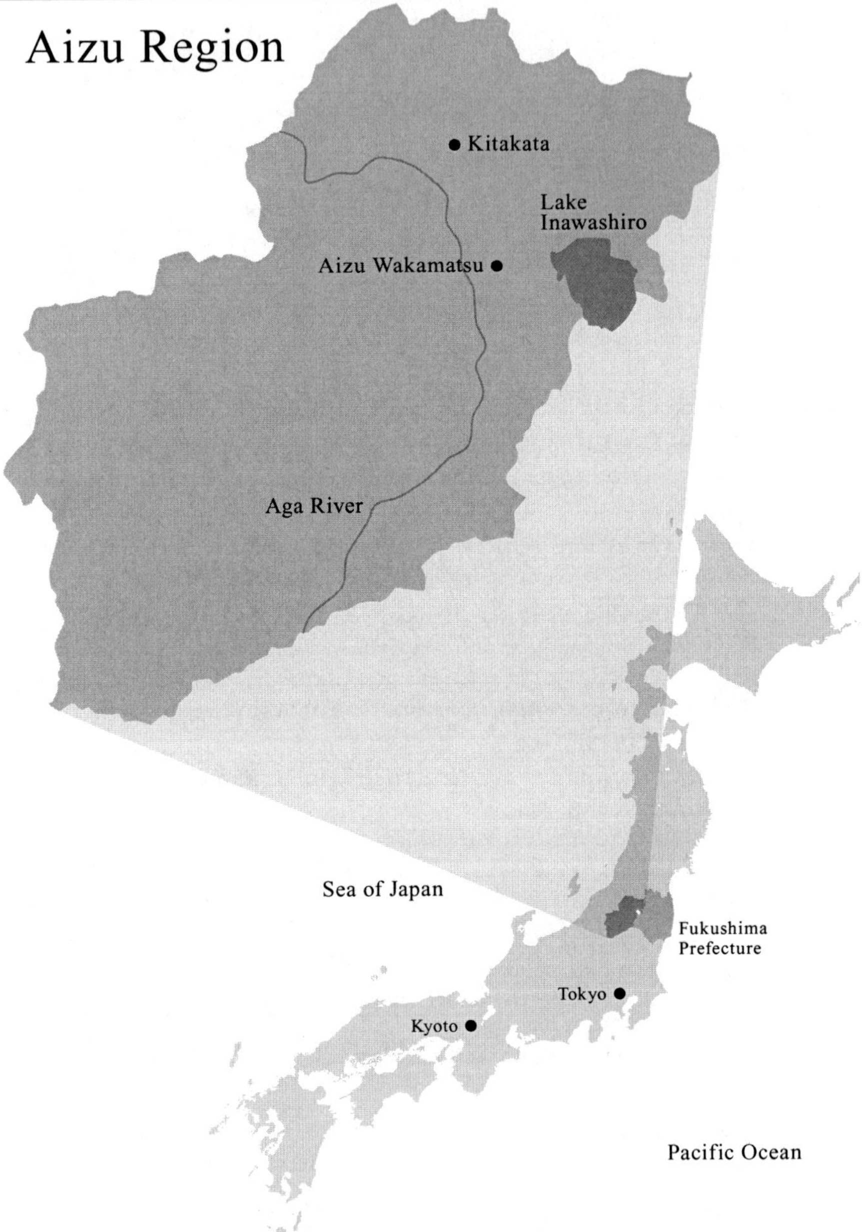
Aizu Region
Kitakata
Lake
Inawashiro
Aizu Wakamatsu
Aga River
Sea of Japan
Fukushima
Prefecture
Tokyo
Kyoto
Pacific Ocean

Introduction

The Trouble with Aizu

Aizu in 1868 reeked of death. Bodies of fallen soldiers and hapless civilians littered the landscape, more than three thousand in all including women and children. This was rather unusual in Japan. Not since the 1630s had war claimed this many lives in one place; not until the 1940s would it happen again. Their deaths were nasty, too, and not just because many of the corpses long lay neglected, "left to be devoured by wild birds and beasts or rot away in a most tragic way."[1] Death in Aizu was especially ignominious because it was tainted by rebellion. Having fought against the imperial will, the people of Aizu died as "rebels" and "enemies of the court." Their demise was soon followed by that of Aizu itself, bringing to a disgraceful end some two and a quarter centuries of domainal sovereignty.

Failures of many kinds carried—or perhaps miscarried—the Aizu domain into modern times. Political overcommitment and miscalculations between 1862 and the winter of 1867 left Aizu outmaneuvered by its rival domains, Satsuma and Chōshū, which seized the imperial cause in a coup. Having thrown its lot in with the ill-fated Tokugawa shogunate, Aizu was shut out of the Meiji Restoration in 1868, then decisively kept out when its samurai army was routed on the battlefield by its rivals, first at Toba-Fushimi in early 1868, then in Aizu itself nine months later. On the late summer day that the newly triumphant leaders of Satsuma and Chōshū declared the new imperial era name "Meiji" and promised to deliver "enlightened rule" to Japan, the scene in Aizu was a stark contrast. There, Satsuma and Chōshū, now proudly flying the chrysanthemum standards as "the imperial forces," were laying a punishing

1. Aizu chōreigikai, *Boshin junnan tsuitōroku,* p. 20.

siege that would last until Aizu surrendered, soon to be dissolved for good. Such failures ensured that the Meiji Restoration in Aizu was far from the hopeful new beginning that it was heralded to be elsewhere in Japan. A badly broken Aizu could barely limp into a new age. As one man put it, Aizu was made a "blood sacrifice" for the birth of modern Japan.[2]

For all that, we find in 1891 another Aizu man speaking dearly of his native place and how it might contribute to imperial Japan (1868–1945), from which it had been so dramatically estranged back in 1868. "The energy that one devotes to his nation," one Wakamatsu Tarō declared, "Must always arise from the passion he feels for his beloved homeland."[3] What may seem like insipid nationalist rhetoric was, in this instance, no mere cliché. By linking Aizu with Japan, the author was doing something rather objectionable, for just twenty-four years earlier, his homeland had been deemed guilty of high treason, "the most serious offense an Imperial subject may commit," as one contemptuous Meiji oligarch judged.[4]

Yet this Wakamatsu Tarō was convinced that the vigor of his fellow Aizu people could be made to serve the national good, even if their recent history of rebellion and failure suggested otherwise. He called upon his fellow *Aizuppo* (a local colloquial meaning Sons of Aizu) to rediscover their past as they looked toward a better future. "Long ago, the name *Aizuppo* evoked awe and respect throughout the realm, but now our spirit has run its course. Come now, you who call yourselves men of Aizu," he beckoned, "Let us be eager to expand the glory of our forefathers."[5] His voice had to be strong, his call uplifting. After all, for someone using the pseudonym "Son of Wakamatsu" to declare his devotion to the nation was laden with heavy historical irony.

It was poignant enough for this one fellow to invoke Aizu's troubled past so earnestly; his wistful attempt to merge region with nation was also strained and counterintuitive given Japan's political legacy. Before a modern imperial nation-state was established in 1868, Japan was long a patchwork of some 260 distinct domains, of which Aizu was but one. Each domain was ruled, under the auspices of the Tokugawa shogunate (1603–1868), by a hereditary lord and his band of samurai retainers who usually governed their land with a decidedly local touch. The eyes of the shogunate in Edo, occasionally watchful but generally wandering, provided a measure of distant over-

2. Craig, *Remembering Aizu,* p. 146.

3. Wakamatsu, "Aizujinshi," pp. 2–3.

4. Brown and Hirota, *The Diary of Kido Takayoshi,* 1:159.

5. Wakamatsu, "Aizujinshi," p. 3. This pseudonym paid homage to the city of Wakamatsu, formerly the capital of Aizu domain and presently the city of Aizu Wakamatsu (population 124,728) in Fukushima prefecture.

lordship but otherwise a domain enjoyed considerable de facto autonomy. The well-established historical subfield of "domainal studies" has suggested as much. In opposition to the earlier "modernization school," which often rendered the Tokugawa period a prelude to post-1868 nationalization, recent English-language historians of early modern Japan have emphasized the locality of the Tokugawa polity and projected a fragmented picture of Japan. By using the domain or a region as a unit of analysis, they have affirmed the importance of domains as postulated by Harold Bolitho and others.[6] Indeed, those who focus on the *bakufu*'s role as a central government, such as Conrad Totman and Kate Nakai, or use the entirety of Japan as an analytical category, such as Ronald Toby, have now become exceptional.[7] Whether historians call it the "*bakuhan* system," the "compound state," or "parcelized sovereignty," Tokugawa geopolitics ensured the primacy of localities for two and a half centuries.[8]

So it stood until the Meiji era (1868–1912), when the Restoration made the nation-state imperative paramount and the previous norm of provincialism politically untenable. The nation-state program drove a fledgling but ambitious government to identify and overcome obstacles of the past. New ideals of national citizenship and belonging, which would later be sanctified within the so-called imperial ideology, were to fold a hitherto myopic and local-minded people into a new Japanese collective.[9] Many Meiji-era nationalists breathlessly critiqued provincial affiliations and affinities as impediments to the modern unity and progress that the nation-state promised.

Scholars, too, tend to think of regions as being historically at odds with the nation. The "making of modern Japan"—or most any other nation for that matter—is often presented as a process by which modern centrality supplants, sometimes violently, deeply rooted regionality. Japanese historians such as Tsukamoto Manabu and Makihara Norio have framed the local-national relationship as being fundamentally antagonistic.[10] Elsewhere around the globe, the idea that nationhood must be superimposed upon extant regionalism have been expressed, for example, in the British context by Linda Colley and in the United States by Elizabeth O'Leary, as well as in general theory about

---

6. Bolitho, *Treasures among Men.*

7. Totman, *Politics in the Tokugawa Bakufu, 1600–1843;* Nakai, *Shogunal Politics;* Toby, *State and Diplomacy.*

8. Totman, ed., *Tokugawa Japan;* Ravina, *Land and Lordship.*

9. Gluck, *Japan's Modern Myths;* Fujitani, *Splendid Monarchy;* Makihara, *Meiji shichi nen no daironsō.*

10. Tsukamoto, *Tokai to ianaka,* p. 141; Makihara, *Kyakubun to kokumin no aida,* p. 10.

modern nationalism, such as Stuart Hall, who drew upon this point from Ernest Gellner.[11]

We have here, then, a seemingly diametric opposition. On one hand was the centrifugal force of provincialism, embodied by former domains, now problematized as an outdated legacy of feudalism. On the other was the centripetal force of the nation-state, a largely novel construct bent on consolidation as Meiji Japan desperately sought its place within a wider world of competing nation-states. The messy multiplicity that regions represented seemed to be at loggerheads with the principles of imperial nationhood, which preached unity and singularity. To bring the two together as Wakamatsu Tarō insisted was no easy task.

Aizu's historical experience invites historians to reconsider the relationship between region and nation not as a collision between the old and the new or the familiar and the unfamiliar, but as an uneasy partnership fraught with both tough contradictions and unlikely complementarities. Aizu and Japan were locked in an awkward embrace that kept them at once separate and mutually reinforcing. Consequently, even as the hopeful patriot Wakamatsu tried to couple the region with the nation, thus bridging the uncomfortable gap between the two, he also took care to affirm the distinctness of his ancestral land—captured in the chauvinistic self-appellation *Aizuppo*—and spoke of it with manifest pride, despite the fact that the imperial viewpoint held his rebel homeland in contempt. Such were the rhetorical and emotional acrobatics that an *Aizuppo* had to perform in order to become a Japanese.

The tensions and complications that gripped this one man, in fact, had their hold on similar efforts in many places. His was one small contribution to a wider effort, made on various fronts in many locales, to establish the region as a meaningful space within imperial Japan. The desire to reconcile one's native place with the greater polity and to recover the value of locality within a zealously nationalizing society was hardly uncommon in the nineteenth century. Those aching to make their familiar homeland worthy of their new nation could be found not only elsewhere in Aizu but throughout Japan and around the globe, too. Wherever the forces of modern nationhood pressed onward, old loyalties had to give way, die hard, or be recast into something relevant and useful. After peasants were turned into Frenchmen, in Eugen Weber's famous formulation, what was left of the peasantry?[12] Having been made Italians, as Massimo d'Azeglio promised, what became of Neapolitans,

---

11. Colley, *Britons*, pp. 6, 373; O'Leary, *To Die For*, pp. 4–6; Hall, "The Question of Cultural Identity," p. 292.

12. Weber, *Peasants into Frenchmen*.

Sicilians, and Sardinians?[13] As the initially fragile illusion of nationhood hardened into reality in modern times, how might local affinity become a meaningful part of that new reality?

Such questions can be asked of just about every society that endured nationalization; in Japan's case, it is in Aizu that this universal problem of harmonizing locality with the nation was especially urgent, complex, and gut-wrenching. What would be "lost" then "found" again along the way was not simply this one place called Aizu, but the greater meaning of regionalism—the belief in regions as a legitimate object of political commitment, a deep source of personal identity, and a worthy community—in a rapidly nationalizing society. Regionalism is not a given; it must be negotiated, defended, and won. This was especially true in a place like Meiji Japan that often assailed provincial norms as it consolidated itself into an aspiring empire. It was truer still in a place like Aizu whose sense of a local self had been so summarily bankrupted.

Recent scholarship on Japanese history has defined regions predominantly in terms of political economy. Whether as a site of protoindustrialization, a node within a shifting web of commercial relations, a discrete mercantilist state, or a struggling backwater, scholars have framed a region or a domain primarily as an economic unit bound by shared commercial interests and macroeconomic experiences.[14] As important as they were, however, economic conditions and practices alone hardly shaped the contours of region. A region must also be captured in less materialist terms as a culturally negotiated space, which is a relatively new approach taken by the likes of Kären Wigen, Marcia Yonemoto, and Mary Elizabeth Berry.[15] This can be insightful because whereas historians have long known the artifice of nationalism, we have been relatively reluctant to see the same when it comes to more intimate localities. Japanese practitioners of the so-called "nation-state theory" (*kokumin-kokka ron*), which emerged in the 1990s in the wake of critics like Eric Hobsbawm, have eagerly taken to exposing the historical shallowness of Japan's nationhood.[16] These scholars, led in part by the historian Nishikawa

---

13. Vincent, *I Miei Ricordi*.

14. Respectively, Howell, *Capitalism from Within;* Wigen, *The Making of a Japanese Periphery;* Roberts, *Mercantilism in a Japanese Domain;* Ravina, *Land and Lordship;* and Lewis, *Becoming Apart*.

15. Wigen, *A Malleable Map;* Yonemoto, *Mapping Early Modern Japan;* and Berry, *Japan in Print*. On the ambivalent power of visual representations such as maps to both unite and divide, see Tsukamoto, *Tokai to ianaka*.

16. Nishikawa Nagao has coedited two volumes that represent this interdisciplinary body of scholarship. Nishikawa and Matsumiya, eds., *Bakumatsu Meijiki no*, and Nishikawa and Watanabe, ed., *Seiki tenkanki no*.

Nagao, have problematized the constructedness of nation-states by revealing the manipulative political and cultural practices that induce nationhood. In sharp contrast to such vigorous indictment of nationhood, however, we have tended to give localities a pass. If anything, we tend to naturalize smaller spatial communities such as regions as being time-honored and organic, especially relative to modern nations, which, we are told, must be actively imagined.[17]

Perhaps this affinity toward locality stems from the fact that regions do not wield the destructive powers of a nation-state, and thus do not provoke the same problem consciousness. Nonetheless, lest we be too enchanted by the romantic, old-time image of the "Sixty-plus Provinces of Japan," regionalism should be viewed as no less an artificial mode of spatial thought than nationhood. By reconceptualizing the region as a fluid, discursive category, historians can call forth three fresh themes: the politics of regional identity construction; difference creation as compelled by nation-state formation; and the primacy of historical memory in forging a community. All these forces help us appreciate a region not just as a bounded political economy but a volatile spatial and cultural product that was tempered in the heat of nineteenth-century nationalization.[18]

Such an awareness of artifice and contingency feeds a healthy skepticism toward many alluring traits that we too readily associate with provincial places. For example, Aizu, as much as any other locale in Japan, has long been said to possess a strong and enduring regional consciousness, best expressed in the proud self-appellation *Aizuppo*. Generations of Aizu locals have celebrated a distinct Aizu identity and a people purported to be "traditional," "martial," "persistent," and "dutiful" like no other, thus suggesting a deeply entrenched tradition of local self-awareness and uniqueness. Proud locals have long sung of *Aizu damashii* (or the Aizu spirit) that presumably animates their community. Yet, by the same token, such breathless discourse has a way of making the region seem more historically aged and embedded than it is, thus inviting historians to dislodge Aizu from such trappings. Indeed, Aizu's seemingly strong regionality is a good place to begin considering why Japanese regionalism has appeared "benign" or "weak" to some observers.[19]

Likewise, a region should also be appreciated as a result of difference creation, which is a core component of the nation-state program. The nation-state logic actively seeks cultural differences in order to clarify and reify

---

17. Anderson, *Imagined Communities*.

18. The historian Kawanishi Hidemichi has been a pioneer in viewing northeast Japan as a constructed spatial category. See Kawanishi, *Tōhoku* and *Tōhoku zoku*.

19. Wigen, "Constructing Shinano," p. 231.

its own normative ideals.[20] Every set of elusive nationalist principles necessarily summons its foil to make itself more manifest; "imperial loyalism" needs "rebels," just as "civilization" needs "barbarity," and "national language" needs "dialects." The often rickety thesis that nationhood is unified and transcendent can best stand by leaning on its antithesis. If ever there were an antithesis to the nation in early Meiji Japan, it was Aizu. One needed to look no further than Aizu to find everything that offended new nationalist sensibilities, including riotous peasants, samurai assassins, gangs of counterfeiters, and people speaking in a provincial tongue, not to mention its recent lèse majesté. And yet, the idea of difference is not unchanging; difference could also be remade into a useful feature of the new imperial culture. Indeed, Aizu's historical experience shows that just the right kind of difference—the kind that would be ascribed to Aizu in due time—could even help cast an apparent misfit into a national ensemble.

Finally, a region can be studied fruitfully as an incarnation of historical remembrance and wishful imagination. If, as Ernest Renan offered, "the possession in common of a rich legacy of memories" is what allows a nation to be, then the same might well be said for a region.[21] In Aizu, however, that legacy was hardly "rich," for theirs was marred by shame and defeat. All the same, war veterans, former domainal retainers, and their descendants sought to re-create their lost homeland by reimagining their past in innovative ways. Fervent revisionist and selective remembrance let them salvage their once-broken history and discover their regional tradition anew. Yet, the homeland that they envisioned was necessarily refracted through the lens of imperial nationhood. That was certainly true of Shiba Gorō, a formerly disgraced Aizu samurai turned decorated general in the Japanese Imperial Army, whose autobiography in translation, *Remembering Aizu*, has recently helped introduce Aizu to a foreign audience.[22] Shiba Gorō and others' poignant reminiscences, rehabilitative historiography, and soothing war commemorations were all designed to reconcile Aizu's tainted past with imperial service and loyalism—the theoretical foundation of the Japanese polity between 1868 and 1945. Such exuberant and purposeful use of historical memory created still more possibilities for making Aizu a worthy and meaningful, if ironic, part of the empire.

---

20. This important function of the nation-state has been discussed in various Japanese contexts, for example, in regional history by Kawanishi Hidemichi, "Tōhokushi no imi to shatei," in gender studies by Ueno Chizuko, *Nashonarizumu to jendā*, and Morris-Suzuki, *Reinventing Japan*.

21. Renan, "Qu'est-ce qu'une nation?," p. 19.

22. Craig, *Remembering Aizu*.

Distance of all kinds separated Aizu from imperial nationhood after the Meiji Restoration. Punitive exile to a remote frontier and administrative reshuffling inserted an undeniable physical distance. Painful reminders of rebellious defeat and historiographical condemnation induced a metaphorical, but no less palpable, sense of distance. Since then, generations of commentators—the learned and the ordinary, famous and anonymous, in and outside of Aizu—have constantly sought to measure that distance, reinterpret that distance, and, whenever possible, shorten that distance. In so doing, they inevitably had to locate the two poles, Japan and Aizu, either of which could be embraced as their *kuni* (or country). Even more so than its English-language counterpart, *kuni* is a highly fluid designation that could be as local and visible as their hometown, and as expansive and unseen as their empire. There were times when a great gulf seemed to separate the two *kuni*; other times they could seem so close as to appear one and the same. In either case, this tension between the two *kuni* produced novel and, at times, deeply ironic and conflicting ideas about regionalism's contributions to modern Japan. Wakamatsu Tarō's clarion call was but one man's desire to recover his homeland within his nation. Having lost his homeland, he had to find it again. In this he was not alone.

CHAPTER 1

Making a Domain, 1643–1868

Landscape and Lordship

No political unit called Aizu has existed since 1868. Today the only reminders of a once proud and prominent domain are but few. One must squint at a map just to see the word Aizu appear as a mere vestigial prefix on the names of several towns and villages scattered across western Fukushima prefecture. By informal custom, Fukushima folks divide their sizable prefecture into three parts: Nakadōri, the most populous and urbanized valley in the center served by the Tōhoku bullet train; Hamadōri, the eastern coastline along the Pacific Ocean that unwittingly received worldwide attention during the nuclear disaster of 2011; and—finally, perhaps—Aizu, the vast expanse of mountains to the western interior, isolated enough to do without the word *dōri* (or pass). Beyond that, the name Aizu carries almost no administrative significance nowadays, as if unworthy of official designation.

This was not always the case. Between the eighth century, when the place name first appeared in classical texts such as the *Kojiki, Shoku Nihongi,* and *Man'yōshū,* and the beginning of the Tokugawa period in the seventeenth century, Aizu developed into a distinct political space. Topography certainly had something to do with this. Formidable mountains delimited Aizu neatly though harshly on all sides, with Lake Inawashiro, Japan's fifth-largest lake, forming the eastern edge. As one Englishman observed in 1868, "In the Aidzu country the hills form a vast fringe of from thirty to fifty miles in extent round the valley in which [the castle town of] Wakamatsu stands. . . . So completely is it hemmed in all sides by hills and mountains that it might almost be the bed of a great lake."[1] Even well before that, in the first half of the

1. Willis, "Report to Sir Harry S. Parkes," p. 6.

seventeenth century, Tokugawa shogun considered the area geographically discrete enough to enfeoff it to four different *daimyō*, or provincial lords, without substantial border adjustments. Once fixed, the borders were guarded with due vigilance. Armed guards and customs officials at nineteen major checkpoints inspected travelers for permits and contraband, leaving them little doubt about their entering a distinct domain.

If the physical environment gave Aizu its seemingly natural space, it isolated the area as well. The mountains, for one, ensured that Aizu be landlocked, an unusual feature among sizable domains on the Japanese archipelago. A mid-nineteenth-century visitor from Satsuma domain in the distant southwest attributed Aizu's economic woes to this trait. "Aizu is quite defensible and rich in paddies, but inaccessible by water," Kimotsuki Kanetake observed, "Whether one heads to Echigo or Mito, one must march overland for three days. For this reason, the domain is greatly poor."[2] For another, Aizu found itself within the Tōhoku region, the harsh northeast of Japan often considered its least developed, most barbarous hinterland where winter comes early and snow falls aplenty. Convention had long deemed the mountainous Tōhoku a physically and culturally liminal space, at least when seen from the bustling plains of Kinnai or Kantō. As another traveler in the late eighteenth century reported, "In ancient times, parts of Tōhoku were inhabited by barbarians [the indigenous Ainu]. Only in the past two hundred years has it become so thoroughly a part of Japan, so people say."[3]

Further away one got from the central basin and deeper into the mountains, more likely one was to encounter shockingly rural hamlets, such as Tajima in southern Aizu. There, as one visitor in 1788 wrote with open disdain, "The residents and their language are terrible in the extreme. There are no saltwater fish, and although there are some unusual freshwater fish called *akabara* and *kajika*, the locals do not know of carp or eel. Salt is scarce." He grumbled on, despite knowing that he had arrived in Aizu just after the devastating Tenmei famine of 1782–87. "The food here is extremely bad. Day after day there is nothing to eat but mountain potatoes and tofu." The scarcity of everyday goods, he deemed, made Aizu "far worse off than Satsuma and Hizen, and it cannot even be compared to the Kyoto region or Chūgoku."[4] There is no shortage of testimonies on Aizu's apparent deprivation. The English visi-

---

2. Kimotsuki, *Tōhoku fūdan*, p. 6.

3. Bolitho, "Travelers' Tales," p. 500.

4. Furukawa, *Tōyū zakki*, p. 15. All translations are the author's unless noted otherwise.

tor William Willis found much the same nearly a century later. "The poverty of the Aidzu country was extreme," he observed in 1868, "The houses were the poorest I had seen in any part of Japan; the farmers themselves were an ill-clad, undersized, and weakly race."[5]

Distanced and lacking though it was, Aizu was hardly choked off from the rest of the Tokugawa world. Serviceable roadways snaked around and between the unfriendly mountains, bearing, if grudgingly, more traffic of all sorts than commonly imagined. The seventeenth century saw a remarkable improvement in road systems throughout Japan, and Aizu, too, benefited. It was then that the five major turnpikes of Aizu were laid, linking the domain with Shirakawa to the southeast, Minamiyama to the south, Echigo to the west, Nihonmatsu to the east, and Yonezawa to the north. The shogunal capital of Edo was about a week's hike to the southwest.[6]

Despite being landlocked, and contrary to Kimotsuki Kanetake's impressions, waterways provided Aizu with still more access. The Aga River connected the Aizu basin with the Sea of Japan to the west and offered Aizu producers a cost-effective means to ship rice, charcoal, tobacco, and lacquerware to the Echigo coast and beyond.[7] The Kinu River could also carry enough cargo southward that the domain used it to ferry its rice to Edo.[8] This network allowed Aizu residents to come into contact with people, goods, and information well beyond their visible realm. Import items, for example, were not entirely unfamiliar to Aizu. An 1842 manifest of goods shipped across Lake Inawashiro to Wakamatsu reveals seafood products, seashell ash (for fertilizer), sugar, and other items that were unavailable locally.[9] As early as 1583, Aizu shoppers in local markets could find imports from places as distant as Kyoto and Ise in central Japan.[10] In turn, goods from Aizu made their way to various destinations. One local gazetteer shows that by the early 1800s, even the relatively uncommercialized southern Aizu exported items like linen, soybeans, tobacco, and silk as far as Echigo, Edo, and the Kantō area.[11]

At the heart of this transportation network lay the castle town of Wakamatsu. This was the domain's administrative and commercial center, built around Tsuruga Castle with its five-storied donjon and its distinctly reddish roof tiles, and by far the most populous and bustling town in Aizu. Visitors

---

5. Willis, "Report to Sir Harry S. Parkes," p. 5.
6. *AWS*, 3:245, 261.
7. *AKJ*, 67: 245–48.
8. Tajima chōshi hensan iinkai, ed., *Tajima chōshi*, 2:583.
9. *AWS*, 3:333–34.
10. *Yanada monjo goyō nikki*, 1583.
11. Shōji Kichinosuke, *Aizu fudoki/fūzokuchō*, 3:208.

remembered Wakamatsu differently according to their personal standards and taste. In 1851 a Takada samurai on official business lodged in Wakamatsu and described it favorably in his travel journal. "The town is finely prosperous," he recorded, "There are rows of shops selling furniture and ceramics. Everything is available here."[12] Coming from a comparably provincial domain, he might have found Wakamatsu to his liking. Furukawa Koshōken did not. The peripatetic eighteenth-century scholar who had earlier chided Tajima noted, "Lord Aizu is a great *daimyō* worth 230,000 *koku,* yet his castle-town is miserable and poverty-stricken in the extreme. As a castle-town it falls far below those of such places as Okayama in Bizen," his hometown in western Japan. That "the appearance of the women is particularly bad" probably did not help.[13]

Such a bleak picture seems unfitting for a domain that possessed, contrary to these images, considerable strategic and political value. In fact, Aizu and its rulers enjoyed a rather elevated position within the *bakuhan* order, for Tokugawa geopolitics rendered Aizu a sensitive space. The area was a buffer cushioning the newly established political base of the Tokugawa family in the Kantō plains against the hitherto hostile *daimyō* of the Tōhoku. Consequently, any *daimyō* enfeoffed to Aizu also held the title of "Ōshū Protectorate" and was technically responsible for carrying out the *bakufu*'s military interests in the Tōhoku against potentially inimical families such as the Satake, the Date, and the Nanbu to the north.

This geopolitical gravity notwithstanding, lordship in Aizu was in flux for a good half century as Tokugawa Japan consolidated in the early seventeenth century. Between 1590 and 1643 Aizu saw three different warlord families—the Gamō, the Uesugi, and the Katō—come and go, none lasting more than two generations. When a scandal brought down the Katō, the *bakufu* could hardly entrust just another warlord to anchor down such a strategic area. This ostensibly explains why Hoshina Masayuki, a grandson of Tokugawa Ieyasu and a younger half-brother to the reigning third shogun Iemitsu, was assigned to Aizu in 1643. It was the Hoshina family, later renamed Matsudaira, that finally provided the administrative continuity in Aizu that would last until 1868.

Not that Lord Masayuki got off to an auspicious start. He began life as an illegitimate child—the result of the second shogun Hidetada's tryst with his wet nurse's attendant—and was kept a secret until he was sent off to adoption at the age of seven. His new family was the Hoshina in Takatō, a minor provincial domain worth only 30,000 *koku*. Despite such a modest beginning,

---

12. *AWS*, 3:287.
13. Bolitho, "Travelers' Tales," p. 499.

we are told, Masayuki soon lived up to his bloodline and devoted his loyalty to the shogunal family, rising to become a principal adviser to the fourth shogun Ietsuna and an occupant of the prestigious Kuroshoin chamber in Edo Castle. Thus Masayuki was rewarded in 1643 as the lord of Aizu and its sizable 270,000 *koku,* making him the second-largest *daimyō* in Tōhoku. Or so goes the standard narrative highlighting the supposedly special fondness between the Aizu domain and the Tokugawa shogunate, which, for some scholars, explains Aizu's ill-fated defense of the shogunate in the *bakumatsu* period.

In truth, this connection between Aizu and Edo may have been more tenuous than has often been presented. Blood ties to the main Tokugawa line per se guaranteed little political security or loyalty, especially in the early years of Tokugawa rule, nor did they preordain the course of any domain's actions down the road. The shogun and *bakufu* leaders were hardly obliged to favor the Hoshina based purely on Masayuki's blood, considering that they readily punished some of Masayuki's kin for incompetence (uncle Tadateru, disenfeoffed in 1625), alleged rebellion (elder brother Tadanaga, ordered to commit suicide in 1630), or purported lunacy (cousin Tadamasa, exiled in 1623). Indeed, Masayuki himself was ambivalent about his Tokugawa pedigree, evidently showing some discomfort about being too closely associated with the shogunal family. In 1668 he declined the *bakufu*'s offer to bestow upon his family the surname of Matsudaira, which officially denoted Tokugawa kinship, and use of the hollyhock Tokugawa family crest.[14] Not until 1696 did the lord of Aizu finally assume the Matsudaira surname and reaffirm the original blood ties between their domainal founder and the main Tokugawa house. Still, even after 1696, they continued to refer to themselves as the Hoshina in some internal documents.[15] Likewise, when the Hoshina family compiled its official genealogy in 1668, Masayuki omitted his Tokugawa origins, emphasizing instead the Hoshina's roots in Shinano province.[16]

Yet scholars persist in coupling Aizu with the *bakufu* so as to romanticize Aizu into a doggedly loyal and tragic servant of the shogunate in Restoration history. Those so inclined often turn to the first article in the Aizu Matsudaira house laws, which Masayuki wrote in 1668 with help from his tutor Yamazaki Ansai the Suika Shintō scholar. The fifteen articles in Masayuki's house laws began by directing his descendants to always look toward Edo for guidance: "Strive in loyal service to the shogun with single-minded importance.

---

14. *AMK,* 95.

15. For example, *AKJ,* 157:161.

16. *AMK,* 95. Some of these practices likely reflected the notion of *omote* versus *uchi* as discussed in Roberts, *Performing the Great Peace.*

Do not pattern your actions after those of other domains. Should you have any second thoughts, you shall not be considered my progeny, and the house retainers need not follow you."[17] These house laws were ceremonially read out loud before the entire Aizu retainer band three times a year.

For all its apparent fealty to the shogunal family, however, the proclamation also rings of overcompensation and betrays the author's anxiety. Masayuki, never hardy and nearly blind in one eye, was at the time fifty-eight years old, and while he himself was in good standing in Edo, he could well have been concerned about the relationship between his family and the main Tokugawa line after his death. After all, even Tokugawa family members could, and did, fall quickly out of the shogun's favor. Such considerations, not to mention the fact his heir Masatsune was then only twenty-one years old, might have led Masayuki to overstate his family's allegiance to the *bakufu* so as to secure for his descendants the lofty position he had gained rather fortuitously in his own lifetime.

The rhetoric of shogunal obeisance did materialize occasionally as various services to the *bakufu*. Some were routine, such as assistance in financing shogunal construction projects, and others less so, such as the three tours of coastal guard duty in 1807, 1810, and 1847 against increasing foreign encroachment. There was, of course, military support in the *bakumatsu* crisis between 1862 and 1868 and the Boshin War in 1868, when Aizu stepped forth as the linchpin in the defense of the old Tokugawa order. Such acts, however, are not to be confused with familial affection or charity. When handed the 1847 coastal defense assignment to the Bōsō peninsula, the then lord of Aizu, Matsudaira Katataka, immediately balked. His memo to the *bakufu*'s prime minister Abe Masahiro presented three reasons for his refusal. First of all, Lord Katataka claimed, his domain's earlier 1810 tour of duty in Miura peninsula proved that Aizu could not afford to serve as the Ōshū Protectorate and provide coastal defense elsewhere at the same time. Second, he argued, it was pointless to "station just four or five hundred men, three hundred kilometers apart no less, to combat huge, castle-like Western warships with our dinghies and cargo ships." Third, he reminded the shogunate that as a so-called familial lord, "unlike the outer lords, Aizu should not have to bear the burden of national defense but rather be the first line of defense against domestic unrest should one be triggered by the foreign threat."[18]

17. *AKJ*, 31:374. There has been some debate about whether 大君 refers to the shogun (read *taikun*) or the emperor (read *ōkimi*), but contextual references to *kōgi* strongly suggests the former.

18. *MG*, 16:236.

Lord Katataka's arguments revealed the domain's fundamental understanding of its duty to the Tokugawa—Aizu could not, and would not, perform shogunal services for free. It took patient cajoling by Prime Minister Abe, a cash payment of ten thousand *ryō* in gold, and a favorable swapping of fifteen thousand *koku* in territory to finally persuade the domain to accept the assignment. Even then, Aizu later demanded for its trouble an additional enfeoffment of nine thousand *koku* in the Bōsō peninsula and nine thousand more in swapping.[19] Even Lord Katataka's official letter of acceptance to the prime minister dripped with reluctance. "Because we have long been assigned as the Ōshū Protectorate, we will be unable to commit too many men to coastal defense," he cautioned. "Furthermore, we are concerned about our samurai who come from the mountains and know nothing of the sea. However," he conceded at last, "Since we have thus been ordered, we shall dutifully do our best."[20]

Upon further review, the Matsudaira's sense of service to the main Tokugawa line stemmed from neither altruism nor kinship, no matter what sympathetic scholars claim. The same could be said about Aizu's most dramatic, and ultimately fatal, political gambit: assuming the position of Kyoto Protectorate in 1862. Initially, not even the weight of the domainal founder's words could move Matsudaira Katamori, then the lord of Aizu, to accept the shogunate's request. At first the young lord sensibly declined the risky and onerous task of snuffing out violent restorationists in the chaotic capital on the *bakufu*'s behalf: "Although our house codes since the days of Lord Masayuki state that we must obey all shogunal commands, I am incompetent and lack the confidence to undertake this unprecedented duty."[21] A senior adviser to Lord Katamori later recalled how Matsudaira Yoshinaga, the lord of Fukui domain and a *bakufu* adviser, ultimately goaded Katamori to take the position. "Lord Masayuki had close blood ties with the shogunal family," Yoshinaga is said to have prodded, "Masayuki would have taken the post."[22] As suggested elsewhere, however, Lord Katamori took on this dangerous task in Kyoto less out of filial piety than a rational calculation of risk and return that revealed his surprisingly ambitious side.[23] In agreeing to wield the *bakufu*'s hammer in the imperial capital, Lord Katamori hoped to try his luck on the grand stage of Kyoto less to serve the *bakufu* than to serve himself and Aizu.

---

19. *AWS*, 5:30.
20. *MG*, 364.
21. Yamakawa, *Kyotoshugoshoku shimatsu*, 1:21–22.
22. Ibid., 22–24.
23. Bolitho, "Aizu, 1853–1868," pp. 1–17.

A similar calculus of domainal self-interest carried the day five years later, in the weeks just before the last shogun, Tokugawa Yoshinobu, restored political power to the imperial court. When many senior domainal advisers beseeched their lord to abandon the hopeless Kyoto post and return home, Lord Katamori reportedly insisted that Aizu not turn its back on the shogunate. "It is inconceivable that Aizu's relationship with the *bakufu* is the same as that of other domains," Katamori is said to have declared. "To share the *bakufu*'s fate is what the domainal founder taught us. We cannot let the main Tokugawa line fall on its own."[24] Katamori's noble words only masked the fact that, by the winter of 1867, his domain was too deeply invested in the *bakumatsu* crisis to have had much of a choice. In the course of acting as Kyoto Protectorate, Aizu had fanned the flames of hatred in Satsuma and especially Chōshū, two formidable foes who were now secretly joining hands to encircle pro-*bakufu* domains like Aizu. By late 1867, Shogun Yoshinobu had all but left Aizu to fight the battles he himself did not care to fight. Besides, hindsight often overlooks the fact that being the Kyoto Protectorate had served Aizu rather well for a good five years until the very last days of 1867. The position had bought Aizu political capital in 1863 when its forces led the ouster of Chōshū restorationists from Kyoto. It brought military glory in the Hamaguri Gate Incident in 1864 when Aizu again routed Chōshū and helped Katamori win, if momentarily, the imperial court's trust, especially Emperor Kōmei's. What sounds like Katamori's heroic and selfless "last stand" was more likely a resolve to roll the iron dice once more and settle the matter on the battlefield.

In the end, neither ancient blood ties nor the supposed tradition of shogunal loyalty decided Aizu's fate. Lord Katamori made his final bet to maximize his domain's returns—with or without the *bakufu*—and to make the most of a dangerous political opportunity that had been presented to him and his domain. While that wager would ultimately fail, it was, at the time, quite sensible given the prevailing politics of domainal self-interest. No matter what the founding father preached, Katamori was committed, first and foremost, to his domain. The fate of his family and his five thousand samurai retainers rested on nothing less.

Building Domainal Solidarity

Self-interested they were, certainly by the mid-nineteenth century and demonstrably earlier, because like most *daimyō*, including even those with

---

24. Yamakawa, *Kyotoshugoshoku shimatsu*, 2:245.

blood ties to the shogunal family, the Aizu Matsudaira had established a distinct political identity based on a deep commitment to their domain. After all, the domain was their charge, their raison d'être, their home base that made their privileged lives possible. Over the course of some two hundred years, both the rulers and the ruled learned the shape of their stead and pondered how the domain was to fit into their political culture and everyday lives. Through it all, they conjured Aizu as a distinct space, even if it was a mosaic patched with many different mental geographies.

When first enfeoffed to Aizu in 1643, the Hoshina were not immediately accustomed to the land of their charge. In this they were like many *daimyō* in the early Tokugawa period who were transplanted afar and frequently as the first three shogun busily shuffled their newly acquired realm. The Hoshina originally hailed from Takatō domain in Shinano province, as did many of their retainers, before they were relocated to Aizu. Masayuki himself might have felt especially out of place in Aizu, since his responsibilities to the Tokugawa *bakufu* kept him mostly in Edo rather than Wakamatsu, making him a particularly absentee lord. His samurai, too, were at first unfamiliar with Aizu, coming as they did from Takatō, Mogami, and elsewhere. The rulers' initial ignorance about their new home lingered in part because the entire retainer band now resided mostly in the castle town of Wakamatsu. Instead of having its samurai manage the land directly, the domain deputized prominent local families called the *gōgashira,* descendants of the native *jizamurai,* who had long governed rural communities before the Hoshina's arrival, to continue administering Aizu's vast countryside.[25] This basic arrangement persisted with only minor adjustments for the remainder of the Tokugawa period and kept Aizu's samurai divorced from the land that made their livelihood possible.

The new rulers would come to know their territory soon enough. For starters, the *bakufu* compelled domains to actively collect and furnish information about the land. In 1605, 1644, 1697, and 1835, the shogunate commissioned projects to map out every domain, county, and village in Japan. *Aizu fudoki,* the first major local gazetteer about Aizu, was presented by Masayuki to the *bakufu* in 1666 and was meant to induce other provincial lords to volunteer information about their own domain as well. In 1646 Aizu produced its first official map, complete with details on the castle town's layout, domainal borders, and economic output.[26] In 1669 the domain began to count its

25. *AWS,* 3:17.
26. *AKJ,* 6:241–42.

commoners annually—42,527 that year—whereas it had previously recorded only the number of its samurai and left the number of commoners as "unknown" in its annual statistics.[27]

To build this self-knowledge, samurai inspectors roamed the countryside every few years to monitor economic productivity, tax compliance, and good behavior.[28] Even the lord himself was known to venture out among the hoi polloi every once in a while. Between 1644 and 1745, the *daimyō* toured the domain seven times, inspecting villages, confirming borders, and lodging at the homes of local notables.[29] The area surrounding the scenic Lake Inawashiro and its hot springs—a major tourist spot in the area today—was naturally a favored destination. An entourage of his retainers accompanied the lord on these trips but, residing now as they did in the castle town, the samurai city slickers seemed uncomfortable with the earthy countryside. In four separate instances, the samurai had to be instructed not to trample on paddies, take fruit from the fields, strike peasants without cause, or seduce the locals.[30] Despite such occasional awkwardness, Aizu rulers actively sought to learn their land and its people and kept a close eye on their economic and moral welfare, taking stock of their physical world and further developing their territorial awareness along the way. That the rulers came to possess a robust knowledge of their land is evident from the sheer volume of gazetteers and histories they compiled.[31] Official historians conferred on Aizu its temporal continuity, geographers its spatial fixity, and ethnographers its cultural unity. This body of knowledge helped to frame their self-portrait squarely within their domain.

The self-cognizance of Aizu as a discrete spatial community emerged not only in officialdom but in more informal ways, too. Even commoners had various opportunities to learn their local landscape and confirm their connection to it. One example is the pilgrimage to the so-called Thirty-Three Kannon Sites of Aizu, which had taken root by the mid-seventeenth century and remains to this day. This tour of famous local Buddhist sites took pilgrims

---

27. Ibid., 34:461. Volumes of *AKJ* after 1669 provide the commoner population but prior volumes simply noted "unknown."

28. Ibid., 123:253.

29. Ibid., 4:165–66; 22:68–69; 71:410–12; 80:74; 90:443–44; 44:370–72, 375; 153:57; for the years 1644, 1662, 1688, 1697, 1705, 1742, and 1745, respectively.

30. Ibid., 71:411; 144:370–71.

31. Major texts compiled or commissioned by the domain include: *Wakamatsu jōka shirabesho,* 1665; *Aizu fudoki,* 1666; *Aizu jinja shi,* 1672; *Aizu fūzoku chō,* 1685; *Aizu ryōnai meisho shōchi,* 1761; *Aizu kagami,* 1789; *Nisshinkan dōjikun,* 1803; *Shin Aizu fudoki,* 1809; *Aizu kasei jikki,* 1815; *Nisshinkanshi,* 1823; *Kyūjin zakkō,* 1839; *Aizu yōgairoku,* 1842; and *Aizu chimeikō,* 1844.

roughly clockwise around the perimeter of Aizu proper, guiding them through towns such as Kitakata, Takada, and Bange, and even into remote mountain temples.[32] The tour became so popular as to earn the authorities' disapproval. One year after *Aizu jiin engi,* a gazetteer on local religious sites, introduced the route in 1665, the domain banned the pilgrimage out of fear that it would threaten agricultural productivity, although this restriction was later loosened to permit visitors during the low season.[33] Participating in this excursion would have allowed even illiterate peasants to gain some firsthand spatial literacy of Aizu.

Primers and other simple, accessible texts widened commoners' imaginary panorama of their land still further. Texts used in schools called *gōkō,* which were operated by the domain and open to commoners, introduced Aizu as a distinct spatial body to its youngsters. Primers such as *Wakamatsu machi annai* and *Wakamatsu yori Edo made dōchūki* furnished a value-laden geography to their young readers. *Wakamatsu machi annai* begins with the couplet, "Tsuruga Castle, ever prosperous for a thousand years / To the east lay Oda Bridge and the Sakurada horse tracks," and proceeds to draw an imagined sphere that stretches outward from the lord's castle, the center of gravity in this domainal universe.

A similar narrative technique shaped other school textbooks, including *Aizu shiki jūrai* and *Aizu jūrai,* which were used as primers in both public and private academies. *Aizu shiki jūrai* takes the reader on a sweeping virtual tour of the domain. It begins with festive springtime in the castle town of Wakamatsu, thus placing the lord and his castle squarely at the heart of the domainal geography. Here, Matsudaira lordship serves as the origin of both space and time, as the domain's spatial center as well as its temporal source through its association with spring, the season of natural beginnings. The text gushes in local pride as it celebrates "the domain's eternality" and "Wakamatsu, which prospers even to its branches," a wordplay on the name of the castle town, which literally means "young pine."[34] It then immerses the reader in a slide show featuring scenic spots and ancient temples, tall mountain peaks and sites of miracles, tracing out the domainal world and touting its special qualities all the while. These texts thus transmitted a distinct local cosmology and a slice of proud self-knowledge to the people of Aizu.

This mental geography of the domain, however fragmentary and piecemeal it was, did occasionally find practical application. These sources of

32. Takamine, *Aizu kagami,* 2:17–19.
33. *AKJ,* 28:277.
34. *Aizu shiryō sōsho,* upper vol., p. 397.

self-identity could lead some to locate themselves within a world as defined by the domainal polity. For example, some business leaders and agricultural elites in Aizu were eager to frame their worldview in accordance with the domain—at least when it suited their interests. Aizu's merchants invoked the principles of *kokueki,* or domainal welfare, as they saw the need to promote a confrontational "us-versus-them" view of commerce vis-à-vis outside competition and argued that the internal had to be protected against the external in a zero-sum economy. This mercantilist concept hinged on an acute sense of domainal self-awareness, and opportunistic merchants were keen to make good use of that self-awareness.

Merchant leaders realized that a domainalist argument was at its most persuasive when discussing strategic exports like lacquerware, an important source of domainal revenue that was considered "the first and foremost export of Aizu."[35] In 1856 Aizu lacquerware wholesalers petitioned the domainal government for special protection to guard their precious cash cow against outside competition. In so doing, they were quick to call upon mercantilist principles. "Recently, major foreign merchants have entered Aizu to purchase directly from lacquer painters and craftsmen," the wholesalers complained to the domain. "They use their own shippers, paying but a pittance to the brokers in Aizu. . . . Local craftsmen are troubled because their selling price is falling. . . . As a result, domestic production is shrinking."[36] To win the authorities' favor, these lacquerware merchants linked their personal commercial activities to greater domainal prosperity and equated their fortune with that of the domain. They saw enough substance in the domainal welfare concept to seize it for themselves and decorate their private interests with public significance.

Some Aizu laborers used a similar domainalist argument to defend their job security against outsiders. In the 1720s carpenters from Sendai, Niigata, and Takasaki began flowing into Wakamatsu, attracted by reconstruction opportunities following a major fire in the castle town. Faced with unwelcome competition, carpenters in Wakamatsu turned to the domainalist strategy in their plea for protection. "It is difficult enough to maintain our livelihood given the shortage of jobs," they cried. "On top of this, carpenters from other places have recently entered our land and are taking away our work. Because wages earned by outsider carpenters will only enrich other domains, we beseech the domain to ensure that we can secure these jobs for ourselves."[37] How the authorities responded to this request is unclear from the records, but in an 1828 case, the

35. *AKJ,* 192:137.

36. *AWS,* 4:89–90; *Yanada monjo kōyōsekibo,* 1856.

37. *Yanada monjo kōyōsekibo,* 1738.

domain seemingly agreed with this basic position, as it instructed Wakamatsu employers to "refrain from hiring foreign craftsmen as much as possible and hire local craftsmen instead."[38] Various members of local society could thus invoke the domain to incorporate themselves into a larger community. By declaring their membership within a greater domainal economy and embracing the "domainal welfare" principle, they reified their own interests into something beyond just personal livelihood. This practice smacks more of opportunism than patriotism, but it nevertheless showed that the domain had gained sufficient currency and gravity to serve as a useful rallying point.

Agricultural productivity was even more obviously linked to the prosperity of the land and could readily be framed in domainal terms. Local agriculturalists were eager to equate their personal labor with the domainal welfare, as they often did through farming manuals. Several agrarian how-to texts circulated in Aizu, the earliest and most famous being *Aizu nōsho* written by Sase Yojiemon, the headman of Makunouchi village on the southwestern outskirts of Wakamatsu, in 1684.[39] In his preface to *Aizu nōsho,* one of the first agricultural texts in all of Japan, Yojiemon affirmed the domain as the basis of his worldview and implicitly directed his manual toward his fellow Aizu farmers. As a man of the soil, he explained, he realized that each land has unique needs. "Standards of other lands are difficult to apply here in Aizu," he explained, "Therefore, I have titled this text *Aizu nōsho,*" and he prescribed practices specific to his native place.

Initially, Yojiemon viewed his work within a narrower scope that was confined to his immediate community of Makunouchi. He explained that he had written his manual because he had in mind "two intentions, one internal [to his family, i.e., private] and one external [i.e., public]. . . . My private intention is to pass this text down to my descendants as a family record, and improve their work. That is my first intention," he declared. "My public intention is to fulfill my duty as the village headman and instruct the untrained peasants in my village. That is my second intention."[40] Despite such a local impetus, word spread about the manual's usefulness, and in 1689 his lord awarded Yojiemon for his good work. Yojiemon then used his reward to establish an endowment and made low-interest loans available to his fellow villagers. By 1720, that fund had yielded thirty-four bales of rice and more than one *ryō* in gold, "much to the benefit of his village."[41]

---

38. Ibid., 1828.
39. Sase, *Aizu nōsho / Aizu nōsho furoku.*
40. Ibid., pp. 5–6.
41. Rinsetsuō, *Aizu kōshiden.*

Emboldened by success, Yojiemon designed his sequel to appeal to a wider audience. In 1704 he compiled *Aizu uta nōsho,* which presented various farming tips as 1,669 pieces of *waka,* or 31-syllabic five-line poems.[42] Yojiemon took this simplified approach after one reader felt that *Aizu nōsho* was "too long" and "too difficult for readers to remember and too easy for them to grow bored." He advised Yojiemon to present his ideas to uneducated peasants in the relatively short and accessible *waka* form. "This will make it easier to remember and readers will be better motivated to learn and profit from it," the man suggested. "It will benefit your fellow farmers greatly."[43]

Accordingly, Yojiemon explicitly expanded his new readership to include all members of his occupation in the domain. Furthermore, the sequel promoted domainal service in a way that the original never did. For example, two lines of *waka* in the section titled "Tribute" encouraged readers to meet their tax obligations to the domain cheerfully:

> In the season of paying tribute
> mortar and pestle should grind on day and night.
> Stop all else to prepare tribute;
> work in this world is the blessing of the lord.[44]

These public service messages were an entirely new addition, reflecting the heightened political bend in the later text. The sequel's mental geography expanded to now encompass the entire domain. In fact, *Aizu uta nōsho* closed with an overtly domainalist postscript: "It has been rightly said that farming is the basis of the realm. In the eighty years since Lord Masayuki settled this land, many wise folks have worked hard for the good of society. How felicitous it is that this has become the beautiful custom of our country Aizu."[45] Yojiemon thus equated agricultural work with broader domainal values and practices and politicized production in expressly domainal terms. For these services, Yojiemon, along with his adopted son Rin'emon who published another agrarian manual called *Makunouchi nōgyōki* in 1713, were honored in two profiles of virtuous Aizu figures, *Aizu kōkōden* and *Aizu zoku kōkōden,* respectively, thereby confirming the public value of their work. Owing to their social position, village headmen like Yojiemon already had a sharp sense of their greater social responsibility. It was an awareness that the domainal authorities could readily leverage and put to more public use. It did not take

42. Hasegawa, *Aizu uta nōsho / Makunouchi nōgyōki.*

43. Ibid., p. 9.

44. Ibid., p. 113. The annual tribute in Aizu, which was about 60–66 percent of the yield, was to be submitted by the thirtieth day of the eleventh month.

45. Ibid., p. 352.

much for the agricultural elites to widen their worldview and make the domain a meaningful part of their self-image.

These self-images were further sharpened by encounters with the outside world. As scholars and common sense tell us, only through dialectic interactions with others can the self be defined. There were some such opportunities even in a seemingly remote place like Aizu. For example, travel, while hardly encouraged by the authorities, was far from unusual. As early as 1652, 117 Aizu commoners applied for travel permits to the famous Ise Shrine in central Japan, which prompted the domainal authorities to prohibit any further pilgrimages until 1660.[46] Despite various injunctions against travel outside the domain—eleven women in 1691 tried to sneak their way out to Ise and landed in jail instead[47]—pilgrimages to Ise remained so common as to earn mention in the local gazetteer *Aizu fudoki.*

No one knows precisely how many Aizu commoners ventured beyond their domain during the Tokugawa period, but several well-to-do peasant tourists in 1809, 1840, 1862, and 1879 provide a glimpse. Their travel journals from 1862 reveal the travelers' awe of cities like Edo and the newly opened treaty port of Yokohama, where the Aizu men were shocked to see Americans and Britons eat beef, and the ancient capitals of Kyoto and Nara, whose merchants were ready to swindle unknowing bumpkins from the distant north. "They'll charge a hundred *mon* for a single amulet," the tourists learned, "Be careful."[48] Despite troubles like overpriced sandals, leaky lodges, and greedy ferrymen, those who ventured out of the Tōhoku mountains managed to gain a greater sense of the realm. Their encounters with the world beyond the familiar also deepened their local roots. The party of four travelers in 1862 identified themselves throughout their journey as "Aizu bumaru," or laborers in the service of Aizu domain, presumably to facilitate their passage. Only outside their domain would they have had the need or the occasion to use such a label that confirmed and articulated their domainal affiliation.

Ordinary folks with sufficient time and means could thus move beyond their own localities and broaden their mental landscape, but no one in Aizu had more opportunities to do so than the domain's samurai. Duty compelled many of them, first of all, to accompany their lord to Edo for his alternate attendance obligation. At any given time, some sixteen hundred Aizu samurai were stationed in the shogunal capital, where they could interact with colleagues from other domains throughout Japan. These men could widen

46. *AKJ,* 12:403. There was a similar prohibition in 1666; ibid., 28:277.

47. Ibid., 20:655–56; 74:492.

48. Sakai, "Kinsei nōmin no tabi," p. 140.

their worldview in ways that most of their countrymen could not. Duty in fact sent them off to places more far-flung than they might have ever imagined. As Western vessels began to broach Japan's shores around the turn of the nineteenth century, the Tokugawa *bakufu* assigned Aizu to three separate coastal defense duties. The shogunate in 1807 asked Aizu to guard Ezo, where Russians had been making unsolicited inroads.[49] As a lyrical introduction to an illustrated scroll of the expedition sang, "Commanded by the *bakufu,* the men of Aizu departed as guardians of the north. Russian brigands, they say, trample these islands, and all is not well in these parts."[50] Two thousand men set off in the first month of 1808, marched up through Tōhoku, and crossed into Ezo four months later, with some continuing as far north as Karafuto.

Ezo lay at the fringe of Tokugawa Japan, and there they were, if not altogether happily. Once in Ezo, the Aizu men encountered no Russians but arctic cold and crippling disease. Teetering on the furthest edge of the realm gave Aizu men cause to reassess and complicate their political allegiance. In 1866 Akizuki Kazuhisa, a scholarly retainer who would negotiate Aizu's surrender in 1868 and later teach alongside Lafcadio Hearn in the Meiji era, spent several months in Ezo as the superintendent of the Aizu outpost at Nishibetsu.[51] There, he mustered the national sentiment to muse:

> To die and bury my bones here would not be so bad
> Since all land from Karafuto on south is imperial land[52]

In 1810 Aizu samurai went to guard the Miura peninsula, which, together with the Bōsō peninsula to the east, bracketed the seaward approach to Edo. They spent an entire decade in Misaki and Kannonzaki, a stone's throw away from Uraga where Commodore Matthew Perry would later land. For all their trouble, however, the Aizu guards once again did not encounter any encroaching foreigners, and neither did the 233 Aizu soldiers dispatched to Bōsō peninsula in 1847.

They would get to see the barbarian threat all too vividly in the form of Perry's black ships in 1853. Even prior to that, however, Aizu men were not entirely unfamiliar with foreigners. In 1739, for example, a squad of Aizu samurai raced to the shores of Sendai when four Russian vessels ventured too close.[53] It was, however, the relatively friendly Koreans whom the Aizu

---

49. *AMK,* 176.

50. Endō, *Aizuhan Karafuto shutsujin emaki.*

51. In 1859, the *bakufu* placed Ezo under the custody of four domains, including Aizu. *AMK,* 225.

52. Akizuki, *Akizuki teiken shibunshū.*

53. *AKJ,* 139:220.

men engaged most frequently and personally. As Chosŏn emissaries made their way overland to Edo for their audience with the shogun, an official Japanese party greeted them along the way, and Aizu samurai were a part of this envoy five times between 1682 and 1764. On three of these occasions, the Koreans paid a visit to the Aizu mansion in Edo, sharing tea and tobacco with the hosts and leaving gifts of black hemp, ink brushes, and the obligatory ginseng.[54]

Most of these contacts, however, were hardly the dramatic encounters that crossed lines of race and civilization that were to come in the *bakumatsu* period and beyond. Their significance is not to be overstated, as opportunities for external interactions in the Tokugawa period were limited in both quantity and quality. Perhaps most important, only the elite service class had any regular chance to leave their homes, to expand and test the edges of their known world. Most ordinary folks, for their part, continued to define their world within what they could see, which was securely nestled in the hills and valleys they knew best. Nor did they have cause to imagine much beyond that.

54. Ibid., 60:644; 98:78–79, 83–84; 107:420–22; 158:179.

CHAPTER 2

Unmaking a Domain, 1643–1868

The Limits of a Community

The idea that Aizu was a singular and coherent domainal community might have been expressed in various places—sometimes explicitly, often circumstantially—but, in social practice, this idea was not often persuasive. Potential for integrity should not be mistaken for much more than that. In truth, many conflicts and discrepancies compromised just how much Aizu meant to its people, or if it meant much of anything at all. As a result, popular commitment to the domain was often capricious and unreliable. Two themes in Aizu's political life—defining "belonging" and domainal service—reveal the disintegrative patterns that diminished the domain's value as an object of affinity and loyalty. This limit would be exposed for all to see in 1868, just when the stakes could not be any higher.

The struggle to define the "rightful place" of the domain's resources reveals competing understandings of "belonging" in Aizu. Both people and goods were on the line in this matter. The domain certainly worried about its peasants staying where they belonged, namely, in the fields and paddies, and sought to tie peasants to Aizu's land. Absconding, a common weapon of the weak, was a problem even before the Hoshina arrived; as many as two thousand peasants abandoned their land and fled Aizu to escape Katō rule in the early 1640s. In fact, one of the first pronouncements that Hoshina Masayuki made upon his arrival was to call on those peasants to return. In 1649 the domain conducted a survey of absconders to learn more about why they fled, and it went so far as to pay them to return to Aizu.[1] Early measures apparently had little effect. In 1652 the domain had to establish an office and a set of regulations devoted to bring-

1. *AWS*, 3:69–71.

ing back absconders.[2] The problem lingered well into the Matsudaira tenure, as evidenced by the official instructions to border patrol in 1721, which threatened to punish guards "who ineptly allow absconders to pass freely" and offered a bounty to anyone who captured peasants on the run.[3] In 1787 the domain tried a softer tact by promising amnesty to those who would return to Aizu to till the land.[4] Fleeing peasants obviously felt little attachment to their native domain or had needs that overrode whatever attachments they might have had. No farming manual or lordly pronouncements could convince these desperate folks to fulfill their duties to Aizu.

The domain sought to stanch the outflow of peasants in order to maximize its tax base and agricultural extraction. It behooved the domain to hoard its labor supply within its borders. Otherwise, not only would land lay fallow, but too many unhappy peasants wandering about could embarrass Aizu in the eyes of its neighbors, not to mention the *bakufu*. Similarly, conservative thinking prevailed in 1652 when the domain prohibited Aizu day laborers from seeking employment outside their domain. This pronouncement specifically cited the potential for labor shortage within the domain as its rationale.[5] However, calls to return to their native land did not operate on the emotional logic of a homeland, that is, the sentimental notion that those born in Aizu belong in Aizu and should stay there through thick and thin. The domain's definition of human "belonging" in this case, which grew strictly out of the elite's economic needs, never evoked romanticized images about staying true to one's local roots or the value of collective solidarity.

The authorities also fretted about excessive outflow of goods, especially in times of shortage. Official economic policies usually presumed that internal commodities belong in Aizu; that is, domestically produced goods were to be domestically consumed. Trade regulations, designed to secure supply and moderate prices within the domain, made various goods illegal for export. Eight contrabands could not leave Aizu without domainal license: women, hawk hatchlings, ponies, candle wax, lacquer, paper, bearskin, and lead.[6] Market conditions rendered other items illegal for export from time to time. In 1721, for example, goods like lacquer base, cedar, straw mats, large game birds, and reindeer skin were ordered to remain within Aizu borders.[7]

---

2. *AKJ*, 12:400.
3. *AWS*, 3:301–2.
4. *AKJ*, 235:288.
5. *AKJ*, 12:400–1.
6. *AKJ*, 31:381.
7. *AWS*, 3:304–5.

Mercantilist policies also sought to limit the inflow of some foreign goods and thus stimulate the consumption of domestically produced goods. In 1790 the county office in Tajima restricted the import of foreign hoes to "seven or eight to ten containers" annually and encouraged consumers to purchase locally made hoes instead.[8] This order was later expanded to ban all hoe imports outright and applied to the domain at large.[9] In 1809 Aizu authorities also prohibited the import of hairdressing oil explicitly in the name of "preventing the outflow of cash from the area."[10] Such measures promoted so-called *kokueki* mercantilism, which aimed to protect domestic producers while guarding the balance of foreign exchange against other domains.[11]

Unfortunately for domainal mercantilism, rarely did this domainal welfare argument prove effective. Even the best efforts of protectionist-minded authorities could not prevent astute opportunists from ignoring official demands and seeking profit wherever they could, whether it was in their domain or not. Some traders smuggled rice out of Aizu regularly, especially in times of shortage when the domain artificially lowered domestic prices. Price control might have helped needy consumers but it also tempted unscrupulous exporters. As a 1713 proclamation openly admitted, "It is most deplorable that rice, though a contraband, is being purchased to be shipped outside the domain. Consequently, there is much disruption on the southward turnpikes. From now on, such activities must be guarded against vigilantly."[12] Domainal records attest to those who braved decapitation and exile to traffic in various controlled items like soybeans in 1653, paper in 1661, whetstones in 1664, bear pelts in 1679, and candle wax in 1701.[13] In all these cases, market demand clearly proved more compelling than domainal demands. To protect its valuable monopsonies, the domain strengthened its border inspection in 1842 and offered to reward anyone who reported illegal trafficking. In each of the twenty-four villages that stood on the domainal border, a villager was assigned specifically to inspect for contraband, and, though a commoner, he was allowed to bear a sword for the purpose.[14]

No amount of armed guards, domainal finger-wagging, or mercantilist rhetoric could prevent people from using the most desirable marketplaces, either.

---

8. Tajima chōshi hensan iinkai, *Tajima chōshi, shiryō hen,* upper vol. 6, p. 202.
9. *Yanada monjo kōyōsekibo,* 1790.
10. *Tajima chōshi, shiryō hen,* lower vol. 6, p. 383.
11. See Roberts, *Mercantilism in a Japanese Domain,* for how a similar impulse took shape in Tosa domain.
12. *AWS,* 3:243–44.
13. *AKJ,* 13:448; 21:20; 25:186; 53:407; and 85:261–62.
14. *MG,* 13; *AWS,* 4:9.

Although there were several markets throughout Aizu, and domainal officials sought to have them all prosper evenly, sellers and buyers alike gravitated to the most favorable markets. This meant letting some markets flounder. In 1701, what used to be a major marketplace at Takada in southern Aizu fell victim to this trend. "Recently, even those who reside in Aizu go to the nearest market outside the domain, and the Takada market has fallen into disuse," county officials complained. They worried that tax receipts were bleeding out of their jurisdiction. "From now on," area merchants were told, "You must conduct business at Takada and not go outside the domain."[15] The domain, for its part, sought to have Aizu folks do business in Aizu; those doing business, for their part, cared more about doing it well than doing it at home.

The rulers and the ruled could diverge greatly on who and what "belonged" in Aizu and how much they valued the domain as a rightful place of belonging that merited their allegiance. The domain did what it could, naturally enough, to keep human and material capital within its borders for the sake of domainal well-being. On the other hand, producers and consumers, also naturally enough, often defined "well-being" much more personally than the domain did and felt little compulsion to subscribe to the domain's definition. When the two interests clashed, official stipulations left more than a few keen-eyed sellers and buyers unconvinced. Whatever lines officials drew to demarcate Aizu as a rigid political economy proved rather permeable in practice. Subjugating individual impulses to greater interests and accepting the domain as one's "proper place" were far less common in Aizu than its administrators would have liked.

Commoners' worldview was usually not defined by their domain, as their commitments and interests tended to be more locally oriented than that. Aizu's commoners had the leeway to be fickle and opportunistic in whether to make their domain a part of their lives. The samurai did not. Being the professional service class, it was both imperative and intuitive for the samurai to frame their world within the domain. For Aizu's retainer band, the domain was at once the means and the end of their being.

In a time of enduring peace, samurai service called for sacrifice of a different sort than what their ancestors had performed on the battlefield. The Tokugawa samurai slashed budgets not bodies, cut corners rather than limbs. Aizu samurai, like many of their counterparts in other domains, subscribed to a service of poverty, and necessarily so. When the domain's fiscal health deteriorated, as it did most elsewhere, the samurai on payroll were asked time and again to make do with less. Even in Lord Masayuki's time, his retainers were

---

15. *AWS*, 3:231.

instructed to pare down luxuries.[16] Samurai in need naturally turned to loans, but in 1667, Masayuki rebuked his men for borrowing money, condemning it as something "practiced only by peasants, townspeople, and servants," whereas indebtedness "does not befit a samurai and must be avoided even at the risk of starving to death."[17] The convention of the day held samurai to be morally above monetary worries, and so went the platitudes, if not the practice, in Aizu. Austerity measures occasionally targeted commoners, too, but it was the samurai who were under the most severe watch. Only the elite are known to have been punished for failing to fulfill the service of suffering. In 1787 the domain reprimanded eight retainers for not suffering enough, as they were found guilty of indulging in luxuries.[18] Thus, samurai were compelled to curb their behavior out of ethical expectations accompanying their elite status and share most personally in the domain's plight. When the domain caught a cold, it was the samurai who sneezed first, not the commoners.

The service elite were also saddled with the burden of representing their domain to the rest of the Tokugawa world, especially when stationed in Edo. Domainal rules made sure the Aizu men understood this responsibility. In 1813 the domain issued the following to its samurai stationed in the capital:

> Constantly strive to maintain the practices of the Matsudaira house and the true meaning of being a samurai. In this place [Edo], it is easy to be influenced by the ways of other domains. Be mindful of your appearance and language, and refrain from fancy accessories. Maintain simplicity as your base, and keep up an appearance of uniform house practice. To imitate shallow ways and to be vulgar is unattractive and unbefitting our house's prestige. Righteousness and sincerity are our values, and you shall uphold our virtues without imitating others.[19]

This warning obliged the samurai to serve as the standard bearer for Aizu as a whole and to defend its distinctive traits. Likewise, when the Aizu forces departed for their coastal defense assignment in 1847, Lord Katataka issued a ten-point command that prohibited the servicemen from gambling, singing, public dining, and other inappropriate behavior so as to maintain not only military discipline but the good name of the Aizu Matsudaira family.[20] These measures ensured that Aizu's elite were inculcated with a sense of domainal ambassadorship and its accompanying responsibility in a way distinct to them

16. *AKJ*, 18:599.
17. *AGK*, 43.
18. *AKJ*, 227:636–37.
19. *AGK*, 90.
20. *MG*, 251.

and no one else in the domain. Failure to discharge that responsibility could have serious repercussions, as one retainer in Edo learned in 1756. He had attended a play and became so engrossed that he forgot his short sword at his seat. He was fired when word got out about this embarrassment. A week later, all Aizu samurai on duty in Edo were ordered not to attend any more *kyōgen*, Kabuki, and other theatrical performances.[21] By contrast, no such restrictions were ever imposed upon Aizu's commoners.

Samurai were sensitive to the state's demands in good part because they were bred to be so. Various social mechanisms, both institutional and informal, conditioned the elite to think domainally from an early age. Education, naturally, was foremost among those means of socialization. The center of the domain's education system was the Nisshinkan academy, which had been in operation in various forms since the 1660s. All samurai boys in Aizu entered the Nisshinkan at the age of ten, with the best and brightest advancing, at domainal expense, to the *bakufu*'s Shōheikō academy in Edo. As a public institution, Nisshinkan left no doubt about its mission. Its charter promised to "ground students in filial piety and develop their talents through received virtue so as to produce men of character who are useful to the state."[22] As a domainal pronouncement affirmed in 1805, samurai children were to be trained to "become vessels of the state."[23] Samurai education sought to breed them in domainal governance and commitment, for that was the duty to which every Tokugawa-period samurai was born.

Even the culture of children's play reinforced disciplinary socialization among the service elite. Peer oversight and communal enforcement formed an integral part of Aizu's samurai youth culture. Samurai boys between the ages of six and nine were organized into "play groups" of about ten boys each. The group met every day in a member's home, and the oldest boy began each meeting by delivering the following commandments to his mates:

> One, you shall not disobey elders;
> Two, you shall bow and pay respect to elders;
> Three, you shall not lie;
> Four, you shall not act in a dastardly way;
> Five, you shall not pick on a weakling;
> Six, you shall not eat outside the home;
> Seven, you shall not exchange words with a female outside the home;
> Eight, what must not be must not be.

---

21. *AKJ*, 94:612–13.
22. *AKJ*, 232:166–72.
23. *AGK*, 83.

After this reading, the leader asked each member if he had broken any of the rules since the group last met. The boys were expected to confess their own violations or report on those of their mates and handed down appropriate punishment as a group.[24]

From an early age, then, the domainal elite were subject to rigorous social-conditioning programs. The samurai were deeply steeped in a culture of stately service and self-discipline. However, this education and socialization that instilled a domainal mentality belonged mostly to the elite. Inevitably, some of this elite sensibility did trickle down in Aizu society. For example, *Nisshinkan dōjikun,* a moral textbook written by the fifth lord Katanobu and used at the Nisshinkan, made its way beyond the samurai students there. Commoner children also read it in some local academies (*gōkō*), and copies of it could be found in the private libraries of several prominent townspeople.[25] However, the privilege of political education was mostly the samurai's, and so, too, was the accompanying burden of having to pattern their lives according to the state's dictates.

All told, the service elite of Aizu were well ahead of their fellow residents in their propensity to think and act "domainally." It could hardly have been otherwise. It was the domain that provided the samurai's education in statecraft, paid them for their public functions, and granted them social prestige according to their family's historical relationship to the lord. This was no mere rhetoric, either, because their socioeconomic reality demanded noble suffering for the lord and the domain, securely embedding sacrifice and self-denial into elite culture as a worthy form of domainal service. As the state's guardians and administrators, samurai retainers were subject to the state's needs and discipline like no one else in their domain. It was they who found themselves most intimately tied into the domainal community.

---

24. *AWS,* 4:312–14. In his autobiography, Shiba Gorō recounted the effect that this practice had on his development as a young samurai growing up in Aizu: "I spent my afternoon with a neighborhood group of young boys called the *asobi no jū.* I owe a great deal to this institution. The spiritual training I received in the company of peers served me well in the difficult year that followed. Indeed, in many ways, I feel I owe my very survival to the values and habits I absorbed unconsciously as a member of that group. I cannot praise it enough." Craig, *Remembering Aizu,* p. 34.

25. *Nisshinkan dōjikun* can be found, for example, in the family archives of Yokoyama Hideo and Fukunishi Morio, whose families are both long-standing merchant families in Aizu Wakamatsu. Aizu Wakamatsu-shi, *Aizu Wakamatsushi shiryō mokuroku,* pp. 68, 139.

Becoming Unraveled, 1868

The mental geography of early modern Aizu was an untidy amalgam of conflicting ideas about what the domain meant to its people. Multiple understandings of the domain's worth—which were sometimes determined by one's status but far more so by the vagaries of individual desires and circumstances—fragmented Aizu's political culture and diluted the meaning of the domain. Those seeking protonational yearnings amid this sloppy potpourri could surely find some if they are so inclined. So, too, could those seeking inklings of a strong local tradition or identity that might have led to latter-day Aizu regionalism. In practice, however, integrative promise seldom yielded either protonational or regional solidarity. Aizu's political practices show that so-called *han* nationalism was so shallow and limited that it cannot be understood as protonational intimations or regionalism longing to become national.[26] Insofar as "*han* nationalism" meant anything, it belonged exclusively to the service elite. More significantly, it was meant to be kept that way. The domain was a limited polity operating in a decidedly premodern environment that did not seek to envelop local society into a cohesive political community. To exaggerate its "nationness" is to flirt with anachronism.

The domainal state's ability to instill a sense of affinity and belonging was restricted in part by the technology of statecraft that was at the rulers' disposal. For example, there was no bona fide national myth that gained currency throughout the domain. While Aizu had a "founding father" construct in Hoshina Masayuki, he was hardly a transcendental icon. After his death, Lord Masayuki was deified as the divine spirit Hanitsu and installed as a Shintō divinity at Hanitsu Shrine near Lake Inawashiro. Domainal ordinances were occasionally delivered in the name of Hanitsu, the rhetoric of samurai service claimed to honor him and his descendants, and it was his house codes that were invoked in times of anxiety like the *bakumatsu* crisis. However, the Hanitsu iconography was not for mass consumption. There was, for instance, no official holiday to honor this figure, nor were there any sanctifying rituals or symbols directed at local society. Aizu's domainal authority did not rest on ideology or myth, and the rulers saw no need to infuse the masses with an imagined collectivity premised on divine genesis or authority. Such an imperative, and its accompanying political devices, would have to await the tail end of the nineteenth century and the coming of a far more sophisticated and ambitious central state.

---

26. Craig, *Chōshū in the Meiji Restoration*, pp. 358–59.

Moreover, efforts to leverage territorial awareness toward political ends were limited at best. While Aizu featured a degree of shared spatial literacy and communality—some measure of "Aizuness," as it were—this self-cognition is more remarkable for what it did *not* do. Domainal awareness rarely secured popular political commitment or spurred the people into action. Aizu lords did not think to systematically cultivate a sentimental concept of a domainal homeland worth serving and protecting. No sustained discourse circulated a shared sense of "Aizuness" until modern times when, ironically, Aizu was no longer. Whatever amorphous sense of local collectivity that might have existed in name hardly served as a political asset in fact.

This was largely because Tokugawa political culture obliged the "people"—the *min*—with no such function. The *min* was political capital only in a passive sense. Of course, the people were expected to pay tribute, perform corvée labor, and generally stay out of trouble. But early modern political culture demanded this and not much else. The domain did scarcely anything to prepare commoners to think and serve in any active, "national" sense because it seldom needed such a thing. Enduring peace and the absence of interstate violence and competition had long obviated the need for a robust citizenry. The domainal state did not compel its people to learn to read, maintain proper hygiene, alter their speech, or condition their bodies and behavior in the name of strengthening their polity. A distinctly premodern, circumscribed definition of the *min* held sway in Aizu as it did elsewhere throughout the Tokugawa world. Certainly, the domain could be as stern and imperious, morally condescending, or downright neglectful as any other state. But rarely did it—nor could it—summon and commandeer its people as thoroughly as modern nation-states do. Instead, the domainal state was content enough to oversee a flock of *kyakubun*—passive "guests" who quietly met the hosts' expectation to be polite but ultimately unhelpful. Fukuzawa Yukichi, the enlightenment thinker who later condemned the detached "guests" that Meiji Japan had inherited, certainly would have recognized just such a people in Aizu domain.[27]

In early modern times, no *kuni* compelled the *min* to become a *kokumin*. A domain—the most familiar and relevant polity for much of Tokugawa society—simply did not need to synthesize the *kuni*, the territorial space, with the *min*, its human corpus, into a *kokumin*, the potent space–body composite. It took a very different kind of polity working under very different circumstances to further marry the *kokumin* with the *kokka*, or the state, to make a *kokumin-kokka*, or a nation-state. As suggested elsewhere, nation-states beget nation-states, and it was not until the mid-nineteenth century, when the

27. Fukuzawa, *An Encouragement of Learning*, p. 17.

nation-states of the West pressed themselves uncomfortably upon Japan that a nation-state became a political necessity in Japan as well.[28] What emerged in domainal Aizu was less the inkling of a nation, or even a distinctly regional people, than a tellingly premodern, uneven collectivity. Domainal Aizu was an unfixed and uncommitted mass of congeries that could easily unravel. And unravel it did, rather spectacularly, in the domain's final days.

This all happened quickly in the year 1868. After Aizu lost first the political contest over imperial restoration at the end of 1867, then the clash of arms at Toba-Fushimi in the first month of 1868, it braced for an assault on its homeland. Unlike most other places during the Meiji Restoration, Aizu faced a very real crisis of the state as a formidable army led by Satsuma and Chōshū came crashing in, eager to settle old scores with their longtime rival once and for all. When lives, property, and dignity were on the line, how would the people of a domain perform? The challenges of warfare and the reactions of a people unaccustomed to stately service exposed the fatal flaw of the premodern *kyakubun* for all to see.

Three eyewitnesses testified to popular wartime involvement most vividly. Dr. William Willis was an Englishman who arrived in Japan in 1861 as the official physician to the British mission in Japan. Having traveled widely during his stay in Japan, Willis had a solid foundation of knowledge for assessing Aizu. When the Boshin War broke out in 1868, Willis accompanied the new government forces on their campaign in the Hokuriku and the Tōhoku regions, treating casualties on both sides of the conflict. Willis stayed with the advancing army as it fought its way through Aizu into Wakamatsu and witnessed the one-month siege of the castle town during which he tended to some six hundred injured combatants. Willis continually reported his observations to his superior Sir Harry S. Parkes, who then added his own comments and forwarded the war reports to London.

In Aizu, Willis figured that he would encounter hardy mountain men putting up fierce resistance to defend their land and lord. What he got instead surprised and perhaps disappointed him. "I expected to have found in the Aidzu country a peasantry possessing the robust constitution of highlanders and strongly attached to their Chief," he wrote, "instead of which I found a weak, half-starved peasantry that looked upon its Chief as identified with a system of cruel and rapacious oppression."[29] Aizu was no Scotland, as the Englishman discovered. Perhaps it is not surprising that Willis found no domainal affinity, much less war fever, among the commoners of Aizu. But even

---

28. Ravina, *Land and Lordship*, p. 200.

29. Willis, "Report to Sir Harry S. Parkes," p. 8.

Aizu's samurai seemed alarmingly unprepared for the crisis at hand: "The estimate I formed of the Aidzu official class was unfavourable. They appeared to me to be very indifferent about things outside of their province and their country, and spoke in a more narrow and bigoted circle than the corresponding classes in other provinces with which I am acquainted."[30]

In Willis's mind, the myopic samurai of Aizu failed to serve the domain when it needed them the most. "The Aidzu men do not appear to have offered any very determined resistance in the open ground to the advance of the Mikado's forces," he noted. Willis gave more credit to Aizu's "hilly country" terrain than its samurai defenders for frustrating the attack. He wrote that an unseasonable chill and the lack of supplies tested the invaders no less than Aizu resistance. In the end, the only things in Aizu that impressed Willis favorably were the "many stories told of the bravery and energy of the Japanese women who were amongst the besieged. They cut off their hair, busied themselves in preparing food, nursing the wounded, and in not a few instances shouldered the rifle, and bore a share in the fatigues of watching."[31] Beyond these samurai women, Willis reported precious few signs of a remarkable fighting spirit or devotion to the domain in its darkest hour.

Contemporary Japanese observers offered similar indictments of Aizu's wartime performance. Another physician, Matsumoto Jun, who was then the head of the *bakufu*'s Office of Western Medicine and later became Japan's first surgeon general, also found himself in Aizu during the Boshin War. While his personal sympathy seemed to lay with Aizu, Matsumoto's report of wartime Aizu corroborated Willis's. Matsumoto, too, saw in Aizu a helter-skelter pack of self-centered samurai concerned more with their own vainglory than with saving their lord and domain:

> Although the imperial forces threatened all corners, Aizu was not without its chance at victory. However, the domain's retainers zealously competed against one another for individual honor. Consequently, they lacked coordination and a comprehensive plan. This was extremely unfortunate. All Aizu samurai are schooled in the martial arts from an early age, and they share, from the highest elders down to the lowliest retainer, a sense of fraternal equality. Yet their thinking is narrow, and they rather seek personal honor than work together. Such men cannot possibly hope to rescue their state on this occasion.[32]

By contrast, Aizu's commoners fared a bit better in Matsumoto's eyes. In the course of treating two hundred Aizu soldiers hospitalized at Nisshinkan,

30. Ibid.
31. Ibid., pp. 3, 6.
32. Matsumoto, *Ranchū jiden*, p. 72.

he needed to provide more nourishment to his patients. He asked domainal elders for permission to feed some beef to the wounded. After some negotiation with the reluctant officials, he was allowed to do so, and when he began to slaughter one cow every other day, "not a few honest and upright peasants came to offer up their cows," perhaps driven by the cash payment for their livestock as much as sympathy for their overlords.[33]

Like Willis, Matsumoto was quick to disparage the samurai leaders in charge during the war. "Among Aizu's retainers, the talented ones had been stationed mostly in Kyoto and many of them died in the battle at Toba-Fushimi. Therefore, there are not many men worth mentioning in the domain today. Those of any ability are at the bottom of the hierarchy and lack the authority to do anything," he lamented. What leaders Aizu had left initially refused to allow Matsumoto to feed beef to the wounded, stubbornly insisting on preserving domainal precedent even under such dire circumstances. "The domainal founder himself prohibited the killing of cows," the elders argued, "The law must not be changed." Matsumoto then had to appeal directly to Lord Katamori for permission. As he finally served his patients some beef, he caught the same elders surreptitiously helping themselves to the beef. "How despicable it was," Matsumoto spat out.[34]

Having been completely surrounded and cut off from any hope of external aid, Aizu finally surrendered in the ninth month of 1868. As Lord Katamori and his men were carted off to Edo as prisoners of war, the common folks of Aizu hardly seemed to miss their fallen leaders. According to Willis, the disgraced lord evoked little sentiment from the people he once ruled:

> With the exception of the guard, not a dozen of spectators had assembled to witness the departure of the former master of the Aidzu province. On all sides a cold indifference was shown, and not even the peasants at work in the neighbouring fields turned aside to witness the departure of the once renowned

33. Ibid., pp. 71–72.

34. Ibid. Matsumoto's *Ranchū jiden*, including his account of Aizu, later received a heavy dose of nationalized reworking. In 1933, the original text was augmented with nationalistic commentaries and rereleased as Suzuki Yōgo, *Rangaku zenseijidai to ranchū no shōgai* (Tokyo: Tokyo ijishinshikyoku, 1933). The revised version contains several polemic commentaries that were not in the original. For example, the offering of cows by the peasants is presented as "a supreme act of honor performed by the peasants from distant villages in a time of national crisis." The Boshin War in Aizu is described as "a fierce all-out battle waged by the entire country [domain] to serve the lord's grace. It was the realization of a citizen-soldiery in which everyone between the ages of nine and eighty rushed to the battlefield." No such words or spirit concerning popular national service appear in his original autobiography in 1902.

> Prince of Aidzu. Outside the official class, I failed to elicit any expression of pity or sympathy either for the Daimio or his chief advisers who accompanied him, the general opinion being that they had caused a cruel and unnecessary war, and that inasmuch as they had failed to perform *harakiri* in the hour of defeat they had forfeited all title to respect.

"Even if Aidzu and his chief advisers received a free pardon," Willis concluded, "It would be impossible to force them again upon the people of their province."[35] The Matsudaira lords, now reduced to prisoners of war, disappeared from Aizu with nary a peep of remorse from the people they had long ruled.

On the victorious side of the war was Itagaki Taisuke, then the young commander in chief of the Tosa army. When the invasion of Aizu first began, Itagaki was nervous about their chances of victory. "Aizu being one of the great domains of the realm," he would later write, "had those high and low combined their will and served their domain with all their might, it could have easily defeated the imperial forces with our less than five thousand men." However, as the invaders fought their way into Aizu, Itagaki saw that resistance was far less than committal: "When I witnessed all the commoners fleeing with their belongings on their backs, I was deeply impressed. . . . The people avoided conflict and scattered, with none feeling any debt to the many generations of lordly benevolence."

Much disturbed by this experience, Itagaki later presented wartime Aizu as an alarming example of what happens to a polity whose people did not identify themselves with it and did not bother to defend their homeland. "Aizu was destroyed despite being known as one of the great domains of the realm because those who gave themselves to their domain were no more than its five thousand samurai." He then asked, "Upon seeing the fall of their country, the people felt no more remorse than did some livestock—how could this be?"[36]

Itagaki's answer to this rhetorical question was that the *min* had been detached from their *kuni* when in fact they needed to be mobilized as a *kokumin*. He thus offered Aizu as a historical cautionary tale in his introduction to *Jiyūtōshi,* where he called upon the Meiji masses to outgrow their *kyakubun* mentality and cultivate a political commitment as a *kokumin* so as to avoid Aizu's tragedy. What he saw in Aizu, then, was a state betrayed by

---

35. Willis, "Report to Sir Harry S. Parkes," p. 5.

36. Uda and Wada, *Jiyūtōshi*, upper volume, pp. 6–7. Local scholars in Aizu have begun to call attention to the so-called peasant soldiers who participated in Aizu's defense, in part to ameliorate the image of indifferent commoners that Itagaki popularized in *Jiyūtōshi*. See Hoshi Ryōichi's comments in Arakawa, *Meiji nisshi*.

"guests," a people whose identity did not rest with their polity, a people who would not come to its rescue, a people who lacked the personal will to dedicate themselves to stately affairs. Rather than rally together to confront a crisis, the people lost their nerve and abandoned their domain. When push came to shove, two centuries' worth of domainal rhetoric and lip service suddenly came to naught. For a modern nationalist like Itagaki, nothing exposed the dangers of apolitical and unpatriotic masses more convincingly than the uncaring commoners of wartime Aizu.

So Aizu domain lived and died with mere "guests." Meiji Japan could ill afford the same fate.

CHAPTER 3

The Death and Resurrection of Aizu

A Place with No Name

At ten o'clock in the morning of the twenty-second day of the ninth month in 1868, a white flag rose over the northern gate of Tsuruga Castle. The flag could barely be called white, for it had been pieced together with scraps of blood-stained bandages. All the same, it sufficed to signify surrender, ushering in at once a bitter ending and an uncertain beginning for a defeated domain and its people.

The end of hostilities marked a jarring shift from the anguish of lost battles toward an unsettling future. "I was [taking refuge outside the city] when the shooting suddenly stopped," Shiba Gorō would later recall, "The stillness, coming after a month of constant gunfire, made us even more uneasy and left us with an eerie sense of emptiness. The cloudless, late-autumn sky, a vault of brilliant blue, seemed incongruous and strange, and the thin wavering line of red dragonflies, survivors of the autumn season, only added to the feeling of despair that gripped us."[1] Aizu had fallen and defeat was in the air; even an eight-year-old boy could sense that much.

At noon on that day, Lord Matsudaira Katamori and his adopted heir Yoshinori, accompanied by five domainal elders, presented themselves in defeat to Nakamura Hanjirō (later Kirino Toshiaki) of Satsuma and Yamagata Kyōsuke (later Aritomo) of Chōshū who represented the victorious allies. Lord Katamori's surrender brought to an ignoble end two and a quarter centuries of Matsudaira rule and six years of Aizu's national prominence as a significant political player—six years during which the domain sought to realize its grandest ambitions then, failing that, to at least protect its sovereignty. It

---

1. Craig, *Remembering Aizu*, p. 60.

ended, too, six months of fierce combat in which those ambitions were summarily crushed and that sovereignty lost. The young lord's great gamble had brought ruin to his land and death to 2,973 of his men. Aizu's instrument of surrender explained responsibility for the colossal failure in these terms: "Whether the lord, his family, and his samurai retainers will live or die is left solely up to the sacred discretion of the imperial court. However, as regards the domain's people, including the young, the elderly, and the women, they are without knowledge or fault from the start. We beg you to forgive them."[2] It was the guiltless people, however, who were left to rebuild their broken land.

The burden of reconstruction fell upon others as well. Defeat brought about a military occupation that would oversee Aizu's postwar settlement. Those now in charge were unlike any that had ruled Aizu for the past two centuries. They were outsiders from distant places whose right to rule had been confirmed on the battlefield. They were, quite simply, conquerors, but as such they also shouldered the conquerors' burden. What they had destroyed in war could not be left to wither away in peace, and it behooved the new rulers to tend to the damage—physical and otherwise—that they had brought upon Aizu. It had been, after all, a civil war, and a measure of civility was expected to follow.

Unconditional surrender soon forced Aizu into a new, entirely unfamiliar structure of rule. Within a week of the surrender, the victors rounded up and carted off the Matsudaira family and their samurai as prisoners of war to Tokyo and elsewhere and replaced them with the Minseikyoku, or the Office of Civil Administration. This was clearly an organ of foreign occupation, as its leadership roster made clear. Its top administrator was the Echizen samurai Murata Yoshisaburō, and his Echizen colleagues headed each of the three inaugural Minseikyoku departments. Three more departments were added a month later, all run by men from Echizen, Echigo, Shibata, and Kokura domains.[3] Aizu was now firmly in the grasp of outsiders and subject to unprecedented external controls. The new Meiji government institutionalized this arrangement for good when it replaced the Minseikyoku in the fifth month of 1869 with Wakamatsu prefecture, then again in 1876 as Wakamatsu was made a part of Fukushima prefecture. Both the Minseikyoku and the prefectural apparatus acted as agents of the central Meiji state, dispatched to Aizu to do

2. Arakawa, *Meiji nisshi*, p. 177.

3. The extent to which locals were allowed to participate in the Minseikyoku has been debatable. Some claim that Aizu men were not allowed back into government service until Wakamatsu prefecture was founded in the sixth month of 1869 (*AWS*, 6:12). On the other hand, Tasaki Kimitsukasa writes that some former retainers, town officials, and village headmen filled some lower posts in the Minseikyoku. Tasaki. "Aizu sensō to chiiki hensei," p. 18.

Tokyo's bidding. The first governor of Wakamatsu was Shijō Takahira, a courtier and a Meiji official who had been in Aizu inspecting the conquered land for the new government when he was appointed governor.[4] All subsequent prefectural governors were Meiji appointees from distant locales who ultimately answered to the imperial government. Never had Aizu been pulled by such a distant and powerful center of gravity.

Once incorporated into this centralized imperial structure, Aizu lost all its sovereignty as a domain. No longer was Aizu a distinct polity as it had been for so long. It was now demoted to an administrative subunit within the national Meiji apparatus as Wakamatsu prefecture. Aizu would soon not even have that distinction. When Wakamatsu prefecture was absorbed into Fukushima prefecture in 1876, Aizu became a nebulous space. Not only did Aizu devolve into an obscure region—a place with no name—it came to be widely scorned as a deeply problematic one. Meiji leaders defined postwar Aizu not by political boundaries or official designations but instead by its recalcitrant character and reputation as a troublemaker, all linked to its recent imperial blunder and subsequent denigration as "rebels" and "enemies of the court."

A bevy of political, social, and economic problems wrought postwar Aizu and distanced that region from the new ideals of imperial unity. The displacement of Aizu was both figurative and literal. Severe socioeconomic problems in postwar Aizu, coupled with its obstinate and sometimes outright defiant former samurai, redefined the region metaphorically as a thorn in the imperial side and posited Aizu as a foil to national collectivity. The Meiji state also displaced Aizu quite physically when it relocated Aizu's defeated *daimyō* and his samurai to the northern tip of the empire in 1869 and also when it redrew old domainal boundaries as a part of its national administrative overhaul. These dislocations estranged Aizu from Imperial Japan as a region that was, in short, antithetical to modern nationhood.

Yet, postwar Aizu also saw other forces—both intentional and unintentional—that could return Aizu to the national fold. Meiji developmentalism recast Aizu's former samurai as a potentially productive national resource, while the Seinan War of 1877 offered an unlikely yet dramatic opportunity for redemption and national service. Through it all, as the distance between Aizu and nationhood was continually recalibrated and negotiated, Aizu was unmistakably reconstituted as a "region" within Imperial Japan, adding new meanings to the place even as it was being physically erased.

---

4. Shijō was technically the second governor of Wakamatsu, but the first to actually serve. Hayashi Kaneyoshi of Awa domain was the first man appointed governor, but he never took office.

"The People Here Heed Only to Fury"

"It is impossible to speak of this prefecture as one might of any other prefecture." So began a Wakamatsu prefectural report to Tokyo in 1870. "The territory under our jurisdiction is vast yet the roads are poor. Its people are temperamental and stubborn, and the *shizoku* [former samurai] here are especially impoverished."[5] What remained of Aizu domain after the war was riddled with so many problems that the report beseeched Tokyo for more personnel and a bigger budget to help restore badly needed order. War and defeat cast a pall over Aizu society, bringing distinctive complications to bear and isolating postwar Aizu as a unique stigma within Meiji Japan.

Aizu was, first and foremost, a physically broken place. Six months of warfare left visible scars all across the landscape. Along the warpath, even the most rural communities were not spared damage at the hands of attackers and defenders alike. Invaders threatened to destroy some villages to coerce cooperation, defenders torched other villages as they retreated, and many more hapless villages were caught in the crossfire. Both sides requisitioned men and materiel on the march, and coming as they did around harvest time, the locals found these demands especially onerous and unwelcome.

Plenty of anecdotes attest to commoners' plight during the war. According to the diary of a young soldier from the village of Hongō, the domain forced both men and women into combat-related labor. Local women were ordered to cook and deliver rice balls to the front, while the men were to dispose of the dead samurai. The unhappy villagers could hardly be blamed for having simply "thrown the dead into a river" and "muttered curses at the dead Aizu soldiers as they sent the bodies floating downstream."[6] As far as these villagers were concerned, this war was not their war. Jinbo Yazaemon, an Echigo samurai dispatched to Aizu to survey the postwar damage in late 1868, found nothing but desolation in the countryside: "Everything has been taken away, even the peasants' farm implements, horses and oxen at stations, craftsmen's tools, and sacred icons in shrines and temples, not to mention cash, crops, and private possessions. No peasant east of Tsu River has the means to continue farming."[7]

It was Wakamatsu—the site of a vicious one-month siege—that suffered the most. A grainy daguerreotype of the castle taken after the surrender succinctly captured the state of the entire city. The crumbling donjon appears unnaturally distorted and crooked, having absorbed the punishment of several

---

5. Nihon shiseki kyōkai, *Ōkuma Shigenobu kankei monjo,* 2:225–27.
6. Endō, *Aizu Boshin sensō jūgunki,* p. 190.
7. Matsuo, "Meiji shinseifu no chihōshihai," p. 14.

thousand artillery shells. At least the castle was still standing, which could not be said for two-thirds of Wakamatsu that had burned to the ground during the siege. Suffering hardly ended with the war. After the surrender, the occupation forces openly helped themselves to the spoils of victory, claiming entire warehouses by marking them with their domain's name. Ransacked goods "flowed out of Wakamatsu on horseback like a never-ending stream" while merchants in turn rushed into Aizu "eager to buy up war booty on the cheap."[8] Even the highest authorities in Tokyo had to concede that their troops had taken excessive advantage of victory. Four days after the surrender, Kido Takayoshi received a report from Aizu indicating that "victories one after another have inevitably brought out an unfortunate streak of arrogance and brutality in the soldiers of the government army." The minister was advised that "henceforth, appropriate measures must be taken to deal with these troops if we are to win the hearts of the people." As Kido confessed in his diary, "I have been anxious about these matters in recent days."[9]

Refugees who slowly returned to Wakamatsu found their city as Jinbo Yazaemon described it: "Although two months have passed since the surrender, burned homes remain lying on the ground. Corpses are left to rot, with no one to take care of them. The ugliness of this sight is unbearable."[10] When Wakamatsu merchants returned to their town, they discovered that merchants from other domains had taken over their homes and shops, conducting business in their place.[11] Economic activity had ground to a halt and was slow to return to normal. Only in the summer of 1870 were the date and location of the regular Wakamatsu market reestablished. Even then, the prefectural authorities had to artificially stimulate trade by offering to exchange unsold goods for a government loan.[12]

Exacerbating the problem was a famine that happened to strike in 1869, when the postwar recovery effort had barely begun. In the summer of 1869, the worst floods in forty years swept Aizu. "Wind and water damage is quite extensive," one government report warned. "In Iwaki and Iwashiro provinces [the latter covering most of Aizu], there is a terrible famine, and the crop yield in Mishima is one-third the normal amount."[13] Oda Kanshi, a Wakamatsu prefectural inspector who toured the prefecture in 1869, described the famine in Yama county. "The people mostly eat the bark of *tara* trees, and

8. Ogawa, *Shigure zōshi*, p. 35.
9. Brown and Hirota, *The Diary of Kido Takayoshi*, p. 122.
10. Matsuo, "Meiji shinseifu," p. 14.
11. *AWS*, 6:6.
12. Ibid., p. 75.
13. Tadami chōshi hensan iinkai, *Tadami chōshi, shiryōshū*, 4:109.

warabi or *kazura* roots. . . . Everyone has the look of starvation about them."[14] All told, 70 percent of the rice crop was lost in the fall of 1869, dealing a severe blow to reconstruction efforts.[15]

The most violent expression of postwar disorder was a peasant uprising that began three weeks after Aizu fell, and it spread quickly. Dr. William Willis was in a village just outside Wakamatsu when the violence erupted:

> Later on in the day I learnt that the farmers were rioting in several places. Towards the night I could hear the wild uproar of multitudes on all sides. There were large fires in different directions. By ten o'clock the rioters had approached a village about half-a-mile from the one I was stopping in; they fired one of the chief houses; they kept up a constant wild cry, and appeared to be in a state of great excitement. . . . [The village headman] told me that in case of attack he could not protect either me or my property.

Willis then fled for Wakamatsu, and he was lucky to have done so, for "on the following morning, I visited the place I had left the previous night. I found my house a heap of ruins. I was told that not a half-an-hour after my departure 400 or 500 people, many of whom had saws, hatchets, and other cutting implements, came to the house and immediately set about sacking and pulling it down."[16] Ultimately, the so-called *yāyā ikki* engulfed 1,200 households in 1,100 villages and destroyed 170,000 *ryō* worth of property, besides the unquantifiable loss brought about by the destruction of land and debt records.[17]

What the victors had on their hands in Aizu, then, was a veritable hotbed of problems. This was no secret, either. At one point the Meiji government asked Ōmura and Shōnai domains to relocate to Aizu and govern it, but both refused on account of the chaos there.[18] The onus of managing postwar Aizu fell instead upon the Minseikyoku, which was established in Wakamatsu a week after the surrender. In the face of unprecedented disorder and social upheaval, the occupiers took a hard-line approach. Nothing short of martial law governed Aizu in the immediate postwar period, and necessarily so. One

---

14. Oda, *Wakamatsuken hōshokuchū junsatsu nikki.*

15. Mishima chōshi hensan iinkai, *Mishima chōshi,* p. 466.

16. Willis, "Report to Sir Harry S. Parkes," p. 4.

17. Tasaki, "Meiji shonen," p. 116. According to Shōji Kichinosuke, whose work has been made known in English through Stephen Vlastos, *Peasant Protests and Uprisings in Tokugawa Japan,* this movement called for village officials to be selected by the villagers, land equity and redistribution, removal of usurers, tax exemption, recalculation of tax obligation, return of confiscated land, and free land rent. Shōji, *Kindai chihō minshū undōshi.*

18. Matsuo, "Meiji shinseifu," p. 19.

of the first Minseikyoku pronouncements, issued in the name of the "Military Occupation Commandant in Aizu," made this abundantly clear: "On the occasion of recent unrest, evil criminals have banded to break into innocent civilians' homes and commit atrocities, sometimes even feigning the name of a domain in the imperial army. Such men must be apprehended at once, and may be cut down on the spot. Even the lowest-ranking soldiers of the imperial army are authorized to handle these criminals without prejudice."[19] Hostile locals were not to be spared, even if they were samurai. The Occupation Commandant also warned against "some samurai who haughtily proclaim their Aizu retainership and loiter around bearing swords [weapons had been confiscated upon surrender]. If they resist arrest in any way, they may be cut down as needed."[20] Basic peacekeeping remained a pressing issue even after the interim Minseikyoku was replaced by Wakamatsu prefecture in 1869. The 1871 roster of the prefectural staff listed thirty-eight constables, making law enforcement by far the largest employee category, as it accounted for more than one out of three employees.[21]

This heavy-handed image notwithstanding, the new government also envisioned itself as a force of liberation, one that promised to bestow imperial benevolence upon a truculent Aizu. This image was first advertised during the war. As the invading forces marched toward Wakamatsu, they presented themselves as imperial liberators to win local support along the way. "His Majesty is kind enough to love you as His children," they claimed to the people of Aizu: "His Majesty has commanded that villages that submit to the imperial forces will have half of their rice tribute exempted. You shall all appreciate His kindness, strive in agriculture, keep up your households, and do your duty. Since you are all the emperor's people, you shall know to despise the enemies of the court [i.e., Aizu], strive to support the imperial forces, put forth your best efforts, and heed the grace of heaven."[22] As self-proclaimed liberators, the new rulers also offered to forgive past errors, at least to civilians. Their first public pronouncement after their victory assured that "innocent people shall not be harmed; if they surrender, even those who have resisted in the past shall be pardoned."[23]

This promise of magnanimous if patronizing saviors had been made in the heat of battle and now had to be delivered in peace. To a remarkable extent, it was. They did so primarily through direct humanitarian aid, especially to

19. Yamaguchi, *Kinsei Aizushi no kenkyū*, lower vol., p. 270.
20. *AWS*, 6:212–13.
21. Based on data reproduced in Tajima chōshi hensan iinkai, *Tajima chōshi*, 3:39.
22. Dajōkan, ed., *Fukkoki*, 2:134.
23. *AWS*, 6:3.

civilian war victims. Immediately after Tsuruga Castle fell, the victors made available what store was left in it. The Minseikyoku released to the needy public sixty bales of rice and ten barrels of soy paste and provided rice porridge service twice a day to the townspeople.[24] The Minseikyoku also distributed cash to the needy, handing out a total of 11,590 *ryō* to the Wakamatsu poor in the first month of 1869 alone.[25] In nearby Odazuki (present-day Kitakata), which had seen especially heavy combat, the branch office of the Minseikyoku there offered cash aid to local war victims.[26] The new government also supported housing. Since many homes were destroyed during the siege, the Minseikyoku subsidized home reconstruction for 1,349 families in Wakamatsu.[27]

Similarly, merchants received direct economic support from the new authorities. In the fifth month of 1869, the Wakamatsu city alderman requested a loan of 10,000 *ryō* to revive industry and commerce in the wartorn city. In turn, the Minseikoyoku provided smaller, six-month loans to small and medium-sized businesses.[28] Even some war captives received handouts. Nonsamurai prisoners of war and samurai women and children who had been detained by the Minseikyoku office in Odazuki were each given the equivalent of a two-man stipend upon their release.[29]

These acts of goodwill appear to have been triggered by new and extraordinary conditions but, in fact, they continued a line of political practice that had been in place since the domainal days. The domain had long provided emergency aid and subsidies in times of disaster, and local society expected no less from their new rulers. One irony in the liberator concept was just how often the liberators were expected to act much like the very authority they had just destroyed. Established expectations regarding lordly morality and munificence proved durable. For instance, the domainal government had often rewarded commoners who demonstrated moral excellence. After the war, the Minseikyoku felt compelled to continue this practice in several ways. In the first month of 1869, the Minseikyoku solicited information about those who had committed "righteous and filial deeds" during the war, such as "carrying their parents on their back or helping out their masters," and advertised its moral authority by rewarding such upright conduct.[30] To demonstrate its

24. Yamaguchi, *Kinsei Aizushi no kenkyū*, lower volume, p. 273.
25. *AWS*, 6:4.
26. Kitakata shishi hensan iinkai, *Kitakata shishi*, 6:15–16.
27. Yamaguchi, *Kinsei Aizushi no kenkyū*, lower volume, p. 274.
28. Ibid., p. 282.
29. Tasaki, "Meiji shonen," p. 135; Matsuo, "Meiji shinseifu," p. 13.
30. Tasaki, "Meiji shonen," p. 121.

filial piety, the Odazuki branch office had area villages identify seniors over sixty years old and presented them congratulatory sake.

More tellingly, when the new government failed to display traditional benevolence, the people noticed. Each winter, five major shrines in Wakamatsu conducted an elaborate prayer ritual, and even amid the rubble of war, town leaders wished to do the same. In the third month of 1869, the Wakamatsu city alderman reminded the Minseikyoku that it should sponsor the event just as the Matsudaira had done in years past. "This being an auspicious precedent," the alderman pointed out, the Minseikyoku was obliged to support the event "upon this occasion of Restoration."[31] Local leaders saw no irony in invoking the Restoration to prod the new government into maintaining the domainal status quo. More often than not, continuity was the norm in immediate postwar Aizu. While the Minseikyoku was a postwar occupation authority composed chiefly of outsiders, it perpetuated many political practices of the previous power holders. The Minseikyoku might have advertised its policies as "imperial renewal," but in substance, it brought little change to local political patterns. Despite the rhetorical implications of "renewal," the Minseikyoku was hardly liberating or innovative. As an ad hoc administration, the Minseikyoku did not arrive in Aizu intent on remaking its people or reformulating its political norms. It had neither the will, the manpower, nor the mandate to fundamentally redefine political life in Aizu.

Instead, Aizu's new administrators were too preoccupied with maintaining order—a task they could barely handle, in part because of Aizu's recalcitrant combat veterans. More than a few samurai, disenfranchised and disenchanted in the aftermath of defeat, turned into agitators. Some became petty criminals, others were more organized; they all touched political nerves. Petulant samurai reinforced Aizu's image as a troublemaker and further highlighted Aizu as a problematic place that flew in the face of imperial authority.

The men who had fought to protect Aizu but failed were detained as criminals and prisoners of war following the surrender. They were disarmed, taken into captivity, and split up into detention camps in Aizu, Takada, and Tokyo. Shiba Gorō was among those sent to the new imperial capital. "We must have looked like a procession of beggars," he recalled, "Men with arms in slings, others limping on crutches, still others struggling to keep up but gradually falling behind, and not least of all, the gray-haired elderly carried piggyback by their attendants. We walked in complete silence, each burdened with his own fate."[32]

---

31. Ibid., p. 120.
32. Craig, *Remembering Aizu*, p. 71.

They were held in so-called Disciplinary Confinement Centers, but some not for long. In the first week of the eighth month of 1869 alone, thirty-seven Aizu detainees in Tokyo broke free; three who were captured were beheaded.[33] Twenty others who escaped captivity in Takada were also caught and beheaded in the same month.[34] Enough captives escaped over time that in the second month of 1869, twenty-eight guard stations were set up along the Aizu border to catch those fugitives as they tried to make their way back home.[35]

Once they escaped and returned to Aizu, many of the runaway samurai found little to do but raise trouble. A number of crimes, including roadside ambushes and armed robberies, were said to be perpetrated by such fugitives.[36] These fallen samurai added to a general sense of lawlessness in postwar Aizu that undermined much-needed reconstruction efforts. As one government inspector reported in 1870: "Those who have surrendered are filled with discontent. In the aftermath of war, they stir up trouble-making commoners, who bring much grief to administrators by burning or stealing official records. . . . These people simply do as they please."[37]

Some rogue samurai did much more. Two types of illicit activities were sophisticated and politically sensitive enough to warrant serious attention from both prefectural and central authorities. The first was widespread counterfeit currency schemes that plagued the prefecture between 1868 and 1872. The second was a series of antigovernment insurrections hatched between 1869 and 1876. Both directly challenged the imperial government's authority, one symbolically and the other physically, and confirmed Aizu's reputation as a place inimical to central authority.

The first cause of headaches for Wakamatsu prefecture was once described as nothing less than "the single greatest problem of all the problems facing the government" in the immediate postwar.[38] Counterfeit production distressed the Meiji government, especially when it discovered that the bulk of the bogus currency was being minted in Aizu by its former samurai. Certainly, counterfeit was produced in several places throughout Japan in the first few disorderly years of Meiji rule. But nowhere was the problem so acute and politicized than it was in Aizu, prompting one aggravated Meiji official to call Aizu "the national breeding ground of counterfeit."[39]

---

33. Dajōkan, ed., *Dajōruiten*, 217, microfilm *tai*-24-1580.
34. Arakawa, *Meiji nisshi*, pp. 203–4.
35. *Tadami chōshi*, 7: 212.
36. Tasaki, "Aizu sensō to," p. 13.
37. Nihon shiseki kyōkai, ed., *Ōkuma Shigenobu kankei monjo*, 1: 226.
38. Ōkurashō, ed., *Meiji zenki zaiseikeizai shiryōshūsei*, 13:77.
39. *Kōbunroku*, vol. 28, microfilm *kō*-004-273.

Currency manipulation began in the domain's final days. Following its defeat in the Battle of Toba-Fushimi and retreat to Aizu, the domain took to a creative means of raising cash as it prepared for defense. According to one record, Lord Katamori returned to Wakamatsu with some Edo goldsmiths. He put them to work in the western enceinte of Tsuruga Castle, where they pounded and stretched one-*bu* silver coins and cut them into three pieces. The domain then designated each piece to be worth two *bu*. One *bu* of silver was thus made to yield six *bu*.[40] This devalued coinage came to be called "castle cash," and some two million *ryō* worth made their way into the local money supply and markets beyond.

The chaos of postwar occupation both necessitated and encouraged counterfeiting in Aizu. Deputy Inspector Okatani Shigetomi testified in his 1869 report *Aizu jijō* that "because the Minseikyoku was remiss, people are publicly and openly making counterfeit in Wakamatsu." Even some unscrupulous Minseikyoku officials were themselves engaged in the counterfeit business. A samurai from Yonezawa domain stationed in Wakamatsu named Kitamura Tokutarō produced counterfeit, purporting to do so with official approval. "Crooked officials make counterfeit under the pretense of official approval, and gullible people accept it as genuine," Okatani reported, "As a result, counterfeit has come to overrun the city." The prefecture was forced to concede as much in 1870: "The entirety of Wakamatsu prefecture has become a nest of counterfeiters. Counterfeit is so extremely prevalent that every person in every household is seemingly connected with this crime."[41]

Since counterfeiting flagrantly challenged one of the government's basic authorities, the prefecture struck back accordingly. Its first governor, Shijō Takahira, made the issue a top priority as soon as he took office in the fall of 1869. The first proclamation of his tenure warned against counterfeit, and four days later, he ordered a round of raids. Governor Shijō advocated a stern approach by explaining, "The imperial court's leniency has only exacerbated the problem. The old laws of the former Aizu domain were ferociously stringent on this matter. Truth be told, the people here only heed to fury and firm resolve."[42] The governor also tagged the crime a political one, condemning counterfeiters for acting "in contemptuous disregard of imperial authority."[43] Shijō requested and received from Tokyo executive powers to punish counterfeiters, and he

40. Okatani, "Aizu rakujōgo."

41. *Kōbunroku*, vol. 1, no. 28, microfilm *kō*-004-273.

42. Ibid., *kō*-004-257. Records of counterfeiting in domainal times can be found in *AKJ*, 85:242–46; 251–52.

43. *Kōbunroku*, vol. 1, no. 28, microfilm *kō*-004-274.

was quick to use them. Of the 123 criminals that the prefecture exiled or executed in 1870, a full 100 of them were counterfeiters. Counterfeiters were down to 20 in the following year, but still represented a remarkable percentage of the 48 total cases of corporal punishment.[44] The zealous governor even requested that troops from neighboring domains be mobilized to catch counterfeiters at border checkpoints. In the eighth month of 1870, 13 domains dispatched their soldiers to Aizu at the Army Ministry's urging and rounded up about 200 suspects.[45] In the end, Governor Shijō proudly reported that some 1,200 suspected counterfeiters had been apprehended.[46]

As Wakamatsu prefecture reported to the central government, the main perpetrators were former domainal retainers who had escaped detention camps.[47] In the seventh month of 1870 alone, the prefecture identified 93 such men involved in counterfeit schemes, leading Shijō to conclude, "Wakamatsu is a veritable den of counterfeiters, and at the root of this problem are the former domainal retainers."[48] He would often be proven correct. In many cases, samurai masterminded a team of peasants who provided the labor, craftsmen who supplied the technical skills, and merchants who traded or knowingly accepted counterfeit. One such operation was led by Suzuki Jōnosuke, a onetime low-ranking samurai. Jōnosuke, after being released from his postwar internment in Inawashiro, organized two residents of Nakaji village to provide funds and supplies to produce fake one-*bu* silver coins. He recruited the technical assistance of a gunsmith in Wakamatsu and set up shop in the mountains, where they made about seven hundred *ryō* worth of counterfeit. They divided the coinage among eight partners, including a Shintō priest. In 1870, four of them—three samurai, including Jōnosuke, and one commoner—were captured and beheaded, and the rest were exiled for seven to ten years.[49]

There were even more elaborate schemes, as some larger operations reportedly involved selling fakes at a discount for authentic cash, exporting counterfeit to Niigata, or colluding with the manager of the Tokyo Tsukiji

---

44. Calculated from Matsuo, "Meiji shonen no gan'akukahei mondai to shinseiken," p. 191, chart 1.

45. *Kōbunroku*, vol. 1, no. 28, microfilm *kō*-004-276 through 281.

46. Ibid., *kō*-004-273.

47. *AWS*, 6:16.

48. *Kōbunroku*, vol. 1, no. 28, *kō*-004-253; list of suspects on *kō*-004-259 through 261. Those who were punished tended to be nonsamurai. For example, of the one hundred punished in 1870, only five were samurai, with the rest being merchants and peasants. Selective punishment may reflect the prefecture's desire not to agitate the samurai population any further.

49. Fukushima-ken, *Fukushima-ken shiryō*, vol. 5.

Hotel to pass off 1,300 *ryō* of counterfeit to Western traders in Tokyo and Yokohama.[50] Aizu-made counterfeit thus made its way overseas, causing one foreign diplomat to complain, if hyperbolically, that thirty million *ryō* in counterfeit had been passed off to unsuspecting foreign merchants. He demanded that the Japanese government "either exchange it for legitimate currency or compensate six million *ryō* in gold for damages."[51]

This may explain why the Ministry of Finance instituted a generous buyback program. Prefectures were to seize the counterfeit, which the ministry then exchanged for legitimate currency to get the fakes off the market. This program fetched 1,396,797 *ryō* of counterfeit nationwide (exchanged for 417,184 *ryō*), and its results confirmed Aizu's reputation as "a nest of counterfeiters." Wakamatsu prefecture was by far the worst offender, having yielded 177,858 *ryō* of counterfeit, or more than 12 percent of the national total. Despite this campaign, the problem seems to have lingered in Aizu. As Sawa Kantoku, the Wakamatsu governor in 1874, testified, "There is still much counterfeit in Wakamatsu prefecture. . . . If the laws were applied to the letter, every resident of the prefecture would have to be deemed guilty."[52]

The counterfeit problem even led to politically motivated violence in Aizu, the most notable being the so-called Tabanematsu Incident in 1869. The Minseikyoku's chief of police and prisons was an Echizen samurai named Kubomura Monjirō. He had led the Minseikyoku's crackdown on Aizu counterfeiters and was reputed to have executed several innocent people in the process. Furthermore, it was said, Kubomura had earned the ire of Aizu men for his frequent slander of the former lord and his samurai. As Kubomura made his way back home to Echizen after the Minseikyoku was dissolved in the sixth month of 1869, he was fatally ambushed at Tabanematsu Peak by two Aizu war veterans, Ban Hyakuetsu and Takatsu Heizō.[53] Ban went into hiding but was soon discovered and committed suicide, while Takatsu escaped and was to make even more trouble later.

The assassination of a high-ranking official was disturbing enough. Worse yet were the whispers of an Aizu insurrection among former domainal retainers. Just two months after the Tabanematsu Incident, two separate groups of Aizu fugitives were discovered to be plotting a rebellion against the new prefecture and perhaps more. One band was led by Kameda Yasubei, a twenty-year-old

---

50. *Kōbunroku*, vol. 1, no. 28, *kō*-004-258.

51. Ibid., *kō*-068-089.

52. "Kengensho sono ta," document F288, Fukushimaken bunka sentā rekishishiryōkan.

53. *AWS*, 6:7; *Kōbunroku*, vol. 1, no. 28, *kō*-062-1084.

former samurai. According to Army Ministry documents, Yasubei escaped the Shiokawa detention camp and hid out in southern Aizu, where he allegedly "recruited defeated soldiers and planned a rebellious uprising." Yasubei and three accomplices—two ex-samurai and one former peasant soldier—broke into a local home and stole cash and clothing and prepared to return to Wakamatsu. They were captured along the way, and in the eighth month of 1869 they were beheaded in Wakamatsu.[54] Later in the same month, four other former Aizu samurai who escaped their detention in Tokyo were said to be planning a similar scheme. When the police raided their hideout in Kanda, they narrowly escaped; the authorities could only warn that "the men might return and plot their rebellion once again."[55] Such extremists were only a small portion of Aizu's former retainers, but they were sufficient to raise the specter of insurrection and did nothing to undo Aizu's reputation as an "enemy of the court."

The most dramatic display of Aizu rebelliousness was the Shianbashi Incident, a plot masterminded by Nagaoka Hisashige who was once a prominent Aizu official. Nagaoka had excelled as a young student at the Nisshinkan and Shōheikō. When the Boshin War broke out, he was detained under house arrest in Edo until 1869, after which he rejoined his former Aizu colleagues in Tonami domain. He later returned to Tokyo and founded a short-lived newspaper company called the Shūshisha and published the antigovernment paper *Hyōron shinbun*. After the paper failed, Nagaoka took up residence in Hongō and began to collaborate with Maebara Issei and Okudaira Kensuke from Chōshū to plan a samurai revolt against the imperial government.

Sometime in October 1876, Nagaoka received a coded message by telegraph indicating that Maebara was ready to begin his uprising in Chōshū. Nagaoka then kicked his own plan into motion. He and his compatriots planned to take a boat from Shianbashi in Tokyo to Chiba prefecture, where they hoped to recruit sympathizers among Chiba's police officers. They were then to attack the Chiba prefectural office and join Maebara's forces as they fought their way north to Wakamatsu. There they would establish their antigovernment base and raise the banner of rebellion.

Nagaoka's gang never made it out of Tokyo. On October 29th, the day after Maebara began his uprising in Hagi, Nagaoka and his thirteen accomplices stole their way to Shianbashi under the cover of night. The *Yūbin hōchi* newspaper reported what happened next:

> At about 1:30 in the morning, fourteen or fifteen *shizoku* boarded seven boats headed for Chiba. Because they were acting suspiciously, the boatman secretly

54. *Dajō ruiten*, vol. 1, no. 217, *tai*-024-1580.
55. Ibid., *kō*-010-0606.

> alerted the police.[56] When four officers arrived and demanded the men's names, the suspects suddenly drew out their hidden blades from their dummy umbrellas and attacked. One officer was killed immediately, two were wounded seriously, and one was cut in the back but managed to report back to the station. The station's officers realized that there was serious trouble and raced to the scene, some holding lanterns and some with nightsticks under their arms. Finally, they captured six of the brigands and sent them off to the third precinct.
>
> Also it is said that at about 3 AM the same day, several tens of officers scoured the Fukagawa area, and found five more suspects rowing a small boat down Sumida River. Ten-odd officers in two boats sandwiched them and tried to force them ashore. Officers along both riverbanks cheered them on as the brigands readied their blades and made as if they would attack if accosted. . . . But then one of them called out to the boat on the left, and yelled, "We're done for; take our weapons." Surprisingly, he then gave up his sword. The officers drew their boats closer and captured the five men. It is thought that the suspects spoke with an Ōshū accent.[57]

During the melee, Nagaoka was badly cut in the waist by an errant comrade but managed to escape. He was soon captured and, in January 1877, he died in prison at the age of thirty-eight. Three more conspirators were caught and beheaded, including Takatsu Heizō, who had been wanted by the government for his role in the 1869 Tabanematsu Incident. Eight others received prison terms ranging from a year to life.[58]

The Shianbashi Incident ended as a false start, managing to incite far less trouble than Maebara and Okuhira's failed rebellion in Hagi. Nonetheless, the dramatic roundup rattled Meiji authorities because it occurred right under their noses in Tokyo. It also revealed a nationwide network of rebellious *shizoku* who could rise up simultaneously across the country. The incident uncovered as well some disturbing patterns of local solidarity, as it was driven in good part by Aizu men's shared enmity toward the Meiji government. The plot was headed by Nagaoka, once a fairly prominent Aizu samurai, and seven of the conspirators were from Aizu. Furthermore, Nagaoka had chosen to attack Chiba because he had learned that there were about sixty Aizu natives working as Chiba policemen, including the deputy police commissioner, and he had counted on their sympathy and support. Regional

---

56. Evidently, the police knew about the plot beforehand. Two young Aizu students who were living at Nagaoka's house informed the police of their patron's plans the night before. Ishii, "Shianbashi jiken no kaiko," pp. 33–36.

57. "Bōto keibuhosa nado o sasshō su," *Yubin hōchi shinbun,* October 31, 1876.

58. Ibid.

fraternity and expectations based on it—naive though they may have been in this case—drove the failed insurrection. For these reasons, some have celebrated the Shianbashi Incident as a distinctly Aizu event and heralded Nagaoka as a tragic hometown hero. In 1916, several prominent Aizu men held commemorative services in Asakusa to honor the five Aizu conspirators who died as a result of the incident.[59] The Shianbashi Incident, along with other signs of Aizu samurai disturbance, confirmed Aizu as an anathema and a thorn in the side of the imperial polity.

Ultimately, no armed uprising occurred in Aizu, and the specter of violently disgruntled Aizu samurai remained mostly that. As it was, that menace materialized mostly in domains that had prevailed in the Boshin War, not in a place like Aizu that had already tasted defeat. Nonetheless, Aizu's defiant samurai presented enough of a threat to make both the Minseikyoku and Wakamatsu prefecture deeply wary about the task of controlling them. Following the Tabanematsu Incident, a government investigator dispatched to Aizu issued this warning to Matsudaira Keisaburō, the infant son of the now-retired Lord Katamori and the putative head of the Matsudaira family: "Among you and your father's men, there are those who have escaped detention and hidden, and from time to time these fugitives perpetrate wanton violence. These rebellious men who assemble to cause trouble must be a source of deep concern to you both, as they reflect poorly on your own positions."[60] In the end, the investigator ordered the Matsudaira to "quickly round up the ringleaders and demonstrate your effectiveness," all but conceding that bitter Aizu samurai do not heed Meiji authority. Yet again it was as if postwar Aizu had somehow drifted beyond the pale and out onto the figurative fringe of the imperial landscape.

"The Most Barbaric Hinterland in the Empire"

Aizu was in fact pushed out to the edge, not only metaphorically but quite physically as well. Beset by myriad problems there, prefectural and central authorities alike began to conclude that remnants of the rebel domain are best rounded up and quarantined. Governor Shijō eagerly pressed the central government into re-creating a domainal polity that could contain Aizu's *shizoku*—but not in Aizu. Rather, he proposed that they be relocated elsewhere under Matsudaira lordship. "The former domainal retainers residing

59. Ishii, "Shianbashi jiken no kaiko," p. 30.

60. Nishi Aizuchōshi hensan iinkai, ed., *Nishi Aizuchōshi*, 5:27–28. Keisaburō was born in the sixth month of 1869 while his father was still in captivity. He was later renamed Kataharu.

in the prefecture are stubborn to the bone. They are the root of all our problems here," he complained, "If we delay the relocation of these men, it would interfere with all aspects of governance. There is no better way to imperialize the people and wash away old habits than samurai relocation."[61] Once a new domain was re-created for them elsewhere, Shijō promised that Aizu "can be swept clean, the counterfeiters eradicated, and the land purified." But as long as disruptive *shizoku* remained in Aizu, there would never be peace in his prefecture and "all the efforts we have made to this day will be for naught."[62]

The governor also argued that physical removal of undesirable domainal vestiges would relieve his prefecture of a major financial onus as well. Shijō was unhappy about having to support Aizu's impoverished *shizoku,* complaining to the central government that "the former domainal retainers are eating up the prefectural budget. Between the surrender last year and the third month of this year, 10,000 *koku* of rice and 160,000 *ryō* have disappeared." Rather than burden his prefecture, the governor proposed, the *shizoku* could be doing productive agricultural work up in northern Japan. "If they can make bountiful that barren land, it would bring great benefit to the empire," he envisioned. Better still, "it is like killing two birds with one stone, for it would benefit the *shizoku* while coming at no loss to the imperial court," he proposed.[63]

As unlikely as the revival of Matsudaira lordship seemed after the war, the idea of recreating Aizu was, by the time Shijō wrote those words, reasonably within the Meiji political purview. After the Restoration and the Boshin War, the Aizu Matsudaira were branded "enemies of the court," stripped of their titles and holdings, and placed under punitive custody of Okayama and Kurume domains. Kido Takayoshi, the Chōshū man in charge of punishments against Aizu, had initially taken a hard-line stance. Kido denounced Aizu as "the greatest villain of all" for its "many years of criminal intent" during the *bakumatsu* years and concluded that "clemency is impossible."[64] Likewise, the lord of Chōshū Mōri Takachika sought to make an example out of his longtime foes. "We must instill fear by punishing the unruly rebels," he argued in 1868, "and make it impossible for others to harbor any rebellious thoughts."[65]

By the following year, however, Kido grew convinced that excessive punishment would "cast doubt on our aspirations for benevolent government"

61. *Kōbunroku,* vol. 1, no. 28, *kō*-004-257.
62. Ibid., *kō*-004-255.
63. Ibid., *kō*-004-248.
64. Nihon shiseki kyōkai, ed., *Kido Takayoshi monjo*, 3:155–58.
65. Tokutomi, *Kinsei Nihon kokuminshi*, 78:5.

and create "a multitude of *rōnin* who would interfere with governance."[66] After he met with a certain Koide Tetsunosuke, an Aizu man who had entered the Buddhist priesthood upon surrender and was "secretly making efforts on behalf of his old country," Kido came to think that "the Aizu men are truly penitent, and they are going to a great deal of trouble to redeem themselves for their treason against the Imperial Government. Their feelings deserve our pity." Thus he concluded, "The Imperial Government now regards everyone in the Empire as equal to everyone else as a matter of course. It would be highly improper to show partiality to any particular group." Kido attributed this conciliatory tone to nothing less than "His Majesty's own wishes."[67]

Consequently, Katamori's infant son Keisaburō was restored to *daimyō* status in the eleventh month of 1869 and given a very modest enfeoffment of thirty thousand *koku* on the northernmost tip of Mutsu province. There they were to set up self-sufficient agricultural communities with support from the central government. This domain would be the new home for Aizu's surviving *shizoku* and their families, where they could reassemble under their old lord and start life anew. The defeated were now given an unlikely opportunity for redemption and a chance to re-create their old polity in a distant frontier.

Their new home was named Tonami to reflect hope for a brighter future. The name is commonly said to be taken from a line in a Chinese poem—"All land south of the Big Dipper is imperial land"—to remind themselves that though they were now in the distant north, they remained still within the imperial realm.[68] Nagaoka Hisashige, the later rebel who was chosen to help lead the new domain, expressed his dreams in this hopeful poem:

> Though ash once gray burns no more
> Heaven has proven kind after all;
> Tonami port in ten years' time
> Shall welcome ships from round the world.[69]

Their hopes were quickly betrayed. Tonami was an oddly shaped domain that was splintered in two, as Shichinohe domain divided Tonami's northern half from the southern half. The Aizu transplants were scattered across this

---

66. Brown and Hirota, *The Diary of Kido Takayoshi,* p. 189; Nihon shiseki kyōkai, *Kido Takayoshi monjo,* 3:156.

67. Ibid., p. 197.

68. Sasazawa, *Shimokita hantōshi,* p. 52. A more iconoclastic and imaginative hypothesis by a local historian, Kasai Tomio, holds that the name Tonami referred to the constellation Sagittarius, which aims its arrow at Scorpio, which supposedly represents Satsuma and Chōshū. Kasai, *Aizu Tonami hanshi,* p. 53.

69. Hoshi, *Tonami ni ikita Aizuhan no hitobito,* p. 102.

vast and unforgiving terrain, which was often frozen and barren. Tonami was nominally assessed at thirty thousand *koku*, but its punishing winter and poor soil composed of volcanic ash meant that it was, in truth, worth only six or seven thousand *koku*. This was a far cry from the days when Aizu boasted as much as 270,000 *koku*. Tonami's paltry output was far from enough to support its *shizoku* population, much less contribute to national prosperity.

They did not yet know this in the spring of 1870 when the Aizu samurai and their families started arriving in Tonami, some by land and some by sea, to begin lives anew. As a clearly sympathetic Ōta Hiroki, the lieutenant governor of the neighboring Hachinohe domain, wrote in his diary, "Though the Aizu families have arrived, they have no shelter, furniture, bedding, coal, salt, or soy paste. At best they manage to squeeze six or seven people into a single tiny farmhouse, just barely shielding themselves from raindrops."[70] Even under more favorable circumstances, samurai who suddenly had to trade their swords for hoes were hardly fit for agriculture; as it was, they had even less of a chance. Tonami's soil was too lean for rice, and the new residents tried their hands at growing dry rice, soybeans, millet, sesame, potatoes, tea, and sweet potatoes. One such makeshift farmer was Arakawa Katsushige, who had just been released from internment in Takada and followed his lord to Tonami with his elderly mother, wife, two sons, and two daughters. He had some luck with potatoes; the three *shō* [1 *shō* equals about 1.8 liters] of potatoes that he planted yielded forty-seven *shō*. But fifty *shō* of buckwheat that he planted were reduced to one *shō*, while twenty *shō* of *kurimochi* was mostly eaten by his neighbor's horse, leaving only one *shō*. The horse also devoured most of the family's daikon radish.[71]

In their hunger, the Aizu transplants ate whatever the land sparingly yielded, including ground kelp, tree leaves, and dog meat. Unsympathetic locals disparaged the disgraced outsiders as "Aizu caterpillars," because they would eat just about anything, and "Aizu pigeon samurai" because they ate soy dregs as pigeons do.[72] Not surprisingly, malnutrition and starvation ran rampant. An 1871 prefectural report found that "many Tonami residents, whether young or old, male or female, are suffering from intestinal parasites, often fatally. Physicians have determined that because their diet is so poor, they cannot digest properly. . . . The afflicted rarely survive." The situation led the report to conclude, "Tonami is the most barbaric hinterland in the empire."[73] Another

---

70. Aomori-ken, ed., *Aomori kenshi,* 6:105.
71. Arakawa, *Meiji nisshi,* p. 103.
72. Ibid., p. 163.
73. Aomori-ken, *Aomori kenshi,* 6:86.

report to the Ministry of Finance conceded in 1871, "Truly, it is no exaggeration to say that these are the most pitiful people in the empire."[74] Tonami was no promised land, as Yamakawa Hiroshi, the domain's administrative leader and regent to the young lord, became all too aware:

> To those who ask of Tonami in the north,
> tell them this;
> It is a land before human time.[75]

Given these conditions, some saw no reason to stay on this desolate, alien land. In the hamlet of Sai, 156 of 272 residents drifted off between 1870 and 1871. A quarter to a third of the population fled Tonami as a whole, including, soon enough, their lord.[76] Matsudaira Katamori and his family left Tonami for the comforts of Tokyo as soon as domains were abolished in the seventh month of 1871, all but abandoning their retainers who had hoped to recreate Aizu in the northern frontier. "The samurai in Tonami were devastated," Shiba Gorō wrote, "The work of developing the land had only begun. Bereft of their mainstay and support, they would have to fend for themselves. Aizu was no more; their dreams of restoring the domain to its former glory had dissipated like the morning fog."[77] In 1872 Tonami was absorbed into Aomori prefecture. By the year's end, Aomori prefecture suspended all developmental projects in former Tonami, and in April 1873, all Aizu émigrés in Tonami were ordered to return to Wakamatsu or disperse to other prefectures as they saw fit.

Tonami proved to be a debacle, but collective suffering also had a galvanizing effect. In the depth of their first winter in Tonami, the Shiba family was reduced to eating dog meat for sustenance. One day, young Gorō reached his limit and could no longer swallow his grisly meal:

> My father noticed this. "Have you forgotten that you are the son of a samurai? In war, when soldiers run out of food, they'll eat cats, dogs, anything to keep on fighting. We came to this miserable, forsaken wilderness because we were hounded by the enemy. If those scoundrels from Satsuma and Chōshū ever hear that the Aizu samurai have died of starvation, they'll ridicule us. Our domain will go down in infamy. This is a battlefield, do you hear? It's a battlefield until the day Aizu wipes the stain from its honor." My father, who was usually soft-spoken, had scolded me with unexpected vehemence.[78]

---

74. Ibid., pp. 43–55.
75. Yamakawa, *Sakurayamashū*.
76. Kasai, *Aizu Tonami hanshi*, p. 106.
77. Craig, *Remembering Aizu*, p. 98.
78. Ibid., p. 89.

Moments like this caused Gorō to conclude that Tonami was a punishment, the kind of venom that the imperial state reserved especially for Aizu. "Let me be absolutely candid and say that Tonami was neither the revival of the domain nor an act of mercy," he declared. "This was an exile, pure and simple, and at no time in our nation's history had an entire domain been subjected to such cruel punishment."[79] Physical dislocation to Tonami became a cornerstone of Aizu's victim narrative, and the émigrés remembered the Tonami years as a powerful collective misery that affirmed their identity as the defeated. The humiliation of being chased off to the empire's edge served to divorce the region from the nation further still.

Meanwhile, the Aizu homeland itself was also subjected to various forms of physical displacement, all designed to eradicate old political loyalties and alignments. The new prefectural authorities consciously set out to destroy material reminders of Aizu's domainal past. Their first target was Tsuruga Castle, for no structure in Wakamatsu was more physically prominent or politically iconic. It had monumentalized domainal authority to those who lived under its literal shadows for almost three centuries. After the war, the castle also cast a figurative shadow as a broken embodiment of defeat. Its decrepit exterior betrayed the sorry state of the entire town, while its silent interior housed the ghosts of many who had died defending it. "The gateway has collapsed and the mounds are in ruin. The pitiful sight is barely tolerable," Governor Sawa Kantoku wrote of the once majestic castle in 1873. "All who pass by cannot help but recall the painful past."[80] The castle stood as a poignant reminder of failed resistance and fallen authority that lingered all too uncomfortably in postwar Wakamatsu.

Immediately after its fall, the castle was taken over by the Army Ministry and placed under the Sendai commandant's jurisdiction. In 1869 some Wakamatsu prefectural offices were built on the castle grounds and the prefecture began to chisel away at the sprawling compound. In 1871, parts of the northern enceinte, the eastern gate, and all the surrounding stockades were torn down. Later in the year, prefectural authorities filled the moat and sold it off as farmland to nearby residents.[81] Other parts of the castle compound were similarly converted, and Arakawa Katsushige, the former domainal retainer who had just returned from Tonami in 1873, took a day job planting mulberry trees on the now desolate grounds where he used to report for duty.[82] A good

---

79. Ibid., p. 98.
80. *MKS*, 2:1035.
81. *AWS*, 6:32–33.
82. Arakawa, *Meiji nisshi*, p. 183.

portion of the old samurai estates surrounding the castle were confiscated, flattened into fields, and sold off for cheap or even given away for free. In 1871 the prefecture disposed as farmland more than twenty-five acres of samurai property abutting the castle.[83]

By 1874 much of the castle and its environs had been taken apart piece by piece so that it barely resembled its old self. When the new prefectural office was constructed elsewhere in the city at the end of 1873, what remained of the castle, including the dilapidated donjon, fell entirely into disuse. In December 1873, Governor Sawa wrote to Iwakura Tomomi in Tokyo, requesting that the entire castle be demolished for good. The governor cited economic and emotional reasons for this: "Rather than leave the castle to wither in wind and rain, dismantling the castle would allow us to at once save repair and maintenance costs, and also ease the saddened hearts of Aizu's samurai and commoners."[84] Governor Sawa must have been planning this for some time, as he attached a highly detailed inventory of the castle compounds to his memorial. Iwakura forwarded Sawa's request to the army minister, Yamagata Aritomo, who approved the demolition in January 1874.

The prefecture's plan, announced in February, called for the forty-six structures left on the grounds to be disassembled and the material auctioned off to the public. Wakamatsu residents had until the tenth of March to submit bids, but the deadline came and went without a single offer, perhaps out of respect for the old lords or simply because few locals had either the means or the need. Finally, more than a month after the deadline, Machino Mondo, the Wakamatsu town supervisor and a former domainal official, organized a bid of 862 yen and submitted it to the prefecture.

Before being demolished, the castle would serve a political purpose one last time. In March 1874, as the buildings awaited their bidders, Governor Sawa asked Colonel Miyoshi Shigetomi, the Sendai commandant, for permission to open the castle for public exhibition. "More than a few prefectural residents have asked to tour the castle before it is taken down," Sawa wrote, "They have asked us to hold an exhibition there. As this helps to advance popular knowledge, I request your permission." Colonel Miyoshi initially declined, saying that "if a large crowd of people enter the castle, they will naturally cause damage to the structures" and "lower their value before any bids have been made."[85] As the two sides discussed the matter, Machino's bid came in, clearing the way for a twenty-day exhibition that ran from April into May.

---

83. *AWS,* 6:41.
84. *MKS,* 2:1035.
85. Miyanouchi, "Wakamatsujō nyūsatsu ni tsuite," p. 4.

For a modest entry fee of two sen, any ordinary person could roam the grounds once reserved for the elite and see for themselves the last great vestige of domainal rulership. Thus, a once rarefied space was opened up to the public in an unprecedented way. Once the last visitor filed out, all the structures were dismantled and carted away or destroyed. By the middle of that summer, nothing remained of the castle that had once stood for so long and for so much.[86] The modern concrete replica that stands today has witnessed none of the historical turbulence that its predecessor did.

Physical demolition of the castle broke one connection between the local people and their old political world. Other physical displacements and manipulations had the same intention but, oddly enough, quite the opposite effect. In an unlikely turn of events—one that surely neither William Willis nor Itagaki Taisuke knew about—the old rulers' removal in 1868 stirred some Aizu commoners to campaign for the lord's return. After Lord Katamori and his family were deposed and detained, about five hundred Aizu peasants walked as far as to Kyoto, Tokyo, Kaga, Kii, and Owari to plead for their old masters' return. Some of them went to Takada domain, where one contingent of Aizu samurai was being detained. In the tenth month of 1869, seven concerned peasants arrived during a heavy snowfall, surprising Arakawa Katsushige who was then being detained in Takada. As Katsushige wrote in his diary, "The Aizu peasants have banded together to petition for the lord's reinstatement in former Aizu domain. . . . Ueda [a Takada domainal elder] met with them. They departed today to continue on to Echigo."[87] Katsushige's diary says nothing of the peasants' motivation or rationale. Was their affinity toward the person of the lord, or to the familiar way of life that he represented? Were the predictable limits of the old ruler better than the unpredictable promise of a new one?

Regardless, these peasants were soon joined by others. Two months later, five village headmen and four Wakamatsu town leaders signed a memorial to the Meiji government, requesting that their old *daimyō* be permitted to return to Tsuruga Castle. "For several hundred years, the Matsudaira family graciously provided virtuous rule," the local leaders explained. "The people of Aizu have knotted their brows worrying about their detained lord,

86. In 1890, Endō Keishi, a former Aizu retainer and the chairperson of the Seventy-Seventh National Bank in Sendai, purchased the former castle grounds from the Army Ministry for three thousand yen and presented it to the Matsudaira family. The land was sold in 1916 to the city of Wakamatsu, which subsequently converted it into a public park, including a velodrome for *keirin* (gambling on competitive cycling). A concrete replica of the donjon was built in 1965 and stands to this day.

87. Arakawa, *Meiji nisshi*, p. 122.

forgetting even to eat or sleep day and night. Last winter, we even went to Tokyo to make our case, holding off a multitude of others who also wished to do the same." The petitioners promised that "if our lord is allowed to return to his homeland at once, the people's sentiments would be soothed, and the farmers and merchants would all feel encouraged to follow their occupation." These local leaders even went so far as to suggest that the people of Aizu were, by nature, temperamentally resistant to outside rulers. "We are a people who have always lived in an isolated land enclosed on all four sides, and we are stubborn in our ways. We are accustomed to the several centuries of benevolent nurturing by Matsudaira lordship," they claimed.[88]

Similar yearning for the domainal past drove the villagers of six hamlets in Yama county to submit the same request in the first month of 1870. The petitioners compiled thirty-four examples of past lordly benevolence, including aid to the elderly and the poor, riparian projects, and emergency relief, as reasons the Matsudaira deserved to be reinstated in Aizu. Their memorial concluded, "We are extremely grateful upon this glorious occasion of imperial restoration. However, the ways of our old lord have seeped into our skin over more than two hundred years, and they cannot be forgotten even for a moment. . . . We respectfully request that you show imperial compassion and pity by allowing our lord to return to his castle at once."[89] The conservatism of the villagers here is explicit, as they used a classic moral lordship argument to try turning back the political clock. Lip service to the Meiji Restoration notwithstanding, the restoration that they really sought was that of their old political life, starting with their old *daimyō*.

The residents of Yoshida, who had cosigned the earlier petitions, were particularly active in trying to restore Matsudaira rule. On two other occasions in 1869, villagers requested, on behalf of "all the peasants in the county, young and old, male and female," that Aizu be returned to its previous lords. They argued that even the imperial government could not ignore the "blessings that the Matsudaira bestowed upon our country Aizu from days long past." Like the earlier memorials, these requests also promised that the lord's return would bring about socioeconomic stability. If only old Aizu could be reinstated, the villagers promised, "The people would feel at peace, and feel motivated to pursue the path of agriculture."[90] The petitioners implied that, by contrast, they could not wholeheartedly devote themselves to the new imperial structure.

88. "Kohankō no gokijō ni kansuru ryōnai minshū no seigansho," pp. 1–2.

89. Ibid., pp. 2–3.

90. Nishi Aizuchōshi hensan iinkai, *Nishi Aizuchōshi*, 5:184–86.

It comes as no surprise that all these requests were denied; still, they demonstrate how some continued to judge governance by the old standards of lordly benevolence. Even after the Restoration, even after a resounding defeat, some could still fathom Aizu as a polity headed by a benevolent hereditary *daimyō*. Some indeed preferred it to the new political reality that was abruptly imposed upon them. More significantly, these pleas revealed a sense of local identity and lordly allegiance that was rarely, if ever, expressed in the domainal days. Some Aizu commoners suddenly discovered this affinity when the previous lords were physically displaced, which provoked an unlikely outburst of sentiments—affection that they perhaps always had in the recesses of their hearts but never had the occasion to know or emote. Only amid destruction and loss did they find themselves as people of Aizu domain and imagine the good old days of lordly rule. A new situation reaffirmed old attachments, though all too late.

Other political dislocations—especially involving administrative borders—also had similar unintended consequences. As outsiders came in and bent long-standing demarcations, some Aizu residents found cause to discover their local solidarity. In the early and mid-1870s, Meiji oligarchs consolidated their numerous prefectures, hopeful that a more integrative administrative framework would induce the populace to adopt a correspondingly integrated political mentality. For their liking, too many prefectures still lived under the shadow of their domainal predecessors. As one prefectural memorial cautioned in 1872, "In observing the ways of various prefectures, the people do not yet understand the great meaning of the Restoration and have not outgrown old domainal feelings." The memorial called for more domainal borders to be displaced by prefectural ones, warning that "should traditionally divisive and feudal practices be allowed to remain, the people are wont to make light of prefectural authority."[91]

Wakamatsu prefecture was one such place. Because it covered the same territory as the old Aizu domain and was even named after the former castle town, it was all too readily identifiable as the successor to the previous polity. In 1876, formal administrative vestiges were eliminated as Wakamatsu prefecture was incorporated, along with Iwasaki, into Fukushima prefecture. Of the three prefectures that were consolidated, Fukushima was the smallest. Yet the new prefecture was named after it, and the prefectural capital was placed in the city of Fukushima, which is geographically biased to the northeast and away from Aizu. This owed, it was said, to the fact that Wakamatsu was the remnant of

91. *MKS*, 2:331.

Aizu, the onetime rebels.[92] Wakamatsu prefecture was now wiped off the map and so, too, was any formal expression of Aizu's domainal past.

Protest began around 1881, or five years after Wakamatsu prefecture's demise. Several local leaders in Aizu started petitioning the Meiji government to resurrect the old prefecture. The petitioners made their case by claiming, first of all, that the Aizu region possessed distinct qualities that set it apart from their new fellow prefectural residents. "The Wakamatsu region is surrounded on all sides by tall peaks and many hills, making for a distinct geography and a distinct people like those of a single discrete country," they claimed. Furthermore, according to the petitioners, the people of Wakamatsu prefecture had been "progressing steadily toward enlightenment and civilization," but after 1876, when the prefecture was merged into Fukushima, everything from commerce, agriculture, education, and infrastructure took a turn for the worse. This, they said, was not because "the people of Wakamatsu prefecture have lost their will or their mental strength"; the problem was that they were robbed of the administrative unity that had long been familiar to them. Therefore, "if a new prefecture that is consistent with geographic reality and the people's desires is immediately reestablished, it would bring nothing short of true happiness and prosperity to the people of this region."[93] This memorial was signed by one Katō Seiki, a commoner from Kita-Aizu county who was a part of a greater movement to have Wakamatsu prefecture reinstated. On the same day, another Aizu commoner, Mure Tarō, directed a similar appeal to Ōkuma Shigenobu. His memorial also argued that the Aizu region was substantially distinct from the rest of Fukushima, and consolidation had brought "a hundred inconveniences and extreme disadvantage to the people" of Aizu. "For this reason the people truly wish for the old prefecture's return," Mure pleaded.[94]

In another memorial, four other commoners also invoked local distinctness to justify Wakamatsu secession from Fukushima. They claimed that "the geographical features and the popular mentality of Wakamatsu, Iwasaki, and Fukushima all differ from one another, so that what might advance in one area might recede in another, what might grow in one area might wither in another, and what might prosper in one area might fail in another." These petitioners went so far as to use the word *kokumin* to refer to the people of Aizu—not to the Japanese, as would have been conventional by this time.[95]

---

92. *AWS*, 6:31.
93. *MKS*, 2:506–7.
94. Ibid., pp. 507–8.
95. Ibid., pp. 612–13.

Their usage postulated *kuni* not as the new imperial nation but as an emerging vision of regional communality that was now gaining greater clarity vis-à-vis its new unwanted neighbors whom the national government had imposed upon Aizu.

All these appeals were unequivocally dismissed by the Meiji government, and prefectural borders would remain as they are today. Yet grumbling persisted. Two years later, twenty people, including the five who had petitioned back in 1881, submitted another, much longer memorial to the Genrōin, the imperial senate. They argued that Wakamatsu was "once a place occupied by a great and heroic domain, and thus has practices distinct from other places." As they pointed out, "Although Fukushima and Iwasaki regions are only several tens of miles away, we have never had much commercial exchange with them. For example, marriages between people of different areas are extremely rare even now." They protested that the people of Aizu were estranged from the rest of Fukushima prefecture, which, they claimed, sought to keep its westerly neighbors at arm's length. They accused prefectural assemblymen from Fukushima and Iwasaki of neglecting the needs of the Aizu region, "killing budgets" that allocate public funds for infrastructural development in Aizu. Thus, the petitioners concluded, "We can no longer contain our love of Aizu and deign to speak out of place. On behalf of the 200,000-plus masses, we beseech you to consider the great task of breaking up Fukushima prefecture."[96]

This emotional plea was more than a requiem for a fallen domain and old loyalties. It was a new political voice that articulated a new consciousness born of new conditions. Whatever awareness these people previously had of themselves as a discrete regional community now found a sharply political expression. It was the climate of modern national consolidation that fostered this local self-discovery. Faced with external violations of unstated but long-understood borders—an insensitive gerrymandering where Tokyo's designs seemed grossly incongruous with established practices—some residents of former Aizu were driven to reaffirm local norms and discover their distinct locality. Both prefectural rule and administrative consolidation had aimed for nation-building efficiency, but those impositions gave rise, most unwittingly, to a sharper awareness of Aizu's regional identity relative to its neighbors and the new nation.

Returning Aizu to the Nation

Postwar Aizu was physically dislocated to the edge of empire. Lawlessness and samurai restlessness figuratively distanced Aizu from the ideals of impe-

96. Ibid., pp. 414–16.

rial unity and set it apart as a problematic place. Some Aizu residents shunted central administrative reforms as an unwelcome violation of local norms by a distant, unfamiliar state. All these instances drove a wedge between postwar Aizu and imperial nationhood. Yet, other developments—one highly planned and the other purely accidental—could help bring Aizu back into the national fold and better locate Aizu as a meaningful region within the imperial landscape.

The Tonami debacle notwithstanding, Meiji statesmen did not abandon the idea of transforming troublesome *shizoku* into productive labor. To the contrary, they pursued that possibility as "national industrial promotion projects." One famous example was the reclamation of Asaka. The Asaka project is intimately connected with Aizu, because like Tonami, it was designed as a productive outlet for *shizoku,* including those from Aizu. The Asaka project gave Aizu's former samurai an opportunity to remake themselves not only as agricultural settlers but as bona fide contributors to a nationally sanctioned scheme.

Asaka was a vast but fallow plain just to the east of Lake Inawashiro that could be made far more productive if properly irrigated. Hopeful ideas about developing that promising land had been around since Tokugawa times, but Chūjō Masatsune was the first to put them to practice. Chūjō, who as a Yonezawa domainal official had long envisioned plans to develop Ezo, was given an opportunity to put his ideas into practice when he was appointed the deputy governor of Fukushima prefecture in 1872. Chūjō then initiated discussions about reclaiming Asaka and soon convinced twenty-five wealthy merchants in the city of Kōriyama to invest 21,670 yen in a new company that would administer the developmental project. This private company, called the Kaiseisha, was founded in November 1873 in the name of "raising economic production and establishing a foundation for the nation's economy."

Chūjō added a national dimension to this otherwise regional venture when he requested assistance from the central government. By so doing, he placed Asaka onto the national economic development agenda. In 1875 Chūjō asked for government funding to build a waterway from Lake Inawashiro that would irrigate Asaka to the east. His request brought Asaka to the attention of Ōkubo Toshimichi who, as the home minister, came to embrace state-led developmentalism. In 1875 the Industry Promotion Office, which oversaw government-sponsored industrial development, was transferred from the Ministry of Industry to the Home Ministry, giving Ōkubo direct control over its activities.[97] The minister made regional development a national priority,

97. For Ōkubo's political motivations behind his interest in industry promotion, see Ōe, "Ōkubo Toshimichi seikenka no."

thus bringing underdeveloped but promising areas such as Asaka into the national purview.

Ōkubo's agenda converged nicely with local interests, as prefectural authorities were also moving in the same direction. In 1873 Fukushima prefectural governor Yasuba Yasukazu first called upon *shizoku* from the former Nihonmatsu domain to settle in Asaka. The governor pointed out that *shizoku* who tried their hands at commerce "have failed and sunk to the depth of despair," indicating that the quick liquidation of the samurai class in the early 1870s was failing. "What is most needed," the governor argued, "is a long-range plan of ten or a hundred years that would provide permanent financial security." Nationally supported agri-industrial communities like Asaka were the answer. Not only that, Governor Yasuba argued, settlers would have an even more worthy goal. "Your efforts would increase national production, build national strength, and expand the nation's prestige at a time of national crisis, when we are about to be humiliated by foreign countries," he pronounced. Official rhetoric eagerly united local prosperity with national gain, glorified relocation to Asaka as "answering to heavenly benevolence" and "loyalty to the imperial court," and extolled future settlements as "the foundation for enriching and strengthening the nation."[98] The hard work of tilling Asaka's soil was defined, at least on paper, as legitimate service to the empire.

This was certainly in keeping with the Meiji leaders' thinking. To prepare for his 1876 trip to the Tōhoku, Ōkubo instructed his lieutenant Sugiura Yuzuru to draft a policy paper on national development projects. In his report Sugiura formally connected the problem of rehabilitating the *shizoku* with developmental projects and suggested that two problems can be solved at once by using *shizoku* labor to reclaim land and establish industry. Suigiura then identified the Kaiseisha's reclamation efforts in Asaka as a useful example of how provincial officials and local capital collaborated effectively. Sugiura concluded, "The Tōhoku region has abundant land but insufficient human capital," and therefore, "the *kazoku* and *shizoku* should be encouraged to relocate there."[99]

On June 5, 1876, Ōkubo saw for himself the promising work that the Kaiseisha had done in Asaka. He spent the night in Kuwano village, the main settlement in Asaka, and liked what he saw. "The sights leave me no doubt about the success here," Ōkubo recorded in his diary, "There are about 120

98. Nōrinshō nōmukyoku, *Fukushimaken Asaka*, pp. 10–13.

99. Sugiura Yuzuru zenshū kankōkai, *Sugiura Yuzuru zenshū*, 4:218–21. On this linking of *shizoku* rehabilitation and industrial development, see Harootunian, "The Economic Rehabilitation of the Samurai."

households that have moved here. Standing in the middle is a grand western-style building [the Kaiseikan, the headquarters of Kaiseisha]. It is a three-story building that offers an excellent view. The scenery is indeed beautiful." The minister was pleased enough to invite the main officers of the Kaiseisha to his inn, reward them five hundred yen, and promise them an audience with the Meiji Emperor upon his later visit.[100] On June 24, now nearing the end of his journey, Ōkubo returned his comments on Sugiura Yuzuru's report. In his approving note to Sugiura, Ōkubo included this impression of what he saw in Tōhoku: "Although I cannot help but sigh at the overwhelmingly untamed land and the ignorance of its people, it need not be said that this land will be of great use in the future, and become the treasure of our country."[101]

In March 1878, Ōkubo officially submitted his plans for developmental projects to the prime minister, Sanjō Sanetomi. The plans drew mainly on Sugiura's earlier work, as they linked the issues of *shizoku* rehabilitation and developmentalism. The minister's request included a nationwide plan to help 13,000 *shizoku* households relocate to industry promotion sites at a cost of 1.759 million yen. The next day, Ōkubo presented Asaka as "the first site in settling the wilds of the Tōhoku" and requested 651,482 yen to help 2,000 households establish their new homes there.

The former samurai of Aizu were to be an integral part of this grand national project. To encourage Aizu migrants, Chūjō had convinced the former lord Katamori, who was then comfortably retired in Tokyo, to relocate to Asaka along with his former retainers and their families. He had also secured start-up capital of 190,000 yen for the purpose. Chūjō hoped that Asaka could succeed where Tonami had failed. But Chūjō had acted without the consent of Governor Yamayoshi, who angrily canceled the invitation to the former lord. Despite this inauspicious beginning, thirty-three Aizu households left their homes in the winter of 1881 and crossed over into Asaka in a blinding blizzard to begin their new lives as agricultural settlers.

The Aizu families each received about four acres of land and eventually settled in four communities, but their daily experience revealed a mountain of unanticipated difficulties and the project's shortcomings. Many of their fields had poor access to water because government construction provided only the main artery from Lake Inawashiro and not the tributary waterways to individual fields. Those needed to be built privately, and three requests for public assistance were all denied. Over two kilometers separated the main waterway from the Aizu settlers' fields, and the settlers could only build half

100. Nihon shiseki kyōkai, ed., *Ōkubo Toshimichi nikki*, lower volume, p. 503.

101. Nihon shiseki kyōkai, ed., *Ōkubo Toshimichi monjo*, 7:146–47.

the distance on their own before they ran out of money. In 1886, thirty-nine yen were finally loaned out to complete the tributary, but because it was too narrow, it failed to provide adequate irrigation. Little wonder, then, that by the turn of the century, eight of the thirteen households in one migrant Aizu community, Nanbara, had declared bankruptcy and lost their land, with many fleeing back to Aizu and elsewhere.

Ideally, the Asaka settlements were to gain economic autonomy after an initial period of government support. In reality, the communities struggled just to stay afloat. One hundred forty area residents described their plight in a letter to their patron Chūjō Masatsune in 1893. "Since their founding seventeen or eighteen years ago," they wrote, "the new villages have yielded little agricultural produce." Furthermore, the settlements seem to have been a dumping ground for itinerants and undesirables. "Villagers do not stay for long, and those who live here one day might leave for another village the next. Settlers who work these lands one year might take their families elsewhere the next. Those who newly join the village tend to be troublemakers and outcasts. . . . This is truly a deplorable situation."[102] Because the settlements depended on the efforts of those who had failed elsewhere, the odds were against them. They struggled just to feed themselves, much less "enrich and strengthen their country," as rhetoric had cheerfully sung.

Ōkubo's assassination in 1878 robbed Asaka of its most crucial patron and ensured that it would not quite come to be as the minister had envisioned. The last official whom Ōkubo met immediately before he died was the Fukushima governor, Yamayoshi Moritaka, with whom he spoke of Asaka's great promise and underscored its significance within the greater purview of industry promotion.[103] In fact, Ōkubo had on his body notes about Asaka when he was fatally attacked. Asaka's potential died with Ōkubo, for his successors greatly diluted what was tantamount to his will. As Itō Hirobumi and Matsukata Masayoshi subsequently budgeted for the project, it was cut by three-quarters and the national government paid only for the irrigation canal itself, leaving reclamation and all other costs to be borne locally. Conceptually, too, the Asaka settlement came to be understood as merely a one-time project, as it was distanced from an overall national vision of a developmental state.[104]

Having put them there, the Meiji government ultimately left Asaka settlers to trudge onward in the kind of dead-end poverty that inspired the novelist

102. Takahashi, *Asaka kaitakushi*, p. 185.
103. Nihon shiseki kyōkai, ed., *Ōkubo Toshimichi monjo*, 9:163–72.
104. Yabe, *Asaka kaikon seisakushi*, pp. 177–78, 187.

Miyamoto Yuriko, the granddaughter of Chūjō Masatsune, to describe in her tellingly titled 1916 novel *Mazushiki hitobito no mure* (*A Flock of the Poor*):

> In the early Meiji era, my grandfather dedicated half his life to developing this new promised land. Settlers from various places came to build this village. They came from the north and they came from the south, all tempted by this newly reclaimed land, all dreaming of happiness. They even left their homeland to gather here. But these people are pitiful wherever they are. Not only were they unable to succeed as they had imagined, they were forced to suffer more than ever. They grew old and lost the courage to move on, and soon had no choice but to end their lives as sharecroppers in this town. That is why today, as ever, they all remain poor.[105]

The novel takes place primarily in "K Village," likely a code for Kuwano, the largest outpost in Asaka where Miyamoto spent many childhood summers. Her description of a struggling Kuwano bears little resemblance to what Ōkubo Toshimichi saw there some thirty years earlier.

Asaka may have failed to achieve the grand vision of its planners, but it did signal an official reinterpretation of the *shizoku* as valuable human capital. Even the former samurai of Aizu were recognized for their potential to do productive work, and in Asaka, the Meiji state gave them an opportunity to prove their worth in a prominent national project. Leaders such as Ōkubo held out hope that Aizu's former samurai could overcome their past and do the country some good for a change. Such a possibility for national redemption was not without its cost. Meiji developmentalism also cast the region into a subordinate position vis-à-vis the nation. Whether Aizu, Tonami, or Asaka, provincial places were understood as promisingly productive spaces but spaces that needed to be made so at the state's direction and patronage. For "the wilds of the Tōhoku" to become "a treasure of our country," there was a price to be paid. The raw potential of the northeast hinterland attracted financial investment from the state—such as it was, in Asaka's case—but it also made regions subject to external exploitation and whimsy. Developmental policies institutionalized and routinized the region's subordination to the center.[106]

The public project at Asaka gave some Aizu families a chance at a new life, but the prospect of redemption also came much more improbably. Where one war brought Aizu defeat and shame, another brought victory and catharsis. For Aizu, the Seinan War of 1877 was a remarkable reversal of fortune and a dramatic opportunity for its once disgraced warriors to win back what they had earlier lost.

---

105. Miyamoto, *Mazushiki hitobito no mure*, p. 28.
106. Makabe and Nozoe, eds., *Minshūshi toshite no Tōhoku*.

As tension mounted between the Meiji oligarchs in Tokyo and their former compatriot Saigō Takamori in Kagoshima after 1873, government leaders grew increasingly concerned that conscription soldiers, who had only been assembled that year, would be inadequate should their services be needed. Just a month before Saigō's uprising in 1877, Iwakura Tomomi consulted the Home Ministry and the Genrōin about actively recruiting former samurai to fill the ranks of the fledgling imperial army in case of an emergency. This stirred some debate in the government as a *shizoku*-heavy military diluted the notion of a civilian conscript army. In a compromise, the government decided to recruit *shizoku* as police officers, then mobilize them as an auxiliary force if hostilities broke out.[107] Chief of Police Kawaji Toshiyoshi looked to Aizu *shizoku* as one source of this manpower and enlisted the assistance of Sagawa Kanbei. A former Aizu domainal elder and a Boshin War veteran, Kanbei had become a police official in Tokyo after the war, and he eagerly helped to recruit fellow Aizu men into the police force as the clouds of another civil war gathered.[108]

On February 15, 1877, Saigō raised his banner of rebellion in Satsuma. The news was received with great delight by Shiba Gorō, who was then a young student in the Army Cadet School in Tokyo. "I hear that imperial orders have been issued to quash the potato samurai of Satsuma," he rejoiced in his diary, "What wonderful, wonderful news." His elder brother Shirō, despite his illness, wrote to Gorō, "This very day I am leaving Tokyo to fight in the government forces in Kyūshū. If I do not seize the chance to take revenge on Satsuma, I shall never be able to face those who rest in their graves in Aizu. Let us meet on the day of victory."[109] Gorō's elder brothers all joined the war, as did Yamakawa Hiroshi, the former leader of Tonami domain, who was

---

107. Fukushima-ken keisatsushi hensan iinkai, ed., *Fukushima-ken keisatsushi*, 1:525; Obinata, "Seinan sensō ni okeru 'junsa' no rinji bibo," pp. 50–66.

108. During the Seinan War, Kawaji personally led the Third Independent Brigade, in which many police officers fought. He wrote of his brigade in "A Spontaneous Piece":

> Six thousand braves joined the day
> Beckoned to the battlefield by arrows and gun-smoke
> Their frosty blades will be put to the rebels
> Their work will be known by all in the realm.

Kawaji, *Ryūsen ikō*, p. 143.

109. Craig, *Remembering Aizu*, p. 141. Shirō later became a political novelist under the nom de plume Tōkai Sanshi and wrote the popular political novel *Kajin no kigū* between 1885 and 1897. He also became one of the first Aizu representatives to the Imperial Diet.

then a lieutenant colonel in the army. "Yamakawa, my brothers, and other men from the same province and domain who had suffered the same fate were together fighting to redeem Aizu's honor," Gorō exulted, "What could be more glorious! Words could not describe my tremendous joy."[110]

As Gorō did, some welcomed the war as a gift from heaven, though not everyone in Aizu shared their enthusiasm. Two weeks after the rebellion began, Fukushima prefecture issued an immediate call for seven hundred new police officers to be dispatched to Tokyo for combat training. "We shall first choose among *shizoku* those who are honorable and trustworthy," they announced, "However, this being an emergency, typical requirements such as body build and age shall not be considered. Anyone fit for combat shall be selected."[111] Even with the lowered standards, the prefectural office had some trouble meeting its quota. It dispatched recruitment officers throughout the prefecture, including Aizu, but they often encountered indifference. "Many of our efforts have come up empty. Conditions are difficult," one prefectural recruiter reported.[112] Area residents needed to be enticed by various incentives, such as a cash payment of five yen and welfare support for family members who were left behind, and a bonus of twenty-five yen to be paid upon discharge.[113]

After an initial burst of alacrity, *shizoku* recruitment in Aizu hit a wall rather quickly. When Aizu men joined the police to fight the war, they were placed in one of two brigades, the Third Independent Brigade or the Shinsen Brigade. The Third Independent, which was created in March, included many *shizoku*; of its 517 Aizu enlistees, 329 were *shizoku*. However, by the time the Shinsen Brigade was formed two months later, most former Aizu samurai wanting to take vengeance on Satsuma had already enlisted. As a result, the Shinsen Brigade had to be composed predominantly of commoners, with only 64 *shizoku* accounting for its 297 Aizu soldiers.[114] The pool of Aizu *shizoku* who were eager to join the fight ran dry, and prefectural recruiters were forced to take many commoners despite its original intent to target former samurai.

Once the Aizu police officers reached the battlefront in Kyūshū, field commanders seemed reluctant to use them. Yamagata Aritomo, who took personal command in the war, limited the Aizu men's actions in the crucial early

110. Ibid., p. 143.
111. Fukushima-ken keisatsushi hensan iinkai, *Fukushima-ken keisatsushi,* 1:532.
112. Ibid., p. 534.
113. Ibid., p. 535.
114. Ibid., p. 537.

phase of the war. During the battles to relieve the besieged Kumamoto Castle, Yamagata designated the police as backups to the regular forces and kept them in the rear. When the Aizu men were finally deployed to the front, they were ordered to fight hand to hand with just their blades. One hundred Aizu soldiers formed the Bare Blades Company (*Battōtai*) especially for this purpose, and they entered combat on March 14, 1877.

Inukai Tsuyoshi, the would-be prime minister, was then a young newspaper reporter for the *Yūbin hōchi* newspaper. He accompanied the government forces along the front and was reporting on the war in Kumamoto when the Aizu men finally joined the fight:

> On March 14, during the Battle of Tabaruzaka, our forces advanced toward a rebel stronghold. We tried to take it, but thirteen rebel soldiers firmly held their ground. Just then, a former Aizu soldier put himself in bodily danger and charged forward, immediately cutting down the thirteen rebels. As he slashed about, he called out loudly, "Remember the Boshin, remember the Boshin!" This may sound like a work of fiction but it is by no means made up. It is said that this Aizu man suffered only slight wounds.[115]

The Bare Blades Company fought hand to hand with the Satsuma forces over two days and suffered staggering casualties—twenty-five killed and fifty-four injured. The company would later become the subject of an eponymous military song:

> We are the imperial forces
> Our foe is the enemy of the court;
> The enemy is led by an incomparable hero
> The men who follow him are stout and fearless
> Though they may be brave
> Of those who dare rebel against heaven
> None have thrived since ancient times.[116]

Their work in the Seinan War allowed the song to forget a central irony; many Battōtai members had only recently been considered "enemies of the court" themselves.

Meanwhile, Yamakawa Hiroshi was a field commander in the Second Independent Brigade, which was moving in to break the Satsuma siege on Kumamoto Castle. There, the Kumamoto commandant, Tani Kanjō, was desperately holding the castle against the numerically superior Satsuma forces. As the Second Independent came up on the Satsuma troops encircling

115. *Yūbin hōchi*, March 17, 1877.
116. Shiotani, "Aizujin to Seinan sensō," p. 140.

Kumamoto Castle, Yamakawa was ordered to hold down the right flank in a defensive position. Yamakawa, however, defied orders and charged through the enemy, his forces becoming the first government forces to reach Kumamoto Castle and relieve Tani Kanjō's besieged garrison.

One historian has simply described Yamakawa's surprising initiative as "a violation of orders" without explaining why he made such a bold and unauthorized maneuver.[117] Yamakawa's action begins to make sense when one considers, first, that Tani Kanjō was Yamakawa's patron who had facilitated his entering the army—for an Aizu man to join the Imperial Army officer corps then was no easy task—and second, Yamakawa's origins as an Aizu samurai and, as such, the emotional baggage he carried into battle.[118] Just before his departure for the Kyūshū front, he expressed his hope for poetic justice:

> Men of Satsuma,
> behold the blade that hangs
> on this warrior of the east;
> see for yourselves—is it dull or is it sharp?[119]

Aggressiveness fueled by bitter memories and thirst for vengeance served Yamakawa well, but not nearly so another former Aizu elder. Sagawa Kanbei, who had helped to recruit Aizu men against their old nemesis, was a veteran of the Battle of Toba-Fushimi and a fierce hawk during the defense of Aizu in 1868. He had urged resisting the Satsuma and Chōshū forces to the death, calling them "villains by the emperor's side" and "a band of criminals, not soldiers of the emperor."[120] His militant fury during the Boshin War earned him the nickname "Kanbei the Demon." Kanbei was on the front lines serving as a platoon commander in Ōita when he was killed in action on March 18. The special enmity that more than a few Aizu soldiers reserved for Satsuma might have accounted for their pugnacity and perhaps for their anomalous casualty rate as well. Overall, 749 Aizu men participated in the war, 463 as police officers; 100, including 86 police officers, were killed in action.[121] The casualty rate for the government forces as a whole was 10 percent, making the Aizu soldiers one-third more likely to die fighting than anyone else.

---

117. Buck, "The Satsuma Rebellion of 1877," p. 445.

118. The Imperial Army leadership was dominated by former Chōshū samurai, and it was not easy for Aizu men to gain rank. Yamagata Aritomo is said to have opposed Yamakawa Hiroshi's commission on the grounds of his Aizu background.

119. Yamakawa, *Sakurayamashū*.

120. Craig, *Remembering Aizu*, p. 16.

121. As calculated from a table in Shiotani, "Aizu hanshi no Seinan sensō sansen," p. 91.

The Seinan War ended in September 1877, with the suicides of Saigō, who had led Satsuma against Aizu in the Boshin War, and his top lieutenant Kirino Toshiaki, who had accepted Aizu's instrument of surrender back in 1868. Their deaths satisfied young Shiba Gorō's sense of vengeance all the more because they came partly at the hands of his fellow Aizu men. As far as Gorō was concerned, the two Satsuma leaders were "arch-villains" who had "made Aizu their blood sacrifice" in the Restoration. "Their violent deaths were the logical conclusion of their actions," as he coolly judged.[122]

Karmic victory had gratified and redeemed Gorō so much that he chose to conclude his autobiography with the Seinan War, though he was, at the time, just another teenaged army cadet observing the war from afar. It mattered little that his greatest accomplishments as General Shiba Gorō of the Japanese Imperial Army, an international hero in Peking during the Boxer Rebellion and the first full general from Aizu, lay well beyond 1877. It was as if that victory in Satsuma was what finally made him a modern man of Meiji—as the title of his autobiography declares—and a full member of the Japanese Empire, bringing a closure that only an Aizu man could know.

122. Craig, *Remembering Aizu*, p. 146.

CHAPTER 4

Chasing Ghosts in Aizu: Identity and Remembrance

Unpacking the Aizuppo

When the publisher Chūō Kōrōnsha released Shiba Gorō's 1942 autobiography, it chose a telling, and perfectly appropriate, title: *The Records of a Man of the Meiji Era*, along with the subtitle *The Living Testament of Shiba Gorō of Aizu*. The simultaneity of the two words *Meijijin* (A Man of Meiji) and *Aizujin* (A Man of Aizu) gives proof to a basic tension that sustains this deeply personal narrative. Shiba Gorō was indeed a man who was born and raised an *Aizuppo* but came of age as a Japanese, embodying at once, if awkwardly at times, those two sets of sensibilities and identity. The title of Teruko Craig's English translation of the autobiography, released in 1999, adds still another important layer of truth to the matter. By "Remembering Aizu," Shiba Gorō truly was relying on retrospection and memory to locate himself within the long and turbulent making of Modern Japan. It was through a recollection of his youth, when he was a disgraced Aizu samurai searching desperately for vengeance and redemption in Meiji Japan, that Shiba Gorō could discover himself as both an *Aizuppo* and a Japanese.

Shiba Gorō was hardly the only person to recover and reaffirm his identity through the act of remembrance. Various forms of identity, whether personal or communal, are crafted out of remembering, and vice versa. The powerful link between identity and remembrance can be seen in many modern-day discussions about regional identity in Japan, including Aizu, which assume that each region possesses distinctive traits, or so-called regionality (*chihōsei*). These traits are said to form the psychological bedrock of the region's people, separating them from their neighbors and adding wrinkles of diversity to an otherwise seemingly cohesive nation. In Aizu, these characteristics are crystallized in the self-appellation *Aizuppo,* or "Sons of Aizu."

Who is this *Aizuppo*? This imagined figure, we are told, is "traditional." One nationwide survey in 1979 characterized Aizu as "the extreme example of traditional Japan" as it came in fifth in the nation among "regions that are strongly conscious of tradition."[1] Fukushima prefecture in general was deemed to possess "a stronger sense of tradition than other prefectures" but even within Fukushima, Aizu was said to stand out for its "strong communal bond that links people within social relations and the region . . . strong reverence for authority such as family and the government . . . [and] a severe sense of morality."[2] These findings led the editors to conclude, "Aizu is the most traditional region in the country, a place where social intimacy and family consciousness are high."[3] Even their fellow prefectural residents regarded their neighbors to the mountainous west as being a different breed. Back in 1913, one local educator pondering the nature of Fukushima folks doubted whether any single quality bound every resident of "such a large administrative unit, especially now in our enlightened days." He could, however, say with confidence, "If there is a place within the prefecture with a decidedly peculiar flavor, it is Aizu."[4]

Differences that supposedly distinguished Aizu have been captured in the notion of "the Aizu spirit." This term began to appear in print regularly in the late Meiji era as a centerpiece of regional identity creation. Its ambiguity allowed it to serve many highly rhetorical and emotionally satisfying functions in the late nineteenth and early twentieth centuries. "The Aizu spirit" was used, for one, to explain the past. "The Aizu spirit"—or lack thereof—was used to scorn the present. And "the Aizu spirit" was used to muster up strength and hope for the future. Most of all, this "Aizu spirit" anchored a local identity that supplemented a national one and expressed a faith that not only did such a place as Aizu continue to exist even after its erasure, an unbroken psychic unity still bound its people, the *Aizuppo.*

The idea of "the Aizu spirit" was bandied about in many contexts, but it was articulated most clearly and obsessively in the official publications of the Aizu Society. Established in April 1912, the Aizu Society (Aizu Kai) was one of many regional fraternities that began to be founded in the late 1880s as people who left their native places, often for Tokyo and other large cities, sought to reestablish and confirm their local roots.[5] As the

---

1. NHK, *Nihonjin no kenminsei,* pp. 122, 22. One through four were northwest Tokushima, northern Kumamoto, eastern Toyama, and eastern coastal Fukushima.

2. Ibid., p. 119.

3. Ibid., p. 122.

4. Hashimoto, "Fukushima kenjin to sono shisō," p. 3.

5. The historian Narita Ryūichi attributes this timing to the need to create regional voting blocs for parliamentary elections. Narita, "Teito Tokyo," p. 206.

society's commentators tell it, several key elements constituted the so-called Aizu spirit. The adjective "stubborn" certainly came up repeatedly. "It need not be said that the people of Aizu have always been known to be stubborn and strong-willed, so to speak," one contributor wrote in 1915.[6] Another concurred, "No matter the hardship, we do not change our ways—this is one distinctive characteristic of the Aizu spirit."[7] The willingness to sacrifice was also heralded as a part of the local mental makeup. "The spirit of sacrifice that has always coursed our veins is something to be proud of," one declared in 1919.[8] Loyalty, too, was said to be a distinctly Aizu quality. Another author in 1920 spoke proudly of "a sense of loyalty that is unique to Aizu" that "emerged from the Aizu spirit and the Japanese spirit."[9]

None is more prominent in this catalog of Aizu virtues than martial valor. The image of Aizu as brave and soldierly recurs ad nauseam. In the inaugural issue of the *Aizu Society Newsletter*, former domainal retainer Kurokouchi Ryō boasted, "It is an indisputable truth that among the 360 feudal domains, none could compare with our Aizu domain, especially in military matters."[10] A 1916 editorial likewise declared proudly that "Aizu made its name known across the realm through its military prowess. Only two domains, Satsuma and Mito, could possibly compare to Aizu."[11] Some, believing martial valor to be "a special characteristic of our domain," considered a military career the most sensible option for Aizu men in modern times.[12] Traditional and stubborn, loyal and brave—such were the supposed hallmarks of an *Aizuppo* driven by his "Aizu spirit."

These introspections into a regional self often beheld nature and domainal history as the font of a purported Aizu psyche. Seemingly every natural factor, from the tall mountain peaks that walled in the Aizu basin—130 in total, according to the Aizu Historical Association's count—and heavy snowfall, was said to have forged Aizu's flinty, rustic character.[13] Former domainal elders invoked the same sort of environmental determinism to explain Aizu in the *bakumatsu* years. "As our domain is nestled between mountains and valleys, our people's spirits are lowly and their minds vulgar. They are stuck

---

6. Satō, "Aizu kishitsu o ushinau nakare," p. 13.
7. Sōda, "Aizu damashii," p. 35.
8. Sawa, "Gisei no seishin," p. 2.
9. Sugimoto, untitled, p. 18.
10. Kurokouchi, "Aizujinshi ni tsugu," p. 11.
11. "Aizujinshi shōbu kishō no suichō," p. 14.
12. Ogawa, "Aizu fujin ni tsuite," p. 24.
13. "Aizuppo," p. 3.

in old ways and are ignorant of the world," they wrote to the *bakufu* in 1868.[14] Other commentators looked to domainal history to account for the *Aizuppo* personality. Shōji Kichinosuke, a prominent historian of the Fukushima region, once characterized the people of contemporary Aizu as "dutiful" and credited this to "the samurai culture of Aizu domain that has been passed down to the present."[15] Forty-two percent of the respondents from the 1979 survey who felt that "the domain's influence remains to this day" might have agreed with Shōji's appraisal. As the survey's editors concluded, "The characteristics of the former Aizu domain seem to shape the people's consciousness" more than a hundred years after the domain's demise.[16] Perhaps more than any other place in Japan, present-day Aizu is said to bear the legacy of its premodern history.

This conceit has remained remarkably static from the late Meiji era through the present. More than a few people have maintained that an unalienable sense of "Aizuness," first forged in domainal days, lives on in modern times. "Truly the *Aizuppo* are by nature brave and true, and we value righteousness above all," the *Aizu Society Newsletter* editors proclaimed in their 1916 mission statement. "This became our true character through the beautiful customs that are unique to Aizu, which have been revered for over two hundred years since the days of Lord Masayuki."[17] Flagrantly deterministic and essentialist language continues to be used in articulating "Aizuness" even today. "Some individual differences notwithstanding," one local writer claimed in 1990, "all who were born, raised, and lived on Aizu soil have inherited the Aizu spirit and made it their living flesh and blood."[18]

Even as this soaring rhetoric made "Aizuness" seem safely inherent, some concerned commentators often fretted that a time-honored spirit that had once prevailed was becoming lost in these modern times. A 1916 *Newsletter* editorial was disturbed by a gap between "the pure Aizu spirit and ill practices of Aizu people today."[19] Spiritual decline resulted partly from the passage of time, as one writer noted. "Since the days of our domainal crisis in the Boshin War, people have scattered and many days have gone by. The old have died and our elders have passed on. Nowadays, many are those who call themselves *Aizuppo* yet know nothing of Aizu," he lamented in 1916. "It is extremely difficult to preserve Aizu thought and the Aizu spirit."[20] In their despondent

14. Dajōkan, *Dajōkan nisshi,* vol. 23.
15. "Kenminsei o kangaeru zadankai," 3.
16. NHK, *Nihonjin no kenminsei,* p. 122.
17. "Aizukaikaihō hakkan no shishu," p. 2.
18. Saitō, "Aizudamashii," p. 141.
19. "Aizudamashii," p. 21.
20. Hashizume, "Aizudamashii no kan'yō," p. 25.

head shaking, some commentators cited a familiar cause that could be traced back to alarmist samurai rhetoric from the Tokugawa days. As one man grieved in 1915, "It is startling to see how much the merchants' mentality has taken over. The domainal spirit that was renowned as 'the Aizu character' is now as empty as a cicada's shell."[21] Consequently, even military prowess—"the foremost characteristic of Aizu men"—was said to be in decline, causing those such as General Shiba Gorō to regret that fewer fellow Aizu men were entering military service each year.[22] Another supposed culprit behind the downfall of the Aizu character was the modern compulsory education system. "Because education is now standardized throughout Japan, we cannot educate our children in the strict and traditional manner unique to Aizu," ran one complaint from 1917. "What's more, the parents are themselves a bunch of Meiji-born weaklings."[23] Rueful nostalgia posited Aizu as a conservative spiritual bulwark being eroded by the tide of capitalism and moral degeneracy in modern Japan. And it was a losing battle in the minds of those who cared about these matters. "The bond among us Aizu people has grown weaker by the year," one man bemoaned in 1924, "The country of Aizu is on the verge of spiritual bankruptcy."[24] All these arguments shared the assumptions of nostalgia; they imagined some ideal to have existed in the past and called for a recovery of that supposedly glorious past.

Singers of this requiem often blamed Aizu's spiritual collapse on a singularly devastating event—the Boshin War. In calling for "a return to the Aizu man's spirit," one commentator from 1928 despaired, "Ever since our defeat in 1868, we have become slaves to circumstances." Defeat, he said, crippled the people of Aizu "just like the Koreans, who have also lost their country." As he surmised, "We the defeated panderers have produced only one thing—a useless sense of diffidence. This diffidence has emasculated the men of Aizu."[25] A similar lament was expressed in a 1916 *Newsletter* editorial, which bemoaned that the Aizu spirit had "constituted the mental character of the Aizu people before the Restoration," but now, in the early twentieth century, "our ways have become undeniably vulgar and our spirit clouded."[26]

All this fretful self-pity misses, if not an emotional truth, then a more remarkable point. Their rhetoric of physical and historical determinism and

---

21. Satō, "Aizu kishitsu o ushinau nakare," p. 11.
22. "Aizujin shōbu kishō no suichō," p. 14
23. Akizuki, untitled, p. 17.
24. Watanabe, "Aete Aizu no senpai ni uttau," p. 9.
25. Araki, "Aizujin no seishin ni kaere," p. 5.
26. "Aizudamashii," p. 20.

the pervasive sense of nostalgia conspired to make "Aizuness" seem much more aged than it in fact was. What these image-makers did not recognize was that "Aizuness" was not something that had once existed and was fading, as they feared; it was something they themselves were creating at that very moment. In decrying "the ephemeral spectacle of an unrecoverable identity," they were in fact constructing that identity for the first time by "deciphering what they are in light of what is no more."[27] Contrary to common claim, the onset of modernity did not bring about the demise of a traditional Aizu spirit. Rather, it was a modern cause, namely, Aizu's defeat in the Restoration and the Boshin War, that both compelled and enabled the construction of a new identity, now articulated as the "Aizu spirit" and the *Aizuppo*. The destructive experience of defeat called for subsequent self-rehabilitation and the creation of a fresh, respectable Aizu. Building up the notion of an admirable and innate "Aizu spirit" intended to solve this problem and relieve anxieties about postwar "diffidence" and "emasculation."

In considering this process of identity formation, then, historians should look not to ancient topography or the domainal past, but instead to a text from the relatively recent Taishō era. In his impassioned submission to the *Aizu Society Newsletter* in 1918, a Wakamatsu resident by the name of Watanabe Tadashi identified what he understood as the duties of an Aizu descendant. He began by reminding his fellow Aizu people that "resentment comes in many forms, but none is deeper or greater than that of a lost country" like theirs. He exhorted the readers to never forget their bitter past and proposed three ways in which this past was to be kept alive in the present. First, he advocated an annual "Aizu Memorial Day" on which every Aizu household would hold commemoration services for the Boshin war dead. Second, he sought to produce a definitive history of Aizu. Unlike official "national histories," this one was to be written from Aizu's perspective and titled *The History of a Lost Country* [Bōkokushi], "to be passed down from one generation of Aizu people to the next." Finally, he called upon Aizu Society members to recount and share, at every major meeting, "the events of the Aizu War, glorious tales of our fallen, and the struggles of our lord and his domainal leaders in Tonami." On these occasions, he suggested, attendees should eat nothing but "*akaza* and bean leaf porridge" to recreate their crushing poverty during their exile in the northern hinterland of Tonami.[28]

---

27. Nora, "Between Memory and History," pp. 17–18.

28. Watanabe, "Aizu kishitsu no yōsei," pp. 9–10. *Akaza* is the weed *chenopodium centrorubrum*.

Watanabe's three prescriptions—remember the war dead, re-create Aizu's past through historiography, and form the bond of fraternity by confirming a collective past—were precisely how a sense of regional self came to be in Aizu after the Restoration. He believed that these memorial exercises would "cultivate the Aizu character," as the title of his treatise promised, bearing further testimony to the instrumental role that collective remembrance plays in forging identity. For modern Aizu survivors like Watanabe, their own soul-searching had to begin with the souls of the dead. In so doing, they were unknowingly answering the question that Ernest Renan had posed in 1882—"Qu'est-ce qu'une nation?"—only Watanabe substituted "region" for "nation."[29] Elements of national formation that Renan had identified—"the possession in common of a rich legacy of memories" and "the will to perpetuate the value of the heritage that one has received in undivided form"—seemed to work just as well for regional formation in Japan. Aizu was what it was remembered to be, no less than France or the Jewry were.[30] That was, in some ways, all it could ever be; after all, by the time Watanabe wrote his words, Aizu no longer existed. And so the postwar generation in Aizu set out to recover themselves and their homeland in the only place they could: the field of memory.

The Dying Wish of an Old Samurai

In June 1923, a most peculiar funerary procession marched through the streets of Wakamatsu. Battle standards and lanterns led several men bearing spears and drawn swords, some in full military regalia. Behind them came a horse drawing a coffin wrapped in rough reed straw and dragged along the dusty street, followed by a Buddhist monk and grieving family members. This strange, mournful march worked its way through the city in broad daylight until it reached Yuzū Temple, where the old man was finally laid to rest. Thus, in accordance with his will, Machino Mondo's body was treated in the same crude manner as those of his comrades who had fallen in the Boshin War and lay forgotten on the battlefield, covered only by some straw.[31]

A grizzled war veteran like Machino Mondo could well be expected to use his death as an occasion to honor Aizu's past, and with such martial defiance, too. Even in death, this old soldier refused to just fade away—a fitting end

---

29. Renan, "Qu'est-ce qu'une nation?" p. 19.

30. Nora, "Between Memory and History," p. 16. "In [the Zionist] tradition, which has no other history than its own memory, to be Jewish is to remember one as such."

31. Aizu shikon fūunroku kankōkai, *Aizu shikon fūunroku*, pp. 34–37.

indeed for a man who had devoted much of his life to the memories of his fallen brothers-in-arms. The former Aizu samurai had lost his sixteen-year-old brother Hisakichi to combat and the rest of his immediate family to suicide while he fought on the Echigo front during the defense of Aizu. Machino began his unofficial tenure as a keeper of Aizu's memory in 1869, when he beseeched the occupation forces to permit the burial of the Aizu war dead, which had hitherto been prohibited. Later, as a founder of the Aizu Veterans Memorial Association (Aizu Chōreigi Kai), he continued to preach the importance of remembering the fallen with the dignity he deemed appropriate. His silent protest in 1923 allowed Mondo to pay one final homage and join, at long last, the spirits of his fellow samurai in style, some half a century after death had first separated them.

In post-Restoration Aizu, unlike anywhere else in Japan, the living were haunted by the war dead. There, a morbid past weighed heavily upon the survivors, who were left to reconcile themselves with the nagging memory of their forefathers' failures in 1868. It was their legacy of misdeed that severed the living from the new ideals of imperial nationhood. Aizu was uniquely subjected to the reification of loyalism and the stigmatization of rebels, a powerful means of difference creation that characterized the making of modern Japan. In response, the guardians of Aizu's local memory began a new battle over two thorny issues: how to properly commemorate the war dead and how to cast Aizu in historical narratives about the birth of imperial Japan, especially the Restoration and the Boshin War. On these two fronts, region and nation could collide head-on and a truce did not always come about easily. The struggle to locate Aizu within Meiji Japan entailed a good deal of conflict and lingering bitterness.

And necessarily so, for the Meiji Restoration was a lengthier and bloodier affair than as is often presented. The Restoration required more than a decade of occasional bloodshed and a year and a half of outright civil war. Not only did this long process leave behind considerable physical casualties—well over five thousand throughout Japan—it created a problem that the country had not encountered in a long time: what to do with the war dead and how to remember them. For historical precedent, one had to look back over two centuries to find men who had died fighting a war in Japan. Further complicating the issue was the matter of "imperial correctness." One had to go all the way back to the fourteenth century to find men who were said to have died for the imperial cause and, conversely, those who were said to have died opposing it.

History did offer some guidance. According to the religion scholar Murakami Shigeyoshi, "In feudal Japan, tradition stipulated that those who fell in battle were to be serviced and their spirits consoled regardless of whether they were friend or foe."[32] Conquerors were obliged, at least in theory, to tend to the ghosts of the defeated. "In looking at Japanese history," writes the religion scholar Sakurai Tokutarō, "the biggest problem facing winners after a large-scale war was to console the dead. In particular, the need to soothe the spirits of the defeated and bring about a peace of mind was the burden of those who had won." To alleviate their guilt, many generals and warlords built memorial steles to honor their enemies' spirits and hosted Buddhist funerary ceremonies.[33] As an ideal—if only as such—there was an expectation that combatants divided in life can and should be united in death, and that victors needed to respect this norm.

The reconciliation of spirits, however, was the least of the Meiji victors' concerns in the Restoration's aftermath. To the contrary, they drew a clear distinction between themselves and the defeated by imposing the imperial–rebel (*kan-zoku*) dichotomy. This was not a new idea, of course. The imperial–rebel binary was an ancient tool of didacticism, a classic way to cast the illusion of political moral clarity necessary to conduct war, especially civil war. But in modern times, more sophisticated institutions and techniques of difference creation polarized and politicized the memories of the dead. On the second day of the sixth month of 1868, while combat still continued in the northeast, the new government held a memorial rite for their war dead in the main ceremony hall of the newly captured Edo Castle. Commander in Chief Prince Arisugawa and General of the Left Sanjō Sanetomi hosted this ceremony, which offered no sense of reconciliation at all. The speech delivered at the event venerated the Satsuma-Chōshū soldiers as "the august imperial forces" who had "served their country just as Kusunoki Masashige had in the days of old." On the flip side were the soldiers of the former *bakufu* who were denigrated as "despicable wayward bastards who gathered like flies" around "the most irreverent Yoshinobu."[34] This polemic language made the righteousness of their own cause unmistakable, while their foes were not spared the indignity of rebellion even in death.

Grave markers bear physical testimony to still another technique of difference creation that clarified the imperial normative. The occupation forces that governed postwar Aizu made sure to reserve honorific labels such as "national service" (*hōkoku*), "spirit of loyalty" (*chūkon*), and "fallen in the line of duty" (*junnan*) for their own dead. In the spring of 1869, when former Aizu

---

32. Murakami, *Kokka Shintō,* p. 186.

33. Sakurai, *Reikonkan no keifu,* pp. 81–82.

34. Yui et al., eds., *Nihon kindai shisō taikei,* 4:61–62. The mirror used at this ceremony later became a *shintai* (divine manifest) at Yasukuni Shrine.

retainers buried their compatriots at Amida Temple in Wakamatsu, they dared to erect a sign that read "To the Spirits of Those Who Sacrificed Themselves to Duty" (*junnan no rei*). The occupation authorities learned of this the next day and ordered it to be taken down and replaced by a simple, generic sign that read "A Marker for the Dead," thus neutering the Aizu dead and denying them the honor of having died for a cause.[35] Similar distinction continued to be maintained even a decade later. In 1878, a commemorative stele was built in Amida Temple for seventy Aizu men who had died fighting for the government in the Seinan War. Their monument could be marked "The Stele of National Service and Loyalty," for they had served the imperial banner against Satsuma. However, when a group of returning Seinan War veterans used their war bonus to build a similar stele for the Boshin dead of Aizu, that monument could only be inscribed matter-of-factly as "The Grave of the War Dead."[36] The privilege of dying for the country belonged only to those who had fought on the "right side," namely, the imperial government, and no one else.

The Meiji government's "imperial cemetery system" (*kanshū funbo*) institutionalized this practice of discriminatory burials and further reinforced difference. The imperial dead from the Restoration War were buried in officially designated memorial sites (*shōkonjo*). In 1873, the Meiji government declared these sites tax exempt and promised to cover all costs related to maintenance and ceremonies.[37] The Home Ministry provided 35 yen to every official memorial shrine (10 for ceremonies and 25 for upkeep) annually, and 6.25 yen for each grave.[38] A catalog produced by Fukushima prefecture in 1879 shows 22 so-called imperial army cemeteries throughout the prefecture, in which 231 men rest. These include sites for 12 Aizu collaborators, whose graves have also been sponsored as imperial cemeteries since 1874.[39] In the ninth month of 1870, Wakamatsu prefecture built a memorial shrine (*shōkonsha*) to honor the imperial war dead interned at Yuzū Temple in Wakamatsu, and the prefectural governor, Shijō Takahira, sponsored a memorial rite at the shrine later in the year.[40] Starting in 1890, Fukushima prefecture provided an official guardian and an assistant guardian to each of these sites and paid them an annual stipend.[41] The

35. Machino, "Meiji Boshin sen'eki junnan," p. 22.

36. Aizu chōreigikai, ed., *Boshin junnansha*, p. 9.

37. Motoyasu, *Gunto no irei kūkan*, p. 86.

38. Ōtsuka, "Kanshū funbo to Meiji seifu," p. 30.

39. *Kangun funbo meisaichō*.

40. Ōtsuka, "Kanshū funbo to Meiji seifu," p. 36; Aizu Wakamatsu shiyakusho, *Boshin sen'eki kūjūnensai*, p. 31.

41. Fukushima-ken kyōiku iinkai, *Fukushima kyōikushi hensan shiryō*, 5:121–23, 126, 128.

highest possible prestige was bestowed upon some of these official sites when the Tōhoku imperial progress of 1876 dispatched representatives to conduct rites for the spirits honored there. Government organizers sent the Fukushima lieutenant governor, Okamura Yoshimasa, to confer imperial gratitude upon the government war dead at the Tōmyō Temple imperial cemetery in Wakamatsu, for they, as their gravestones tell it, had fought for "imperially loyal domains" and died "quelling rebel brigands" who had "resisted the imperial will."[42] Imperial donations underwrote a large stone monolith in their honor, which stands to this day.

No such niceties were forthcoming for the Aizu dead. When the war ended, their bodies lay exposed and scattered throughout Aizu proper. Wartime conditions made burial difficult on both sides, but especially for the defenders who were in constant retreat. A few were fortunate enough to be given a makeshift burial or at least have their heads taken back by considerate comrades, but most could only be left where they fell. Those on the run felt great pain and guilt for having abandoned "the bodies of our loyal compatriots," which one combat veteran recalled as "the most painful thing" he had to do during the war.[43]

Meanwhile those trapped in Tsuruga Castle could do no better. As the pounding siege continued, "The dead amassed by the thousands and soon made a mountain. There was neither the time to collect them nor the ground in which to bury them. Some were thrown into empty wells in the castle compound. No words can express this tragedy."[44] The end of hostilities did not relieve their plight, for the government forces classified the Aizu dead as criminals and prohibited formal burial services for them. Consequently, "all the bodies were left to be devoured by wild birds and beasts or to rot in a most tragic way," as Machino Mondo described.[45] A few days after the surrender, one surviving Aizu samurai, Kawahara Katsuharu, saw the remains of his less fortunate comrades strewn along a stream outside Wakamatsu. "They were bloated like rotten daikon," he recalled, "All their clothing, including their underwear and socks, had been stolen and they were all completely naked. This was a horrible and unbearable sight."[46]

Deeply disturbed by this state of affairs, Aizu samurai under captivity dispatched Machino Mondo and Takatsu Heizō—the would-be perpetrator in

---

42. Nakamura, *Seigun funboshi,* p. 22.
43. Kurokouchi, "Aikyō," p. 5.
44. Boshin senshisha chōreigikai, *Boshin senshisha chōreigikai shuisho.*
45. Machino, "Meiji Boshin sen'eki," p. 287.
46. Kawahara, "Omoide," pp. 39–40.

the Tabanematsu and Shianbashi incidents—to the occupation headquarters for permission to bury the dead. Repeated requests were denied each time. Finally, as Machino recalled rather heroically, he and Takatsu resolved to "make one final attempt, and if we failed, to kill the enemy commander then ourselves." The government commander Sannomiya Yoshitane finally permitted the two to hire local outcasts (*eta*) to collect the bodies and bury them outside Wakamatsu in a cemetery for criminals. Machino and Takatsu protested, whereupon Sannomiya tacitly allowed the bodies to be interred at Amida and Chōmei temples, which happened to be near the outcast quarters in Wakamatsu. A Wakamatsu sake brewer named Hoshi Sadaemon provided a thousand *ryō* to hire the *eta* and cover other expenses. Although the Aizu men "remained bitter that our compatriots who had died fighting for our domainal country were to be disposed like animal carcasses or criminals,"[47] the gruesome task of gathering and burying the rotting corpses began. By then more than six months had elapsed since hostilities ended.

As the story has been told, the Aizu men were dismayed at the laborers' careless handling of the remains. Ban Hyakuetsu—later of the Tabanematsu Incident—who, as the Hawking magistrate, was allowed to directly interact with outcasts, negotiated with them. In exchange for higher pay, he got the workers to handle the bodies more reverently and to stop complaining of the awful stench. Under the watchful eyes of armed guards from the occupation forces, what remained of the bodies was moved using whatever implements could be found, including "bathtubs, bedding, and wooden shelves, into which several body pieces were stuffed."[48] Kurokouchi Ryō, then a young son of a domainal retainer, went to Amida Temple hoping to find his father's remains. "Their clothing was already rotten and could not be recognized," he later described. "The bodies had decomposed, their eyes had rotted away, and the juices that ran from the putrid flesh were a bizarre, shiny mix of brown, light blue, and gray. The bodies released a powerful, unique stench everywhere. Words cannot possibly describe this extreme misery." Under these conditions, he and his mother could not find his father's body among the 1,281 interred at Amida Temple and 145 at Chōmei Temple. They could only "walk home dejected."[49]

Initial prohibitions against burials and memorial services notwithstanding, the Meiji government afforded increasing leeway to its former foes over time. Two months after the mass burial in the spring of 1869, the occupation

---

47. Machino, "Meiji Boshin sen'eki," pp. 20–22.
48. Shiba, "Senshisha sōin maisō no koto."
49. Kurokouchi, "Aikyō," p. 6

authorities sponsored a funerary rite, and in the eighth month, formal services were conducted at Amida and Chōmei temples.[50] Later in the year, the occupation authorities appointed Ban Hyakuetsu the official supervisor of burials. He visited sixteen major battlefields throughout Aizu and gave the dead proper funerary services, carefully recording his activities in *Senshi no bosho soezu*, a meticulously illustrated catalog of each and every grave that was likely meant to console grieving survivors.[51]

In 1876 the Meiji government finally lifted the ban on commemorating *bakufu* soldiers who died "having momentarily lost sight of the imperial will and opposed the emperor in the year of the Boshin," though services were only to be performed privately by "kin and comrades" and not by the government.[52] In 1883, when plans were made to honor the seventh anniversary of the Seinan War dead at Amida Temple, local organizers used the occasion to also hold a memorial service for the Boshin dead. Two of Lord Katamori's sons attended the services, and the event was punctuated by merrymaking on the streets of Wakamatsu, which were lit up by "countless lanterns and scores of dancing girls" from the Nanukamachi entertainment district.[53]

Greater leniency on commemoration corresponded to increasing political clemency that was gradually granted to wartime foes. In 1870 all domainal retainers were pardoned, as was Katamori himself two years later; the former lord was even promoted to full third court rank upon his death in 1893. Even Kayano Gonbei, a domainal elder and the official fall man ordered to disembowel himself upon Aizu's surrender, was posthumously included in the 1889 general amnesty that accompanied the constitutional promulgation. No longer considered criminals, their dead comrades too were now eligible for commemoration, at least locally if not nationally at a place such as Yasukuni Shrine.

Perhaps most instrumental in institutionalizing Aizu's wartime memory was the Aizu Veterans Memorial Association. This organization was formed in September 1914 by Machino Mondo and sixty-five like-minded war veterans and their family members. The Home Ministry recognized the group as a government-approved organization in 1917, thus making it a leading guardian of local memory in Aizu. The association's concern with maintaining the old domainal order is apparent from the fact that Matsudaira Takeo, the second son of Katamori, was its director and Machino Mondo its chairperson.

---

50. Miyasaki, ed., *Aizu Boshin sensō shiryōshū*, p. 207.
51. Ban, *Senshi no bosho soezu*.
52. *Tokyo nichinichi shinbun*, August 20, 1876.
53. *Kaiyō zasshi*, no. 8, October 7, 1883, p. 5; no. 11, October 28, 1883, p. 4.

The memorial association worked to improve both the material and symbolic status of Aizu's war dead. Its mission statement declared in 1914: "Forty-six years have passed since the Boshin War, yet today there are still those who were only buried temporarily and have not been given a proper reburial. They are left out in the cold among wild weeds, with no one to pay respect to their spirits with incense and flowers. Their spirits cry, sad and empty, for they can plead only to the wind and insects." Until the dead were properly recognized, the organizers insisted, "they cannot avoid becoming unattached spirits. How can they possibly rest, knowing that they lived as loyal retainers yet died as unattached spirits?"[54] The association promised to permanently maintain the graves of the war dead at Amida Temple, Chōmei Temple, and Mount Iimori, collect the remains that were scattered about Aizu and inter them at Amida Temple, permanently maintain sites related to the White Tiger Brigade at Mount Iimori, and hold regular ceremonies for the war dead. The group first performed these services in 1916 and continues to do so today.[55]

Organizations such as the Aizu Veterans Memorial Association operated on the conviction that memories of fallen Aizu soldiers were being unfairly sullied and that they deserved to be remembered with greater dignity. Anguish and resentment at disparity between the government dead and the Aizu dead often fueled an angry remembrance of Aizu's past. In 1883 a local weekly, *Kaiyō zasshi*, publicized a movement to give proper burial to the Aizu soldiers who died in the Battle of Shirakawaguchi, the first major battle in the Tōhoku phase of the Boshin War. What motivated the six organizers was their perceived slight at the hands of the government: "As for those who died in the battle on the government side, the imperial court has been particularly generous with them. Not only have they received accolades and prizes, memorial shrines have been built for them so as to teach the people about the glory of dying for their country." But what of the Aizu men? "Once in the past, we Aizu domain erred on whom to follow and opposed imperial authority. This crime is on record as history, or so it is now understood." As a result, their bodies were to be left on the field and their spirits neglected. The organizers begrudged "those who died for the imperial cause and are honored in grand memorial shrines and whose kin enjoy preferential treatment" and

54. Boshin senshisha chōreigikai, *Boshin senshisha chōreigikai shuisho.*

55. Today, biennial Buddhist ceremonies are held at Amida Temple on April 23 and September 23. The ceremony lasts about an hour and is attended by about ninety people. A smaller service is conducted at Chōmei Temple on the same day. The Mount Iimori ceremonies are held the following day in a Shintō style. This is supposedly because the Aizu Matsudaira conducted Shintō funerals.

wished to see their own dead "feel the same kind of comfort and be able to rest with a smile."[56]

Those committed to protecting the memory of Aizu's dead often understood this function as a special duty toward their native place. For them, to remember was to affirm their regional selves, even if it sometimes meant affirming themselves as losers on the margins of history. As one commentary on the seventieth anniversary of the Boshin War ran, "To transmit the painful memories of the Boshin War to posterity over a hundred years might not be important to people from other domains. But for us, the people of Aizu, it is something that we should never forget; nay, it is something we cannot forget."[57] Some commentators grew quite passionate in explaining their unique sense of mission that their homeland demanded. "We Aizu people must pass down our accumulated blood and soul to our descendants and endow them with the spirit of loyalty and righteousness," Watanabe Tadashi exhorted in 1918. "That is how we must cultivate the Aizu spirit and do our utmost for the sake of our descendants and the empire."[58] The Yamakawa brothers certainly considered the remembrance of their long dead comrades a part of their continual service to their lost domain, one that did not end with the physical demise of that domain. Yamakawa Hiroshi first compiled a formal list of the Aizu war casualties to commemorate the seventeenth anniversary of the war, which he, along with his younger brother Kenjirō and others, continued to edit and update well into the twentieth century.[59]

In carrying out their duty to remember and fortifying their sense of regional self along the way, the keepers of Aizu's past inevitably had to confront the nation as rebels. At first glance, this seemed like a losing battle. Aizu's past clearly flew in the face of imperial nationhood, for they could not deny that Aizu was a rebel domain that had once dared fire upon the "inviolable" chrysanthemum standard. Revisiting the Boshin past necessarily put them face to face with the distasteful reality of rebellion. At the same time, however, nationhood also offered unlikely redemptive possibilities, and the arbiters of Aizu's memory eventually learned to take advantage of them. This they did by manipulating remembrance to make their once disaffected past better align with a national imperial narrative.

Early attempts to reconcile Aizu's tainted past with imperial nationhood were awkward and not usually successful. In 1872 a certain Kawashima Jūrō

---

56. *Kaiyō zasshi,* no. 3, September 2, 1883, pp. 6–7.
57. *Aizukai zasshi* 51: p. 56.
58. Watanabe, "Aizu kishitsu no yōsei," p. 10.
59. *Kyū Aizuhan Boshin senshisha meiseki*; *Kōtei Boshin junansha meibo.*

submitted a memorial asking the Meiji government to make the Tokyo Shōkonsha, the precursor to Yasukuni Shrine, more inclusive by opening it up to the losing side of the Restoration war. "Even those who opposed the imperial will should be treated equally, for their duty was nonetheless weighty," he implored. "That they answered to the national crisis should be recognized at the Shōkonsha. Those who died, though they may have momentarily lost their direction, should be treated equally to all others at the Shōkonsha."[60] But the Tokyo Shōkonsha was the culmination of a series of institutions and practices devoted to honoring the Chōshū dead since *bakumatsu* times and was a monument to their memories.[61] It would not easily make room for its foes.

Even after the Shōkonsha became Yasukuni Shrine, the Aizu dead continued to be excluded, though not for lack of effort at inclusion. In 1906 Okada Haruhashi, a former domainal retainer in Wakamatsu and a nephew of an Aizu soldier killed in the Yamato Disturbance of 1863, petitioned the Imperial Diet to have 2,542 Aizu war dead recognized at Yasukuni. When his request was denied, Okada isolated 19 Aizu men who had died suppressing the Yamato *ikki* and the Hamaguri Gate Incident of 1864 and asked to have those men instated at Yasukuni, arguing that they had fallen in the line of imperial duty. He also secured a letter of support from the Ministry of Education's Historiographical Association (Shidankai) and prepared a formal document that exalted the Aizu dead as patriots.[62] This second request was also denied but this did not deter Okada from resubmitting a similar request the following year, this time to the prime minister and the army and navy ministers.[63] Finally, in 1915, 32 Aizu soldiers killed in action during the Hamaguri Gate Incident were enshrined at Yasukuni, for they had fought to protect the imperial compounds in Kyoto during that conflict.

However, it took nearly a century and completely different political circumstances for the Boshin war dead from Aizu to finally make their way into Yasukuni Shrine—though as something of an asterisk. In 1965 an annex called the Chinreisha was quietly added to the Yasukuni compound to recognize "the spirits of those who had died in wars and incidents since 1853 but had not

---

60. *MKS*, 2:62–63.

61. On commemorative practices in *bakumatsu* Chōshū that later developed into Shōkonsha and Yasukuni, see Kobayashi and Terunuma, *Shōkonsha seiritsushi no kenkyū*.

62. *Aizu nippō*, May 30, 1908, p. 4. The document was titled "Junkoku shishi hyōshō tsuiroku no seigan."

63. *Aizu nippō*, June 8, 1909, p. 2.

been enshrined at Yasukuni."[64] It is here that those who had hitherto been excluded for their anti-imperial stance, such as the Aizu soldiers of the Boshin War and Saigō Takamori, are now commemorated.

Kawashima and Okada's efforts were in vain but their argument that Aizu had acted in the national interest informed and encouraged later efforts. Subsequent attempts at rehabilitation scoured Aizu's past for evidence of imperial service and made creative uses of it. Thus they sought redemption for the one-time rebel domain, if at the occasional expense of the truth. This was the strategy often pursued by local organizers of Boshin War anniversary commemorations in Aizu. From the thirty-third anniversary event in 1901 to the fiftieth anniversary in 1918 and on to the seventieth anniversary in 1938, the prevailing logic, language, and imageries gradually gravitated toward the imperial nation.[65]

The thirty-third anniversary, hosted by the county supervisor and the mayor of Wakamatsu, marked the first major, area-wide commemoration of the conflict. As such, the event still retained familiar domain-centric sensibilities. The address by Machino Shigeyo understood Aizu exclusively as an independent domainal entity and judged its past solely on standards of the old polity. In a familiar refrain, his keynote speech attributed Aizu's fateful actions in the Restoration to its special qualities cultivated under the "two hundred-plus years of education provided by past domainal lords."[66] He never explained Aizu in terms of Imperial Japan, perhaps rightly fearful that to do so would evoke the problem of Aizu's rebelliousness. Nor did early commemorations in Aizu give any more consideration to the spirits of the enemy than the government commemorations did, paying respect only to their own losses. This silence perpetuated the clear split between Aizu and the imperial side.

Time would bring about greater sophistication in commemorative techniques, one that would embed Aizu more comfortably within empire. Later organizers in Aizu consciously worked to appropriate the nation's prestige and confer it upon themselves by projecting Aizu's past through the lens of imperial service and loyalty. The fiftieth anniversary event in 1918 was shrewdly softened by a sense of goodwill and rapprochement that had been absent in the previous event. Unlike the earlier service, this one offered prayers for both the Aizu dead as well as "the western forces," and in so doing, brought all combat-

---

64. Moriya, *Yasukuni Jinja hyakunenshi,* p. 617. One interpretation of the Chinreisha is that it served as limbo for World War II Class-A war criminals, who were first brought into the Chinreisha in 1965 and then elevated to Yasukuni Shrine in 1978.

65. These dates reflect the Buddhist schedule of death anniversaries.

66. Wakamatsu shiyakusho, *Wakamatsushishi,* upper volume, p. 618. The thirty-third anniversary was held on September 16, 1901, in Wakamatsu.

ants, dead or alive, into the national embrace. The new conciliatory tone was set by the chairperson of the commemoration committee, Matsumoto Tokimasa, whose opening remarks addressed "the spirits of men from both the eastern and western armies who died in the Boshin War." "Although they engaged in battle and minor differences can be seen between the two sides," he announced, "they differed not at all in sharing the utmost sense of loyalty to the emperor and their country."[67] The governor of Fukushima prefecture, Kawasaki Masakichi, struck the same propitiatory note. "Though the dead had fought on opposing sides, they all acted out of the passions of patriotism and they were united in their spirit to serve the imperial throne. Their greatness should forever be held up as a mirror for the entire nation."[68] The two opposing sides of the Boshin War, which had fought so bitterly in life, were now deftly united in death under the banner of nationalism and loyalism.

Inviting the spirits of the government forces seemed to run the risk of highlighting Aizu's imperial faux pas. But in fact the prestige of imperial service was craftily transferred to the Aizu side, successfully transforming the event into one of hopeful reconciliation that centered around, and reconfirmed, transcendental nationhood. Contemporary ideals of the imperial nation were applied, truth aside, to Aizu's past so as to whitewash uncomfortable divisions. Knowing that imperial loyalty and national patriotism trumped all, later commemorators argued that everyone, regardless of domainal affiliation, had acted out of those incontestable virtues and created a "win–win" situation out of something that had, in truth, been quite different. The new modern myth of Aizu as a loyal-minded and earnest yet ultimately tragic loser was now in the works.

The same rehabilitative logic also carried the seventieth anniversary event. There, the rhetoric that forcibly linked Aizu's past with imperial nationhood was made shriller still. In his speech, the mayor of Wakamatsu, Sase Takeshi, went so far as to declare, with no visible irony, that the two purposes of this commemoration were "One, to honor the spirits of the Boshin war dead everywhere, and two, to promote the spirit of imperial loyalty and patriotism."[69] The mayor conveniently lost sight of the fact that they were gathered to remember those once deemed to have fought against the imperial will. The representative from the Aizu Society who attended the event also took the opportunity to justify Aizu's *bakumatsu* conduct by nationalistic, perhaps even anachronistic, standards. "The samurai of the *bakufu* and various domains believed to be act-

---

67. *Aizukaikaihō* 10: p. 69.

68. Ibid., p. 68.

69. Wakamatsu shiyakusho, *Wakamatsushishi,* upper volume, p. 628.

ing for the sake of the state," he assured the crowd, "As far as the great principle of imperial service was concerned, Aizu was no better or worse than any other domain."[70] Now, at a time when the entire nation was desperately toiling in the name of empire, Aizu's past could readily be made to do the same.

What happened between the thirty-third anniversary and the seventieth was not so much that time's passing simply made people forgive and forget the undeniable violence and passions of the Boshin War. Rather, those same actions were newly reinterpreted to provide deeper emotional satisfaction for all, even the losers. In early commemorations, military service and subsequent deaths could only be understood and accepted, mournfully, in limited domainal terms. This older mentality was personified by the stubborn stalwart Machino Mondo. Machino always maintained that the men of Aizu had fought "for the sake of their lord and country" and died with "only loyalty and patriotism in mind." For Machino, however, loyalty was due only to Lord Katamori and the only object of patriotism was Aizu, for "lord" to him meant the *daimyō* and "country" meant the domain.[71] In Machino's mind, he and his fellow Aizu samurai had fought to protect Katamori, the only lord they knew, and Aizu, the only homeland they knew; was that not good enough?

It was not good enough, according to Meiji standards, which is why later commemorators chose instead to bring Aizu's past into alignment with imperial nationhood. This approach, unlikely enough, offered better redemptive possibilities for Aizu. Imperial nationhood, when reduced to idealized rhetoric and imageries, proved malleable and hospitable enough to permit such creative remembrance. Thus Okabe Seiichi, a historian on the Ministry of Education's Restoration Historiographical Committee and a guest speaker at the fiftieth anniversary event in Aizu, could speak of the Boshin War as "the most meaningful expression of the nationalist spirit," which he cheerfully presented as a contest only in how to best serve the emperor. "Although one side happened to be called 'imperial forces' and the other side 'rebels,' this was mere formality. In their spirit to loyally serve the imperial throne and to offer their lives to the state, they were one." The killings, looting, and chastening that had been done in the name of the emperor were now washed out by the glare of imperial glory; even a professional historian like Okabe was blinded by it. By 1918, Aizu sympathizers like him could freely synthesize region and nation in the most maudlin terms: "May the snow atop Mount Bandai never melt, may the Hibashi River flow for all seasons, and may the good name of the Aizu samurai—the last bastion of Old Japan—forever live

---

70. Ibid., p. 631.
71. Machino, "Meiji Boshin sen'eki," pp. 22–23.

on alongside our empire."[72] This was heady rhetoric and its appeal was obvious. The ideals of imperial and national service—once safely extracted from their contemporary politics and reality—allowed both sides to claim legitimacy and justify their sacrifices in a more satisfying way than any bloody, divisive remembrance could. This was true especially of the losing side, which found much to gain from such an uplifting reinterpretation of the past.

The Birth of a Traditional Aizu in Modern Japan

War and defeat prompted an anguished self-assessment about a lost homeland, and, at the same time, also provided the tools to assemble a new and worthy Aizu. Features that were said to constitute the "Aizu spirit"—from "strong-willed" and "selfless" to "loyal" and "soldierly"—in fact come straight out of wistful retrospection upon the Boshin War. These operative terms were intentional results of commemorative efforts to cast Aizu's recent transgression in a better light. It was the recollection of defeat that birthed an Aizu identity, not Masayuki or the many mountain peaks. Aizu's modern self-image was less the product of history itself than the politics of reconciling that history with imperial nationhood and the struggles to find a proper place for Aizu within a national narrative. Of course, many of Aizu's supposedly distinct qualities sound suspiciously familiar and formulaic, even banal. But war and defeat made them something more than the usual platitudes. Haunting memories of the Restoration experience gave these otherwise generic values a unique emotional charge and immediacy in Aizu, making them even more useful and effective for local identity creation. In short, Aizu's modern identity discourse is best understood as an allegory of its Restoration history, one that would have been neither necessary nor possible without the trauma of the *bakumatsu* years. This was a history that could only have been written in the mid- to late Meiji era, and no earlier than that.

By the same token, inasmuch as "Aizuness" was a modern expedient with a shallower heritage than its advocates claimed, historians should be careful not to haughtily dismiss it as an "invention of tradition" or some such. To do so would be to discount the emotional needs that were, at the time, quite real. Heartfelt contemplation of "Aizuness" guided those who had been mentally and literally dislocated toward a respectable place in a new, unfamiliar world. Besides, in imagining and reimagining memory, they were doing nothing that a historian does not do. If in the process they resorted to chauvinistic imageries and essentialist thinking, they could hardly be blamed.

---

72. *Aizukaikaihō* 10: p. 69.

This project to create a new Aizu identity let an estranged people negotiate the tricky problem of difference—rebel versus subject, local versus national—in modern Japan. In reenvisioning a brighter past for their ancestors, the arbiters of Aizu's memory managed to counteract some of the nation-state's discriminatory inclinations, such as the one that Ueno Chizuko has identified: "The *kokumin* were separated into 'those who had the honor of dying for their country' and 'those who did not have the honor of dying for their country.' Only the former were qualified to be *kokumin*."[73] Like the Japanese women on Ueno's mind, Aizu soldiers, too, were long denied "the honor of dying for the country"; they could not become bona fide *kokumin*. In death, however, they could gain what they did not have in life, for the altar of memory posthumously conferred upon them "the honor of dying for their country." That honor had to be earned over time, but it was possible to secure a better place within national remembrance for Aizu's war dead and, by extension, for their living progeny. Of course, it is only proper to concede here that, in Aizu's case, difference stemmed from conduct, which is perhaps less deterministic or compelling than, say, race, religion, gender, and other common sources of difference that discriminatory nationalist practices often bring to bear. Difference defined by what was essentially bad behavior may well have been easier to negotiate and overcome than difference based on more visible, self-evident markers. Still, it is also worth noting that, in a relatively unified polity like Japan, seemingly minor points of difference could appear that much more glaring, and thus plenty daunting to those, as in Aizu, who sought to surmount them.

Difference that could not be countered by a fanciful vision of equality before the emperor could be explained away through another means. This is where the notion of "tradition" became particularly useful. Aizu apologists regularly invoked Aizu's "traditional qualities" to explain its conduct in Restoration history. It was not rebelliousness, so their argument ran, but good old-fashioned values that motivated Aizu. It was, they claimed, not lack of imperial loyalty but surplus of tradition that made Aizu take its hard-line stance throughout the Restoration struggle. Aizu was thus renovated into a venerable storehouse of traditional values, doggedly guarding its wares against the times, even at the expense of itself. Those who had died protecting this traditional Aizu could now be said to have "beamed the final flash of feudal values" and "crystallized *bushidō* unique to Aizu."[74] In 1917 Okabe Seiichi, the sympathetic historian, defended Aizu soldiers as having "expressed to the very end the *bushidō* spirit." He praised Aizu as the sole keeper of that fading

73. Ueno, *Nashonarizumu to jendā,* p. 34.

74. Suzuki, "Aizu kifū no han'yō," p. 6.

martial tradition, arguing that the vaunted Way of the Warrior "survived only in the fields of Aizu," where the last true samurai of Japan made their last stand in 1868.[75] Historical claims to "tradition" thus became Aizu's ticket back to respectability in modern Japan. When the Aizu Veterans Memorial Association called for better historiographical treatment of Aizu in Meiji times, it argued that *bakumatsu*-period Aizu was "the final bloom of feudal society," and as such, "its historical meaning is important and must be made a part of Japanese history."[76] This logic astutely recognized that rebellion might not have a place in national history, but tradition does.

By making such claims to "tradition," one-time rebels could find parity with modern nationhood and place their homeland on the same plane as their country. The image-makers of Aizu understood that they could reach their goal quicker by hitching themselves onto the rapidly accelerating vehicle of Japanese patriotism. Kurokouchi Ryō, a former domainal retainer and an editor of the *Aizu Society Newsletter,* based his local boosterism on the premise that "love for the homeland was originally a part of love for the country. Among those who have loved their homeland, none have not loved their country as well. Therefore, for me to speak of my love for my homeland is to speak of my love for my country."[77] He could then dare assert this equivalency: "Our Aizu spirit is indeed the spiritual essence of our divine country Japan."[78] Articulations of "Aizuness" readily drew upon national idioms, and in the process, Aizu folks could appropriate much of that prestige for themselves. "The Aizu spirit goes hand in hand with the martial spirit, and complements the Japanese spirit and *bushidō,*" one man exuberantly wrote in 1916. "It is one and the same as the Imperial Will as handed down through the Imperial Rescript on Education and the Imperial Rescript of 1908 (*Boshin shōsho*)."[79] He eagerly equated region with the nation and offered that the best of Aizu was the best of imperial Japan. What made Aizu great could also make Japan great.

Or, perhaps, even greater. Some went so far as to prescribe the Aizu spirit as an antidote for what ailed the nation. One Aizu man in 1924 warned of "encroachment of contemporary thought"—that is, Westernization—upon Taishō Japan. His solution was "to blow forth the mighty wind of Aizu *bushidō* from atop Mount Bandai and cast away in one fell swoop the shallow lightweights and arrogant weaklings who have corrupted all of Japan. This is

75. Okabe, *Boshin sen'eki ni tsuite.*
76. Sakuragi et al., *Aizu chōreigikai dokuhon,* p. 64.
77. Kurokouchi, "Aikyō," p. 12.
78. Kurokouchi, "Aizujinshi ni tsugu," p. 13.
79. "Aizudamashii," p. 22.

the most urgent of our duties as people of Aizu."[80] The local historian Sōda Sanpei had something similar in mind when he compiled in 1917 various episodes about Aizu women's tragic and self-sacrificial conduct during the Boshin War. He presented their gruesome tales of group suicide as testament to traditional values in Aizu and, by extension, the value of a traditional Aizu in these modern times. The commendable actions of these women under duress, he argued, were "the natural result" of conduct befitting "womanly women" (a phrase that he chose to present phonetically in English) whom the author "wishes to hold up proudly to the rest of the world." These model women of old Aizu were then contrasted against the self-indulgent women of Taishō Japan, who were obsessed with what he disparagingly called "female self-actualization" as advocated by Western writings.[81] Such vigorous, if questionable, claims to tradition helped Aizu discover its niche within the national body of moral and aesthetic values, giving Aizu yet another positive counterbalance against its negative historical baggage. Thus, even a place like Aizu could not only find parity with the nation, it could even offer to better the nation. Aizu could furnish "tradition" just when modern Japan sorely needed it.

Once again, region and nation found unlikely compatibility. It was not that new visions of the nation had to overcome old visions of the region. Nor was it that the peculiarity of the region had to wiggle itself into the totality of the nation. If nation was a local metaphor, the reverse was also true; locality could become a national metaphor.[82] Identity rhetoric managed to inflate Aizu's value and conflate it with the nation, even in a region as historically problematic and marginalized as Aizu. Indeed, by the time Machino Mondo's strange funeral took place in 1923, men like him were, literally, a dying breed. Many of his contemporaries, and much of the younger generation, were content with a different vision of their homeland, one that had made peace with its own past and with imperial nationhood. They were discovering new, more amicable ways to remember past losses and sacrifice in terms that complemented the empire, not defied it. In so doing, they gladly participated in the "strange forgetting of the history of the nation's past: the violence involved in establishing the nation's writ." In Aizu, this forgetting permitted not only "the beginning of the nation's narrative" but a region's, too.[83] Selective remembrance helped to script an appealing narrative that offered unlikely

80. Suzuki, "Aizu kifū no han'yō," p. 8.

81. Sōda, "Boshin no eki," p. 8. This is similar to Nihei, *Aizu retsujo no kagami,* in content and structure.

82. Confino, *The Nation as a Local Metaphor.*

83. Bhabha, "DissemiNation," p. 310.

redemption for the onetime rebel domain. Aizu's modern myth rendered it into a loyal if tragic servant that was dutiful to a fault and a stout keeper of Japan's finest traditions.

A new reconciliatory rendering of the Restoration neutralized domainal partisanship of that conflict when, in truth, that partisanship had caused much acrimony and bloodshed and brought about the many violent deaths that made these commemorations necessary in the first place. New imageries gently wrapped Aizu's cruel fate in the comforts of an idealized nationhood that did not exist when the men fell in the mountains and fields of Aizu. Their new death portraits, depicting them as unwavering and loyal to the very end, were presented to help their spirits rest easier knowing that they had died as patriots, not rebels. Jubilant remembrance insisted that their ancestors had sacrificed themselves for the sake of national unity and imperial glory, even if neither was what they had in mind when they took a bullet or a blow back in 1868. Now, if Aizu domain could be demonstrated to have acted for the sake of the imperial nation all along, then all its suffering could be made more palatable and their progeny more redeemable. This was precisely the task entrusted to revisionist local historiography, which was expected to bring a curative sense of imperial virtue to Aizu's troubled past.

CHAPTER 5

Healing through History: Rehabilitative Historiography in Aizu

"A Bent Brush and Flurrying Words"

A history quiz show on Japanese television in 2008 posed the following question: What made Aizu domain finally surrender in the Boshin War of 1868? The correct answer, viewers were told, was that the human excrement that had built up in Tsuruga Castle during the siege became too much to bear and caused the Aizu defenders to flee. Upon hearing this, the mayor of Aizu Wakamatsu, Kanke Ichirō, lodged a complaint against TBS, the broadcaster in Tokyo. To him, this was yet another instance of the dominant center misrepresenting and besmirching Aizu history. TBS producers visited Aizu Wakamatsu a few days later to apologize in person, but the mayor stood his ground. "The people of Aizu Wakamatsu cannot accept this apology," he declared as he turned them away, then quoted a classic Aizu maxim from the domainal days: "What must not be, must not be."[1]

This smalltime political performance was in fact a part of a deeper local tradition. It turns out that this incident was just another battle in a long, ongoing history war in Aizu. In 1986, Aizu Wakamatsu refused a request by the city of Hagi in Yamaguchi prefecture—the former castle town of Chōshū domain—to become "sister cities" because, it was said, bitter feelings toward Chōshū still lingered in Aizu even 120 years after the war. In the aftermath of the 2011 nuclear disaster in eastern Fukushima, Hagi sent 2.3 million yen in donations and 14 tons of provisions to Aizu Wakamatsu, whose tourism and agriculture suffered greatly from misperceptions about radiation risks. Even when Mayor Kanke visited Hagi to thank the city—becoming only the second

1. Asahi.com, "TBS ga Aizu ni shazai: rekishi kuizu bangumi mondai de," March 31, 2008.

Aizu mayor to visit Hagi in modern times—he refused to even discuss the possibility of formal reconciliation between the two old rivals.[2]

The past hangs heavily in Aizu in a way that it does in few other locales in present-day Japan. Obviously, this is not to say that other places do not care about their history, but many Aizu people—often with family roots to the old domain, but not necessarily—do continue to engage in an identity discourse that is highly retrospective. These are people who eagerly link their present selves with the distant past and can be rather proud and sensitive about that past. Perhaps this is because the past is the one thing they have for sure. Aizu today finds itself in a quiet, though not uncomfortable, stasis that is rather typical of an isolated Japanese interior. If Aizu tends to look backward rather than forward, it only seems natural.

These people today who take their local history quite seriously and personally are following a long line of predecessors. This tradition was firmly established in the early Meiji years, when the survivors of a fallen domain began to search for redemption and resist the charge that they were nothing more than disgraced rebels. For them, too, a new beginning for Aizu had to start with its past, which may have been the hardest place to start. Scars of defeat, left indelibly upon cemeteries and gravestones throughout Aizu, also marred the pages of Meiji-era history books. The field of historiography became the new battleground where opposing remembrances of the Restoration war now clashed. Here, the defenders of Aizu's memory hoped to have better luck than they had on the battlefields of 1868, for, as Aizu's combat veterans and their descendants saw it, there was a great deal of rehabilitating to be done.

That much is obvious from the vigorous objections that rose in Aizu over how Meiji-era official histories and textbooks treated their old domain. Those who saw Aizu as a historiographical victim made their displeasure known time and again. An *Aizu Society Newsletter* editorial in 1918 accused the business tycoon Shibusawa Eiichi of using "a bent brush and flurrying words" and "greatly misrepresenting both Aizu and Kuwana domains" in his recent biography of Tokugawa Yoshinobu. Shibusawa's historiographical libel "has in turn misled other historians," as the editors claimed.[3] In 1937, when the renowned journalist Tokutomi Sohō stepped forth to support Aizu's historiographical cause, he confirmed what many in Aizu had long known. "Restoration histories written to this day can be said to be the history of Satsuma and Chōshū," Sōhō

---

2. See http://sankei.jp.msn.com/affairs/news/110717/dst11071712000008-n1.htm (accessed July 17, 2011).

3. "Aizujin no tokushoku," p. 6 . They are most likely complaining about Shibusawa's 1918 biography of shogun Yoshinobu, *Tokugawa Yoshinobukō den*.

observed, "It might also be said to be the history of the old *bakufu*. But it cannot be said to be the history of Japan."[4] Such complaints, just two among many, lamented Aizu's cursed place in the annals of Japanese history.

Especially vexing to the guardians of Aizu's past were the labels "rebel" and "enemy of the court," the stigma Aizu had long suffered since its political missteps and military failures of the *bakumatsu* period. Nothing quite touched Aizu nerves the way those words did. "As an Aizu man, I feel great displeasure when I read histories about the Boshin War written by people from other prefectures," complained Sōda Shūson, a frequent contributor to the *Aizu Society Newsletter*. "These works contain phrases like 'the rebel army,' 'enemy of the court,' 'resisted the imperial forces,' 'erred in their direction.' . . . It is unbearable to see these phrases in recent elementary and middle-school textbooks." In an article calling to "take back Aizu's honor," Sōda bristled, "More than fifty years have passed since the Boshin War, yet the words 'rebel forces' are still used to describe Aizu domain. That this is so evident in textbooks makes me unbearably angry."[5] A fellow Aizu man, Kobayashi Yūshichirō, shared this agitation. "I see how this great domain Aizu is presented as an 'enemy of the court' in Restoration histories," Kobayashi decried, "How brave was what came before the war; how tragic was what came after."[6] For them, the persistent use of the imperial–rebel polemic signified the historiographical tyranny of the victors and reminded them, in the most demeaning manner, of their shame and defeat.

Complaints were grounded in a good measure of truth, for not a few history books did indeed use the sort of language that Aizu veterans found insulting to the memory of their struggle. It was certainly standard practice, with only a few exceptions, for Meiji-era history books to refer to the Satsuma-Chōshū coalition as the "imperial forces." As for Aizu, it was commonly presented as the foil: "rebels." Such was the case for private history books such as *Kokushi ran'yō* written in 1874, *Naikoku shiryaku* in 1874, and *Meiji seishi* in 1892, official histories such as *Meiji shiyō* in 1876, and classroom textbooks including *Shōgaku shiryaku* in 1877.[7] The same goes for *Zoku kokushiryaku* of 1873, which, despite being coedited by a former Aizu retainer, Ogasawara Katsunaga, denigrated the Aizu men as "rebel soldiers."[8]

---

4. Tokutomi, *Kinsei Nihon kokuminshi,* 78:5.

5. Sōda, "Meiyo no kaifuku o kisu," pp. 3, 4.

6. Kobayashi, "Aizuron," p. 66.

7. *Kokushi ran'yō* 16, pp. 26, 27; Ishimura, *Naikoku shiryaku,* 2:10; Dajōkan shūshikan, *Meiji shiyō,* 1:12, 96; Fujimoto, *Shōgaku kokushiryaku;* Sasuhara, *Meiji seishi.*

8. Ogasawara et al., eds. *Zoku kokushiryaku kōhen,* 1:6.

It was not only the labels that bothered some in Aizu. No less hurtful to them were phrases and expressions such as "[Aizu] resisted the imperial forces," "[the court] chastised Aizu," "pacifying the northeast," "the northeast rebellion," and "the Aizu rebellion." Not surprisingly, these usages were most glaring in so-called official histories, which were commissioned by the Meiji state. The Dajōkan's *Fukkoki,* which one modern scholar has called not a work of history but a "record of the glorious triumph of imperial restoration,"[9] used unabashedly partisan language, especially to describe combat. On offense, the imperial forces were said to "go forth and smite" while Aizu soldiers invariably "invaded" and "ambushed." When the tide of battle turned, the imperial forces were described as having "not had the advantage" and "drawn back their defenses," while the rebels were prone to "get smashed and run away."[10] Restoration narratives were typically framed as a stark imperial–rebel binary, reifying the former as the norm and prosecuting the latter as deviant.

Little wonder, then, that those who cared about Aizu's historical legacy mistrusted "official" historians. In 1915 an unhappy Sōda Shūson wrote, "It is quite dubious whether the Restoration Historiographical Agency [Ishin shiryō henshūkyoku in the Ministry of Education] is capable of producing a fair and accurate history that people of Aizu desire." He doubted that the official organ could offer "a clear, historical perspective and a nuanced presentation of how Aizu domain contributed to national politics during the *bakumatsu* years . . . and how, once the situation became untenable, it took on the soldiers of the entire realm all by itself."[11] Hirosawa Yasutake, a nephew of Hirosawa Yasutō, a Boshin War veteran and later a dairy magnate in Aomori, shared this suspicion. "The Restoration Historiographical Agency . . . perpetuates the old tendency to write histories that favor victors at the expense of the losers," he complained.[12] Affronted by the perception that "loyal deeds of us, the Aizu samurai, have been ignored," Hirosawa took matters into his own hands by producing and publishing in 1923 his own account of Aizu political activists in the *bakumatsu* period called *Bakumatsu Aizu shishiden kōhon.*

All this was par for the course in the stilted imperial historiography common in the Meiji era. Textbooks openly advertised their polemic and didactic purpose. Whether it was *Kokushikiyō* hoping to "induce love and loyalty for the emperor among readers" or *Nihonshiyō* declaring that "children will be

---

9. Ōkubo, *Nihon kindai shigaku no seiritsu,* p. 351.
10. Dajōkan, *Fukkoki,* 15:324–25.
11. Sōda, "Aizushi hensen no gi," p. 12.
12. Hirosawa and Sōda, eds., *Bakumatsu Aizu shishiden kōhon.*

taught to respect the ruler, love their country, value intense loyalty, and fear rebellion," they affirmed the intentions of the Ministry of Education, which, when soliciting manuscripts for classroom texts in 1887, specified, "Children must naturally absorb the passions of patriotism and imperial loyalty through their study of history. Manuscripts that fail to do this sufficiently must be so improved."[13] Soaring paeans to imperial loyalty was an obligatory part of Meiji historiographical orthodoxy, perhaps even its raison d'être.

The same imperial principle governed official histories. Works produced under government patronage, like *DaiNihon hennenshi, Kinsei shiryaku, Fukkoki, Meiji shiyō,* and *Kokushigan,* were written from the so-called imperial restoration historiographical viewpoint (*ōseifukko shikan*). This viewpoint held that warrior rule was the exception in Japanese history and that Satsuma and Chōshū triumphantly restored the normative default in 1868.[14] This imperial conceit guided official historiographical organs like the Dajōkan's History Section (Rekishika, established 1869), Historiographical Agency (Shūshikan, 1877), the Department of History (Shigakka, 1888) at the Tokyo Imperial University, and the Restoration Historiographical Committee (Ishin shiryō henshūkai, 1911). Works like *Taisei kiyō*, a project coordinated by Iwakura Tomomi that fixed history into "unending imperial succession and unchanging role of rulers and the ruled," and the Tokyo Imperial University's *Kokushigan,* which was an "imperial narrative linking history and myth," all reduced Japanese history to imperial history.[15] As for who could participate in this official production, the Meiji emperor authorized in 1888 four, and only four, former *daimyō* houses to write family histories chronicling their contribution to the Restoration: the Shimazu of Satsuma, the Mōri of Chōshū, the Yamanouchi of Tosa, and the Mito Tokugawa, whose historians, despite being affiliated with the shogunal family, were long known for their Mito School loyalism.[16] Those like the Aizu Matsudaira were, for obvious reasons, excluded from this endeavor.

All this added up to a severe disadvantage for Aizu, which, as the nationalist narrative deemed, had clearly violated the cardinal principle of imperial loyalty. In this Meiji paradigm, Aizu was doomed to be but a cautionary tale. Or so it seemed, until the guardians of Aizu's past began to make their case in the late nineteenth century. Their efforts at national inclusion were bolstered

13. Okamoto, *Kokushikiyō;* Hara, *Nihonshiyō;* Monbushō, *Shōgakkōyō rekishi hensan shuisho.*

14. Ōkubo, *Nihon kindai shigaku no seiritsu,* p. 346.

15. Kōjida, "Nihonshi no tanjō," pp. 136–37.

16. Miyachi, "Bakumatsu Meiji zenki," p. 554.

in part by the times. The classic imperial–rebel split had become less useful in the modern world system. Historical reminders of internal divisiveness, especially bloody conflict, became less desirable in a modern nation-state like Meiji Japan, which existed alongside other competing nation-states. It behooved nationalists, at least once they achieved a measure of security, to forget past conflicts or, better yet, to reshape them so as to render its basis, the imperial throne, not only inviolable but demonstrably inviolate.

Aizu's historiographical rally came on three fronts. Leading the charge were late Meiji and Taishō-era chroniclers of Aizu, including combat veterans and former domainal leaders, who narrated Aizu's *bakumatsu* experience from their perspective. They were followed by outside commentators, journalists, and historians who sympathized with Aizu's historiographical plight. Finally, local activists stormed what they viewed as the final bastion of the winners' history: school textbooks. Collectively, they worked to loosen Aizu from the iron grips of the imperial–rebel vice and cast it instead into the forgiving embrace of patriotic service.

The first volley was fired by the Yamakawa brothers—Hiroshi the army officer and Kenjirō the Yale-educated physics professor—who sought to rehabilitate Aizu's image by recovering and advertising Aizu's history of imperial loyalty. The Yamakawas came from a long line of domainal elders and played leadership roles in the *bakumatsu* crisis. In 1898 Kenjirō became the financial adviser to the Matsudaira family, whereupon he discovered official domainal correspondences and Matsudaira household records, including four imperial letters from Emperor Kōmei thanking Lord Katamori for extending Aizu's services to the court as Kyoto Protectorate.[17] Kenjirō and Hiroshi then used these documents to produce a history of Aizu's tenure as the Kyoto Protectorate. Hiroshi died of illness in 1898, but Kenjirō continued to work on the manuscript and soon made the most of it. In 1902 he showed Miura Gorō—a powerful behind-the-scenes politico, formerly of Chōshū—his completed manuscript and the imperial letters from Emperor Kōmei. When Kenjirō indicated that he would go public with this material, Miura was disturbed enough to consult Itō Hirobumi and arranged an imperial gift of thirty thousand yen to the financially strapped Matsudaira household as hush money. In return, Kenjirō was asked to withhold publication of the documents, which would have undermined the official designation of Aizu as rebels. In 1911, after Itō Hirobumi had died, Kenjirō distributed copies of the

17. Official domainal correspondence between Wakamatsu and Kyoto is now available in Aizu Wakamatsu-shi, ed., *Bakumatsu Aizuhan ōfuku monjo* (Aizu Wakamatsu: Aizu Wakamatsu-shi, 2000).

manuscript privately among former domainal retainers.[18] This work later became *Kyotoshugoshoku shimatsu*, which remains to this day the most comprehensive narrative of Aizu's services as Kyoto Protectorate.

Miura's payoff also came to naught because another former Aizu official, Kitahara Masanaga, did in 1904 what Miura had prevented Yamakawa Kenjirō from doing in 1902. It was then that Kitahara, who had led Aizu's defense of Bonari Peak during the Boshin War and later became the mayor of Nagasaki, published his *Shichinenshi*. Kitahara was evidently in cahoots with Yamakawa Kenjirō, as Kenjirō wrote the preface to Kitahara's work. *Shichinenshi* presented the pivotal seven years between 1862 and 1868 through Aizu's eyes. It directly challenged the official history of the same period, the *Fukkoki*, by advertising Aizu's record of imperial service during that time. Kitahara became the first to put into public circulation the four letters written by Emperor Kōmei to Katamori that Miura Gorō had sought to suppress. Kitahara also detailed the imperial audience in 1863, when Katamori paraded 1,888 Aizu soldiers before a grateful Emperor Kōmei to show that Aizu was willing and able to flex its muscle for the court. Such evidence of Aizu's imperial dedication emboldened Yamakawa Kenjirō to declare in the preface, "Those who devoted themselves to national matter since 1862 are not to be separated by their imperial loyalty. There was only the difference between the 'pro-*bakufu*/pro-emperor' side and the 'anti-*bakufu*/pro-emperor' side. Many histories of the Restoration written by 'anti-*bakufu*/pro-emperor' hands fail to tell the truth of the matter."[19] Another preface went so far as to suggest that *Shichinenshi* was the true official history, praising it as "the history of our country, not merely the history of Aizu domain."[20] This, too, was taking a glove to the face of officially sanctioned narratives such as the *Fukkoki*.

Even those who had once opposed Aizu on the battlefield began coming to its aid in this historiographical fight. When Hiraishi Benzō, a colonel in the imperial army and a grandson of an Aizu retainer killed in the Boshin War, wrote *Aizu Boshin sensō* in 1917, he managed to get not only a prominent figure but a former foe to write the preface to his book. Itagaki Taisuke, the elder Meiji statesman writing just two years before his death, looked back with much forgiveness upon the war he had fought as a young man. The former Tosa commander, now eighty years old, wrote, "Labels such as 'imperial forces' and 'rebel forces' have been used to indicate difference, but this is only formality. The two sides were united in their will to offer their loyalty to the imperial

18. Kinseki, "Yamakawa Kenjirō no hataraki," p. 22.
19. Kitahara, *Shichinenshi*, 1:1.
20. Ibid., p. 3.

court. Therefore, whenever anyone examines the deeds of the Tōhoku domains carefully, no evil can possibly be found." It was neither advancing age nor discontent with domainal cliquishness that made Itagaki offer this olive branch. Rather, his forbearance was motivated by the spirit of national unity, "a viewpoint that will help cultivate our national character and bring beauty into our national history."[21] For this aged warrior, it was now enough for history to convey "beauty" and "national character," rather than sheer veracity or lessons in imperial loyalism. This sensibility also drove much of the rehabilitative historiography in post-Restoration Aizu.

The stewards of Aizu's past eagerly sought validation from outsiders such as Itagaki. They found another ally in Okabe Seiichi, a member of the government's Restoration Historiographical Committee, who also expressed his sympathy for the losers. As a scholar of *Taiheiki*, a chronicle of another imperial conflict in the fourteenth century, Okabe was especially sensitive about historiographical manipulation of imperial loyalism. "Traditionally, the loser's history has returned to dust," he wrote, "The Northern-Southern Courts Period, for example, is barely knowable through glimpses from the *Taiheiki*. Likewise, the history of Aizu domain is about to return to dust. As a member of the Restoration Historiographical Committee, I hope to preserve the loser's historical records."[22] In 1917 Okabe won still more goodwill in Aizu by writing a five-part series in the local daily, *Aizu nippō*, titled "On the Boshin War." Here, he did his best to relieve Aizu from the burden of its past. "Labels like 'imperial forces' and 'rebels' are mere formalities," he argued, "To dwell upon these labels obscures our understanding of historical truth."[23] Okabe thus highlighted the artifice and evanescence of the imperial–rebel dichotomy that informed conventional narratives.

Perhaps the most prominent figure to come to Aizu's rescue was the journalist and public intellectual Tokutomi Sohō. In 1936, he was in the midst of writing what turned out to be his seventy-six-volume masterpiece *Kinsei Nihon kokuminshi* as a serial in the *Mainichi* newspaper. When local activists learned that this work would be sympathetic to Aizu's predicament, they organized an ad hoc "Aizu Association for Sohō" and invited the journalist to speak in Wakamatsu. Sohō accepted, and in May 1937, he delivered a speech that helped unshackle Aizu from the heavy chains of rebellion. "No one in Sendai or Aizu has ever opposed the emperor," he pronounced before a crowd of 1,800 packing Wakamatsu city assembly hall. "It is wrong to refer

21. Hiraishi, *Aizu Boshin sensō*, preface.
22. Okabe, *Boshin sen'eki ni tsuite*, p. 16.
23. Ibid., pp. 56–57.

to them as 'rebels.'" He offered the contemporary party difference between the Seiyūkai and the Minseitō as an analogy to the warring sides in the Restoration and called for an overdue reconciliation. "Today, seventy years have passed since the Meiji era began," he declared, "To continue speaking of 'imperial forces' and 'rebel forces' in print is terribly mistaken."[24] Local papers reported that Sohō's words turned the hall into "a cauldron of emotions" and he left to an exuberant chorus of "Sohō sensei banzai! (Long Live Master Sohō!)"[25]

In Wakamatsu, Sohō was preaching to the choir but he also conveyed the same message to a national audience in *Kinsei Nihon kokuminshi,* which he presented as "an accurate history, a history that does not give imperial loyalists the name of 'rebels.'" Here again he defended the Restoration losers. "The *bakufu* side certainly had no intention of rebelling against the imperial court," he insisted, "The Satsuma-Chōshū side tricked the *bakufu* side and forced the label 'rebels' upon it. From a balanced, historical judgment, both the imperial forces and the so-called rebels were compelled to improvise according to circumstances. Neither was black or white.[26] Sohō also condemned the Meiji government's punishment of Aizu after the war in a chapter he called "The Problem of the Tōhoku Settlement."

These encouragements gave the guardians of Aizu's memory the necessary ammunition to undertake their most important task: textbook revision. Early to mid-Meiji-era school texts varied widely in portraying the Restoration war, but the inconsistency ended when textbooks were standardized in 1903. Government-issued history texts like *Shōgaku kokushi* and *Shōgaku Nihon rekishi* earned Aizu's ire in the early Shōwa years for their openly didactic treatment of Aizu. "Our motherland Aizu is tainted with the name 'rebels' in the annals of national history," one commentary decried, "It is obvious that schoolchildren all over the country who read *Shōgaku kokushi* will all mistakenly think that Aizu domain was a rebel army that resisted the imperial standards. . . . This is a most painful matter."[27] To alleviate this pain, Ugawa Hisae, the son of an Aizu retainer and an Imperial Army Cadet School faculty member, began a text revision movement. In 1940 Ugawa and twenty-eight other Aizu men formed the "Association for Publicizing the Imperial Loyalism of Aizu Domain." Its mission statement made the following eight demands:

---

24. Tokutomi, *Ishinshi ni okeru Aizu,* pp. 6–7.
25. Hayakawa, *Fūgetsutei kaisō,* p. 71.
26. Tokutomi, *Kinsei Nihon kokuminshi,* 78:1–2.
27. "Aizuhan zokumei setsujoku to Ugawa sensei," p. 26.

1. Remove the words "imperial forces" from elementary school textbooks;
2. Remove passages that suggest rebellion such as "Aizu resisted the imperial forces";
3. Include the fact that Lord Matsudaira Katamori was presented imperial gifts for his loyal service to Emperor Kōmei;
4. Include the fact that Lord Katamori was pardoned. This omission is unnatural because textbooks already mention that Saigō Takamori was later pardoned and given court rank;
5. Indicate expressly in the history of the Restoration that there were only the two sides: "pro-emperor and anti-*bakufu*" and "pro-emperor and pro-*bakufu*," and that there were no rebels;
6. Indicate expressly that Aizu domain had a special tradition of imperial loyalty since the days of Lord Masayuki;
7. Although textbooks indicate that "Aizu colluded with the various Tōhoku domains," Aizu was not in fact a member of the Tōhoku alliance;
8. In this time of crisis, national unity must be cultivated. It is time to sweep aside all inappropriate references such as "imperial forces" and "rebel forces."[28]

These demands synthesized the various historiographical calls that had long been made in Aizu—break up the imperial–rebel binary, denature rebellion through claims of shared loyalism, and create a history of imperial loyalty in Aizu, all in the name of unified nationhood. Ugawa and his colleagues approached the Ministry of Education several times in 1940 with their request, which was met with surprising ease and speed in December of that year. In June 1941, schoolchildren nationwide were issued new textbooks, which now featured a specious line about how then-Emperor Kōmei wished for the court, the *bakufu*, and all the people to come together to overcome the challenges facing *bakumatsu*-era Japan. Because an imperial call for national unity resonated naturally with contemporary events in wartime Japan, the government acceded to the Aizu claim on three other points as well. Whereas the text used to state, "Former *bakufu* retainers, along with the domainal retainers of Aizu and Kuwana *raised disturbance* upon hearing news [about Yoshinobu surrendering his land and office]" to describe events leading up to the Battle of Toba-Fushimi, it was now tempered to say, "Aizu and Kuwana *became anxious* upon hearing the news." As for the line "the Lord of Aizu Matsudaira Katamori *colluded with* northeastern domains, holed up in Wakamatsu Castle, and *resisted the imperial forces*," the phrase "colluded with" was replaced by "in conjunction with" and the last phrase about resisting the imperial forces was redacted altogether. Finally, the section on the Meiji Restoration was given a far happier ending. After describing the civil

28. Hayakawa, *Fūgetsutei kaisō*, pp. 124–25.

war, the text now concluded, "Later, the court gave consideration to Katamori's earlier efforts to protect Kyoto and strive in loyalty. It pardoned him and awarded him full third court rank."[29] Clearly, Ugawa chose a most opportune time for leveraging contemporary political imperatives to recover his former domain's honor. Prevailing conditions had made Aizu a rebel in the early Meiji era; prevailing conditions could remake Aizu yet again in the early Shōwa era.

There were two main historiographical strategies for making Aizu's past more palatable in modern times than what the imperial–rebel conflict paradigm had wrought in the early Meiji years. One was to depoliticize the Restoration war by reinterpreting it as the latest in a long series of clashes between regional cultures within Japan. This line of argument rendered the difference between the warring sides as one not of imperial loyalty but of long-standing internal geopolitical tension. The sympathetic historian Okabe Seiichi took this approach in his 1916 newspaper serial. In it, he embedded the *bakumatsu* strife within a long, historical rivalry between eastern Japan and western Japan stretching from prehistory to the modern present. He claimed that "the Boshin War was the final clash in the continual struggle between the two great cultures" of east and west. Okabe made Aizu the representative of a martial eastern culture, arguing that Aizu defenders "expressed to the very end the *bushidō* spirit, which is the essence of Kantō culture," while Satsuma and Chōshū spearheaded western Japan.[30] Thus he made labels like "imperial" and "rebel" less germane to Restoration history. A similar approach favored by the Aizu Veterans Memorial Association also sought to deimperialize the war through a subnational interpretation, and in so doing, escape the imperial–rebel ideology that was so unkind to Aizu. As the association's mission statement began, "In looking back, the Boshin War emerged not from the principles of imperial reverence, *bakufu* preservation, or the court-*bakufu* alliance, but as an armed struggle between the east and the west."[31] Hope in the objectivity of geography still finds expression in present-day Aizu historians' practice of calling the Satsuma-Chōshū side the "western forces" and the Aizu side the "eastern forces."

But the geographical argument could only take so much sting out of the war. It still entailed conflict, and more important, it did an unsatisfactory end around on the point of imperial loyalty. More emotionally fulfilling and politically useful was to collapse the imperial–rebel binary and insist that Aizu

29. Ugawa, "*Shōgaku kokushi* ni tsukite," pp. 10–14.

30. Okabe, *Boshin sen'eki ni tsuite*, p. 8.

31. Boshin senshisha chōreigikai, *Boshin senshisha chōreigikai shuisho.*

had been no less imperially loyal than its foes. One crucial step toward this goal was to establish a historical tradition of imperial service in Aizu. To this end, Hoshina Masayuki, the progenitor of the Aizu Matsudaira line and, unlike his descendant Katamori, safely ensconced in the distant past, was brought out of storage and buffed into a shiny paragon of imperial dedication. The arbiters of Aizu's past seized upon Masayuki's interest in Shintō and ran with it, undeterred by the pitfalls of interpretive anachronism. To that end, much was made of the fact that Masayuki hired Yamazaki Ansai, the founder of the imperialist Suika Shintō, as an adviser, and the fact that Masayuki, as well as all but one of Aizu's lords, was given Shintō death rites. All this was then associated much too freely with imperial loyalty, until Masayuki was transformed into the fount of Aizu's newly minted imperial tradition. "So-called emperor-centrism was at the core of Lord Masayuki's spirit," Tokutomi Sohō declared in recklessly contemporary language, "Lord Masayuki was an estimable Japanese nationalist and his mind was always on the imperial court. . . . There is here in Aizu a tradition of imperial reverence."[32] As hazardous as it is to call anyone in the seventeenth century a "Nihon shugisha," it was a necessary and useful part of crafting a tradition of imperial loyalism in Aizu.

Once Aizu's founder exhumed as an indisputable loyalist, his more recent and most problematic descendant Katamori was gained a new possibility for redemption as the rightful inheritor of this supposed tradition. As Sohō continued, "Aizu's so-called imperial loyalism was not made overnight in the Keiō era (1865–68). It dates back to Lord Masayuki's days, and those who came after him followed in his footsteps. . . . Aizu's imperial loyalism was handed down by its ancestors. Its principle of court-*bakufu* union was handed down by its ancestors.[33] It was this purposefully constructed "spirit of imperial reverence" that allowed one local educator in 1937 to conclude, "The Boshin War was fought under the one umbrella of imperial loyalty, between the progressives and the conservatives. There is no need to think of it in divisive terms like imperial and rebel, loyalty and resistance."[34]

This tact also helped to absolve Katamori's guilt as an "enemy of the court," an emotional baggage that had weighed heavily on his men after the war. It was, after all, their own military inadequacies that burdened their lord with that crime. When Katamori died in 1893, his Aizu keepers gave him the unusual posthumous name Masane (忠誠), written with the same characters as for "loyalty," so as to allow their lord, at least in death, some relief from that burden.

---

32. Tokutomi, *Ishinshi ni okeru Aizu*, p. 14.

33. Ibid.

34. Maeda, "Aizuhan no sonnō seishin," p. 10.

It is no coincidence that the Yamakawa brothers chose to begin their revisionist *Kyōtoshugoshoku shimatsu* with a hagiography of their former lord that was titled not after his tainted living name "Matsudaira Katamori" but the pristine posthumous name "Lord Minamoto no Masane." This transformation unloaded the laden Matsudaira surname and transported their ill-fated lord all the way back to the pure, original warrior surname Minamoto. Nor was it by chance that the text, dedicated to detailing Katamori's imperial services in the capital, concluded with this defensive description of the fateful Battle of Toba-Fushimi:

> When [Satsuma and Chōshū troops] were stopped and questioned [by the Aizu troops guarding the imperial grounds], they suddenly opened fire. Our samurai training could not allow us to let this pass without retribution. That is how the dream of imperial-shogunal union, which our lord had worked so hard for so long to realize, fizzled. The Boshin disorder was now upon us; how unfortunate this was.[35]

Once Katamori was made a dutiful, honor-bound, and tragic imperial servant who was forced into fighting, the same redemptive possibility opened up for his domain and his people. Indeed, this myth of loyal but star-crossed victims of fate—the myth of lovable losers, as it were—became a powerful way to reimagine Aizu in modern times. Nothing embodied this process and its fruitful results better than the boys of the White Tiger Brigade.

Making the Poster Boys of Aizu

Most Japanese, if they know nothing else of Aizu, will surely know of the Byakkotai, or the White Tiger Brigade. The plight of these teenaged samurai soldiers during the Boshin War has become an enduring symbol of Aizu's historical tragedy. These youths are the poster boys of Aizu—sometimes quite literally—celebrated in history books, morality tales, and souvenir shops alike. However, they could not have achieved their star status without decades of politically conscious manipulation. The apotheosis of these young samurai demonstrates once again how locality was harmonized with nationhood so as to make, most ironically, national heroes out of regional rebels.

After its defeat at Toba-Fushimi in the first month of 1868, Aizu braced for an all-out invasion. Lord Katamori called upon his samurai to "wipe away the stain on our domain" and "make our domainal might known in full."[36] In the third month, as its beaten soldiers returned home from Kyoto, the domain reorganized its military to defend its home territory. This was done by age; about

35. Yamakawa, *Kyotoshugoshoku shimatsu*, 2:267–68.
36. Yamakawa, *Aizu Boshin senshi*, pp. 491–92.

1,200 men between the ages of eighteen and thirty-five were organized into the Vermillion Sparrow Brigade (Suzakutai), 900 men ages thirty-six to forty-nine joined the Blue Dragon Brigade (Seiryūtai), 400 men older than fifty composed the Black Warriors Brigade (Genbutai), and boys between sixteen and seventeen became the White Tiger Brigade.[37] More specifically, the White Tiger Brigade consisted of 326 boys further split into two units of upper-ranking samurai sons, two units of middle-ranking samurai sons, and one unit of lower samurai and nonsamurai sons.[38] Forty-five boys made up the second upper-samurai unit, which was led by the forty-two-year-old commander, Hinata Naiki.

The White Tiger Brigade, being the greenest of the bunch, was designed mainly as a backup force. This changed abruptly on the twenty-second of the eighth month. As the invaders quickly pierced Aizu's perimeter defenses and rushed toward Wakamatsu proper, Katamori himself mobilized for battle and set up his field headquarters at Takizawa village, which lay on the northeast edge of Wakamatsu. The second upper-samurai unit of the White Tiger Brigade accompanied their lord to Takizawa as his personal escorts. As defenses grew desperate later in the day, however, the boys had to be called up to the battlefront. They scrambled through a cold, steady rain—early signs of a seasonal typhoon—and reached the front at Tonokuchihara in the evening of the twenty-second. There, they joined the Aizu defenders and took on some 2,600 attackers in a fierce firefight overnight but eventually yielded to superior firepower and crumbled. The morning of the twenty-third brought still more rain and the ominous news that the unit captain Hinata, who had gone to fetch provisions, was missing.[39] Tired, wet, hungry, and reeling, the boys now scampered over marshland back to Wakamatsu in smaller makeshift packs.

One batch of boys had nearly made it back to the Takizawa headquarters when they were ambushed by the enemy and had to turn away. They evaded pursuit by crawling through an irrigation channel that led them out onto

---

37. The names are derived from classical Chinese cosmology and correspond to the guardian spirits of the four directions. These official samurai forces were supplemented by about three thousand commoners between the ages of twenty and forty who were recruited for defense, as well as hunters, *shugendō* priests, and sumo wrestlers, for a total force of more than seven thousand.

38. Gotō, "Byakkotai no meibo," pp. 1–5. According to Yamakawa Kenjirō, the *ashigaru* unit of the White Tiger Brigade did not even carry firearms. Kenjirō himself was fifteen years old at the time and too young to join the White Tiger Brigade. Yamakawa, "Aizu rōjō yodan," p. 181.

39. Hinata, along with the rest of the White Tiger Brigade, eventually made it back to Tsuruga Castle, where they endured the siege for a month until the surrender.

Mount Iimori (elevation 372 meters), which overlooks Wakamatsu from its eastern edge. There, as is now commonly told, the boys saw flames and smoke rising from the castle town, which had just been stormed in the morning. The young soldiers, some nineteen in all, then took their cause to be lost and decided to kill themselves, which they did mainly by stabbing each other or themselves in the throat. One boy who failed to do so properly, sixteen-year-old Iinuma Sadakichi, survived to tell the tale for posterity.

The fall of 1868 brought many deaths to Aizu, some comparably tragic, some equally premature. No less tragic was the mass suicide by the women of the family of a domainal elder, Saigō Tanomo, where twenty-one women killed themselves, along with a two-year-old, when their city was invaded.[40] Neither were the five women of Shiba Gorō's household, who also killed themselves so that their men could fight unburdened by the thoughts of those they left behind.[41] They were among some 230 women who died this way during the Aizu War, as thousands more fell all around them in battle. Yet it is the story of the White Tiger Brigade that has emerged and endured above all others as the emotional climax of the war, as creative narrativity imbued them with just the right octane of pathos and politics.

The constructedness of their narrative is betrayed by sources. When traced over time, textual records reveal uncertainties, inconsistencies, and improvisations even in the most basic details surrounding the episode. For starters, we cannot even be sure about the number of boys involved. Today we are told that there were nineteen boys who met their grisly end atop Mount Iimori that day. But this was not always so. For the first twenty years after their deaths, it was commonly understood that sixteen boys had killed themselves because that was the number that the lone survivor Iinuma Sadakichi initially reported. As a result, early history texts such as *Zoku kokushiryaku kōhen* in 1875 and *Fukkogaiki* in 1876 presented sixteen boys, as did early local biographies of the brigade, such as *Byakkotai eiyū kagami*, written just months after their deaths in 1868, and the *Byakkotai jūrokushi den* in 1887.[42] Early commemorative services also assumed that sixteen had died. Their first memorial site, named the "White Tiger Brigade Stele," was built in 1871 by a former domainal retainer named Ōtake Shūzō at Kanpuku Temple in Sannohe, Tonami domain. He dedicated this stele to seventeen boys, including Iinuma the survivor. On the seventeenth anniversary of the Boshin war dead

40. Saigō, *Aizu hanrō Saigō Tanomo jijoden* Seiunki, pp. 61–67.

41. Craig, *Remembering Aizu*, pp. 16–17.

42. Ogasawara, ed., *Zoku kokushiryaku kōhen*, vol. 5; *Fukkogaiki Byakkotai eiyū kagami;* Sekiba, "Byakkotai jūrokushi den."

in August 1885, sixteen boys were praised for their suicide by a group of teenagers who performed a sword dance in their honor.[43] On this occasion, Sahara Morizumi, a local scholar and schoolteacher, composed a poem that numbered the boys at sixteen. His Chinese-style poem became one of the most popular lyrical celebrations of the White Tiger Brigade. A group of Aizu diaspora in Tokyo followed the same convention in 1883, when it organized to sell five hundred stone tablets commemorating the boys. On these tablets, sold for forty-eight sen each, were carved the phrase "loyal retainers and righteous samurai" and the names of sixteen members.[44]

Uncertainty about the number began to set in when, sometime around 1887, plans were made to construct a larger site at Mount Iimori to honor the boys. Names of three other boys surfaced as locals prepared for construction, and Iinuma Sadakichi then reportedly let on that three other members of the unit had gotten separated from the main group of sixteen but then found them dead on Mount Iimori, whereupon they followed their cohorts to death.[45] What caused Iinuma to suddenly recall three boys he had earlier omitted was never made clear; for most of his life, he was reticent about his wartime experience. Nonetheless, nineteen graves were ultimately erected atop Mount Iimori in 1889, and in the following year, Sahara had to amend his poem to feature nineteen boys in all.[46]

Such a mysterious revision notwithstanding, many sources continued to put the figure at sixteen even well after 1887. Another biography, *Byakkotai yūshi retsuden* by Nihei Yoshitami in 1895, and Kitahara Masanaga's revisionist *Shichinenshi* from 1904 counted sixteen boys, as did the historical encyclopedia *Kokushi daijiten* in 1908.[47] Yamakawa Kenjirō, a longtime champion of the White Tiger Brigade's memory, also maintained the figure at sixteen as late as 1927.[48] Likewise, a poem published in a special issue of the journal *Shin*

---

43. Yoshimura, *Bykkotaishi jijinsha ni kansuru chōsa keika.*

44. *Kaiyō zasshi* 33, pp. 6–7.

45. Yoshimura, "Byakkotai jijinsha ni tsuki," p. 236; Bannai, *Shinsei Byakkotaishi.*

46. Bannai. Some sources indicate that the three boys who were later added—Ikegami Shintarō, Itō Teijirō, and Tsuda Sutezō—had not in fact killed themselves but died under different circumstances. This inconsistency can be seen textually. According to Yamakawa Hiroshi's roster of the war dead *Senshisha meiseki*, the three were killed in action in three separate places, while a similar record compiled by Katō Chōshirō, *Senshi junnan jinmeiroku,* indicates that the three were killed in action near the Takizawa field headquarters.

47. Nihei, *Byakkotai yūshi retsuden;* Kitahara, *Shichinenshi,* 4:302–4; Yashiro, *Kokushi daijiten.*

48. Yamakawa, "Aizu rōjō yodan," p. 181.

Tōhoku in 1926 that was dedicated to the White Tiger Brigade featured just sixteen boys.[49] Other sources could be rather careless and imprecise about the number of boys involved. One work from 1905, *Kokin bushidōdan*, a didactic collection of samurai heroics, first spoke of sixteen boys, then of nineteen just a page later without any explanation.[50] In 1910 the linguist Ueda Kazutoshi edited a pictorial Japanese history book for children in which he lauded the White Tiger Brigade but referred ambiguously to "some boys numbering in the teens."[51] Even school textbooks were far from authoritative in this regard. One early reference to the White Tiger Brigade in a textbook counted twenty boys who "disemboweled themselves and died," killing poor Iinuma Sadakichi in the process.[52] When the young soldiers appeared in the new government-issued textbooks in 1903, there were only sixteen of them. There remained only sixteen until 1941, when the figure was finally raised to the now commonly accepted nineteen.[53]

Over time, generations of storytellers took artistic liberty with the boys' experience for drama's sake. They added as literary embellishments many touching, performative details, some clearly unknowable to posterity. For example, the boys have been made to recite poetry appropriate to their dire straits as they prepared for death. In one rendering, they sing the imperially loyalistic "On the Spirit of the Universe" (*Seiki no uta*), and another loyalist poem attributed to Kusunoki Masashige, "Seven Lives for the Nation," which is itself a dubious conceit.[54] Elsewhere, including a *biwa* musical composition from 1894, they are said to have recited, in addition to "On the Spirit of the Universe" and "Seven Lives for the Nation," a poem about the self-sacrificial death of Zhang Xun (*Chōjun seshi no shō*) and Xiang Yu's poem of suicide at Gaixia (*Kōu gaika no kyoku*), with some boys supposedly reading *waka* composed and given to them by their mothers as keepsakes.[55] At other times, the

---

49. *Shin Tōhoku*, 17:30.

50. Kubo, *Kokin bushidōdan*, pp. 189–90.

51. Ueda, ed., *Nihon rekishi gadan*, p. 174.

52. Tsubaki, *Shōgaku kokushi kiji honmatsu*, lower volume.

53. Monbushō, *Kōtōshōgaku dokuhon*, vol. 4; Monbushō, *Shōgaku kokushi*, lower volume pp. 102–3. The White Tiger Brigade was first introduced in government textbooks in the 1903 Japanese primer. It appeared for the first time in the history textbook in 1921.

54. Yamanouchi, *The White Tiger Band*, p. 14. Several people have written different versions of "On the Spirit of the Universe," including Wen Tianxiang, the Mito scholar Fujita Tōko, and the Chōshū loyalist Yoshida Shōin.

55. Nakamura, *Byakkotai jiseki*, p. 16; Yoshimizu, *Seishin kyōiku teikoku biwa renmashū*, p. 32. Zhang Xun died protecting the city of Suiyang against the rebel An

boys were made to exchange inconceivably noble and selfless declarations as they prepared to die, all of them fantastic.[56] Still other works, as is common when dealing with young samurai heroes, fetishized the boys' youth. One work from 1909 used the hackneyed descriptor "bishōnen" to eroticize the young soldiers as "truly an attractive group of beautiful young boys," while Richard Heise, a German-language instructor in Japan, delighted in using a sensual touch in imagining how "the twenty, underdeveloped bodies fell forward" to die a "beautiful death."[57] Heise was so deeply enamored with the boys as to have himself buried next to them at Mount Iimori in 1940.

What fuels the emotional appeal of the White Tiger Brigade episode is the boys' tragically jumping to the conclusion that their castle had fallen. Conventional tellings of the tale have held that the boys mistook the flames rising from the castle to mean that Aizu had lost and their lord was dead. This derives mainly from Iinuma Sadakichi's testimony, in which he recalled the boys having said to each other, "Our lord is in Tsuruga Castle, and it is up in flames. The path before us is blocked by our enemies. Our duty is done. We should all kill ourselves swiftly and join our comrades in the netherworld."[58] In reality, the siege had just begun that day and the castle was not to fall until a full month later. This purported misunderstanding became a key emotional refrain in many dramatized representations, including Sahara's poem and the "Byakkotai" *waka*, which was popularized through the official elementary school primer. Accordingly, most visual depictions of the suicide scene show the castle in the distance, covered in smoke and flames. The boys' false impression has served to underscore their youthful naiveté and selfless loyalty to the lord while deepening the poignancy of their demise.

Yet, this much-celebrated detail, too, is suspect, for the historical record makes the idea of a blazing castle quite improbable. We know that the boys died on the twenty-third of the eighth month. We also know that the western forces entered the castle town proper on that day but that they did not set up their artillery on Mount Oda until the twenty-fifth or the twenty-sixth.[59] Therefore, the boys were long dead before the bombardment of the castle even

---

Lushan. Xiang Yu was the king of Chu, who killed himself rather than be taken captive by his rival Liu Bang, the founder of the Han dynasty.

56. Tsūzokukyōiku kenkyūkai, ed., *Tsūzokukyōiku kōen shiryō*, p. 317.

57. Nakagawa, ed., *Kinsei eijin hyakuwa*, pp. 242–44; Heise, *Uber Loyalitat in Japan*, pp. 16, 19. *Uber Loyalitat in Japan* was more recently translated by Seno Fuminori as *Nihonjin no chūseishin to shinkō* (Tokyo: Shisōsha, 1997).

58. Hiraishi, *Aizu boshin sensō*, pp. 126–27.

59. The local historian Nakamura Toshi indicates the twenty-fifth while Bannai indicates the twenty-sixth. Nakamura, *Aizu no kindaika o kangaeru*, p. 7.

began. Although the invaders did torch some of the town as they entered Wakamatsu, it is unlikely that whatever fire and smoke the boys saw from Mount Iimori could have been taken as the fall of their castle. Despite what popular versions of the story claim, the boys saw something less than the end of their world as they knew it from their position atop Mount Iimori that day.

Most of these factual uncertainties and artistic embellishments are innocuous enough; few popular tales are free of such defects. But the seemingly mundane detail about the state of the castle reveals a more remarkable problem behind the evolving meaning of the boys' deaths. It is on this central question—why did they kill themselves and what did they die for—that the narrative transformation of the White Tiger Brigade assumes greater political implications.

While the White Tiger Brigade is now presented as having died out of patriotism, self-sacrifice, and samurai ideals, early records indicate something far less glorious. Consider one of the first reports on the event, an 1869 account from the newspaper *Terikarafu:* "The enemy had already rushed upon the castle and smoke filled the sky. No one would come and save them. Each decided that his time was up. They then all agreed that rather than be taken by the enemy, it is better to move to another spot where they can gaze upon the castle and die."[60] A comparably mundane rendition, perhaps based on the *Terikarafu* account, was given in *Wakamatsuki.* The author, Nanma Tsunanori, an Aizu official and accomplished Confucian scholar, wrote in 1876: "The enemy had already rushed forth to the castle's edge. Smoke and fire covered the sky. They could not even hope for a rescue, or so they each decided. They discussed that it would be a shame if they were to be taken by the enemy's hands. They decided to move to another spot where they can gaze upon the castle, prostrate, and die."[61] What comes across here is hardly a sense of heroism under fire; it is, rather, a sense of surrender to their overwhelming reality. Hurting and miserable, and with the enemy blocking their only path home, the boys are shown to have lost hope. Early records presented the boys' deaths as mere capitulation; they do not even mention the burning castle. This is probably why the introductory comments to another early biography, *Byakkotai jūrokushiden* from 1887, use the matter-of-fact phrase "committed suicide" (*jisatsusu*) to describe the boys' actions.[62] Initial reports portrayed the boys as worthy of the readers' sympathy, certainly, but hardly as the model of lordly self-sacrifice that they would soon come to be.

---

60. *Terikarafu,* April 13, 1869.
61. Nanma, *Wakamatsuki,* pp. 10–11.
62. Sekiba, "Bykkotai jūrokushiden", p. 316.

Later mythmakers would make sure that the boys achieved loftier status. Other accounts added a more noble twist to what had simply been a mass suicide by suggesting that the boys killed themselves to "die a good death" rather than suffer the shame of defeat. Sahara Morizumi's poem ended on this point, as he lauded the boys' deaths as "a deed far more virtuous than that of Tian Heng and his men," a classic tale of self-sacrificial resistance from Chinese history.[63] The eponymous *waka* in school primers also used the boys to advertise the virtue of dying a good soldierly death:

> To witness the end of their lord,
> up they climbed on Mount Iimori;
> Only to see that the castle has fallen
> and flames that scorched the sky.
>
> "Our duty as vassals is done," they said,
> "Come, we shall die with resolve";
> Side by side with mind at peace;
> This is their tale of dying by the sword.
>
> So it has been told, now a tale of beauty;
> How sweet are petals that fall.[64]

So, too, did another poem from 1909, which attributed this rationale to the boys: "To surrender would be the warrior's shame. To live on as cowards is not what we wish."[65] Initial portrayal of beaten submission was now being replaced by that of a dignified death befitting a proper samurai retainer. Indeed, the poem's use of the descriptor "tale of beauty" (*bidan*) discloses its purpose: to idealize and celebrate spiritual aesthetics of soldierly death. The emphasis here is more on the self-serving act of avoiding personal shame than on lordly or stately service.

Other renditions reified the boys' suicide into a *junshi*—the warrior practice of a retainer committing suicide to follow his lord to death—by insisting that they did not merely give up but, rather, willingly gave their lives to Lord Katamori. This vision of a model retainer is put forth by Hiraishi Benzō's account of the brigade in his 1917 *Aizu Boshinsensō,* where the boys, standing atop Mount Iimori, are said to have "looked at each other

63. Tian Heng was the king of Zi who killed himself, and was followed by five hundred of his men, rather than submit to the Han.

64. Monbushō, *Kōtōshōgaku dokuhon,* vol. 4; Shōnen ongakukai, *Shintei gakkō gunka.*

65. Nakagawa, ed., *Kinsei eijin hyakuwa,* pp. 242–44.

and said, 'The castle is about to fall. Now is the time to give our lives to the lord.' They knelt, bowed toward Tsuruga Castle, slit their bellies, and died."[66] Hiraishi quoted Iinuma Sadakichi, who recalled his compatriots as having agreed to "kill ourselves swiftly and join our comrades in the netherworld."[67] This presentation evokes the spirit of *junshi*, as does Tatsuno Jirō's *Aizu Byakkotai jūyūkyūshi jitsuden* from 1907: "The castle has already fallen and our cause is lost. Though we are young, we received great affections from the lord and so each of our deaths must be made to serve the lord. We must see our lord on his path and pay respect to him again in the netherworld."[68] Later texts underscored *junshi* even more emphatically, as one account from 1936 did in melodramatic terms: "Ah, the great Tsuruga Castle has fallen, and surely our lord has met his end in the castle. Our work is done, except to swiftly end our lives so that we may accompany our lord in death."[69]

A logical corollary to the *junshi* ideal was the politicized ideal of bodily sacrifice to the domainal state. Another lesson that came to be imparted by the reworked narratives was that these boys could not, and should not, have lived on without their domain and that their fate was intertwined with the domain's to the very end. This is the main theme that Sahara Morizumi sounded in his rendition of the tale. The key quatrain in his poem reads:

> Gazing southward, smoke arises from Tsuruga Castle
> Stunned they pause, swallowing bitter tears
> The state has fallen and nothing is left
> Slitting their bellies, the nineteen warriors perished.

Shichinenshi echoed the same point about casting one's fate with the state in its recreation of the same scene: "They said to each other, 'What good are our lives now; let us slit our bellies for the sake of our domain.' After bowing toward the distant castle and paying their final respects, they stabbed each other and fell side by side, passing like the morning dew."[70] The boys were now reimagined to have been driven by loyalty so intense that they could not live on without their lord and state. According to this sensibility, the (supposed) fall of the castle necessitated the fall of the young soldiers.

Even more patently manipulative and anachronistic were subsequent efforts to nationalize and imperialize the White Tiger Brigade. This grew increasingly common after the turn of the twentieth century, and indeed it

---

66. Hiraishi, *Aizu Boshin sensō*, pp. 170–71.
67. Ibid., p. 260.
68. Tatsuno, *Aizu Byakkotai jūyūkyūshi jitsuden*, pp. 1–2.
69. Akitsuki, "Byakkotai Aizuhan fujin no junnan ni tsuite," p. 5.
70. Kitahara, *Shichinenshi*, 4:302–4.

became nearly impossible not to speak of the White Tiger Brigade in such political terms. The Ministry of Education, for instance, called upon schoolteachers to use the episode to instill a sense of imperial service in young pupils. The teacher's guide to the Higher Elementary School Reader from 1904 instructed teachers to "demonstrate the White Tiger Brigade's fierce sense of loyalty and bravery, and ensure that students likewise carry out the Imperial Will and offer their brave services to His Majesty."[71] One account of the brigade aimed toward children, *Shōnen kagayaku Byakkotai,* also pushed the boy soldiers as lessons in imperial loyalty and praised their illustrious conduct as the result of a long tradition of imperial service in Aizu domain.[72] Both usages are plainly ironic, but also sensible because Japan was then engaged in yet another imperialist war. Some, like Takahashi Tansui in 1909, associated the White Tiger boys' service to the domain with service to the emperor so readily as to declare, "If the same red-blooded passion that was devoted to the domainal nation had been devoted to our present empire, our armies in the Sino-Japanese War and the Russo-Japanese War would have been even more ferocious."[73] Ahistorical conflation of domainal devotion with national devotion came just as intuitively to Tatsuno Jirō, who wrote, "The White Tiger Brigade shows that while many speak of patriotism and imperial loyalty, those who truly love their country without regard for themselves are as rare as stars at dawn."[74] All these renderings necessarily forgot the inconvenient truth that the White Tiger boys were rebels fighting the forces of the imperial court. And so what began as a mass suicide out of desperation was, over time, made into an honorable *junshi,* a nod to samurai aesthetics, sacrificial duty to the domainal state, then—in a final irony—the ultimate lesson in imperial loyalty.

The boys of the White Tiger Brigade accomplished nothing on the battlefield but they eventually performed great service to Aizu as they—or, rather, their newly constructed image—offered redemption for their homeland after the war. The thick layers of pathos that were laid upon their deaths effectively masked the stain of Aizu's rebellion. The overtly manipulative emotional appeal of the boys transcended political partisanship, as their story practically dared any reader not to feel sorry for the young soldiers, their rebel status notwithstanding. One version of the tale, in fact, argued explicitly that

71. Nihon shoseki, ed., *Kokugo dokuhō kyōjuhō oyobi kyōjuan,* p. 138.

72. Takagi, *Shōnen kagayaku Byakkotai,* p. 526.

73. Takahashi, *Sōzetsu hizetsu Byakkotai,* p. 2.

74. Tatsuno, *Aizu Byakkotai jūyūkyūshi jitsuden,* p. 1.

their dramatic deaths made up for their rebelliousness. As this *biwa* song from the late Meiji era pleaded:

> Guilty though they were of resisting the throne
> how can we not be touched
> by the merit of their fiercely loyal spirit?[75]

And so the troubadours implored their audience to overlook the boys' and, by extension, Aizu's imperial lapse. Reconstructed as a piece of tragic drama, the episode assumed a life of its own, allowing the boys to escape the captive context of rebellion. In the process, Aizu, with whom the tale was intimately connected, could also gain a measure of reprieve.

Now reborn as paragons of imperial heroism, the boys came to personify the best features not only of Aizu but of an imagined "traditional Japan." Here again the White Tiger Brigade's narrativity helped Aizu find redemption in modern, national terms. The boys were made to embody virtues now long lost and were then offered as an antidote to contemporary moral ills. The local writer Tatsuno Jirō made just such use of the White Tiger Brigade as he explained the impetus behind his hagiography in 1907. "As I observe the youths in our society today, I see neither resolve nor principles. I see only mental debauchery and repulsive actions that make me want to vomit," he complained. "I introduce here the soldiers of the White Tiger Brigade and their infinite beauty in order to induce some improvement in the minds of people today."[76] He thus prescribed the boy soldiers of Aizu as a spiritual elixir for twentieth-century Japanese society. Similarly, the White Tiger Brigade made for a useful and welcome contrast to ever-encroaching foreign values. One Aizu man who viewed a film about the White Tiger Brigade in 1927 lauded the tale for having "cast *bushidō* like a life jacket to the weaklings who are now drowning in the violent currents of foreign thought." As he concluded, "The film was greatly successful in saving them from spiritual drowning."[77] Yamanouchi Tamenosuke, a writer who in 1939 introduced the boys to a foreign audience in the English-language book *The White Tiger Band,* did much the same. He began by acknowledging, "We have to thank the advanced foreign countries for their help given us when our country was still young." But Japan now needed something more. "The time has come when we must look into our essential line of conduct more thoroughly on the

75. Biwa no ie, ed., *Kokin biwa kashū,* p. 3.
76. Tatsuno, *Aizu Byakkotai jūyūkyūshi jitsuden,* pp. 1–2.
77. Suzuki, "Byakkotai no eiga to kokuminsei," p. 17.

basis of our history, for our ancestors have taught us by their brilliant deeds." For this spiritual recovery, he turned to the selfless boy soldiers of Aizu.[78]

Overseas recognition conferred still more laurels upon the White Tiger Brigade, further sealing the bond between Aizu and Japan. Various foreigners were attracted to the episode, including Arthur Lloyd, a British missionary who arrived in Japan in 1877 as a professor at Tokyo Imperial University. He was moved by the boys' deed to compose a lengthy poem about it, which was published in 1938.[79] Richard Heise, a professor of German at Hitotsubashi and Gakushūin Universities, was another fan of the teen soldiers. Heise waxed poetic about them in his *Uber Loyalitat in Japan*, praising the boys of Aizu as an exemplar of Japanese loyalty. "Rather than shamefully live out the rest of their unfortunate lives under their enemy's rule, they thought it far more beautiful to die as free Aizu youths," he gushed forth, lauding them for their "loyalty and love of their lord and homeland."[80] Sir Robert Baden-Powell, the British founder of the Boy Scouts, also considered the White Tiger Brigade worthy enough to extol them as a model for young boys at the Boy Scouts Inaugural Jamboree in London in 1920.[81]

Individual fascination aside, state-level foreign recognition elevated the boys' status to its pinnacle, allowing Aizu to stand tall as the best of Japan to the rest of the world. Benito Mussolini, who had apparently learned of the White Tiger Brigade from the poet and Rome resident Shimoi Harukichi, was inspired to name an elite thousand-member force of his army after the boy soldiers of Aizu.[82] In 1931 Mussolini ordered the Italian ambassador to Japan, Pompeo Aloisi, to consult the mayor of Rome and the Roman Municipal Museum on a suitable gift to honor the White Tiger Brigade. They chose an old stone column that had recently been excavated in Rome, and Ambassador Aloisi arranged for the sculptor Dario Canperotti to fashion the column into an 8.3-meter, 25-ton pillar inscribed with the words "Rome, the cradle of civilization, pays its undying respect to the White Tiger Brigade by presenting this century-old column marked with the Fascista Party seal, which expresses the glory of ancient Rome. 1928 AD the sixth year of Fascista."[83]

78. Yamanouchi, *The White Tiger Band,* p. 1.

79. Lloyd, "The White Tigers," pp. 20–34.

80. Heise, trans. Yūki, *Doitsujin no mitaru Aizu Byakkotai,* pp. 16, 22.

81. Anzai and Tasaki, eds., *Aizu shokaidō to Ōshū dōchū,* pp. 127–28. Baden-Powell visited Japan for six days in April 1912. Uehira et al., *Shōnendan no rekishi,* p. 77. Baden-Powell's impressions of Japan are in Baden-Powell, *Boy Scouts beyond the Seas,* pp. 86–100.

82. *Yūkan Aizu nippō,* August 6, 1932; Iimori, *Byakkotai seishin hiwa.*

83. Japanese sources render the sculptor's name as デユリオ・カンペロテイ.

On the back read the inscription: "To the spirit of *bushidō*." This pillar was presented to Aizu in December 1928 by Ambassador Aloisi in a ceremony at the Mount Iimori site with Prince Takamatsu, Prime Minister Tanaka Giichi, and Konoe Fumimaro in attendance. As the Italian ambassador then remarked, "The restoration in both Japan and Italy was marked by glorious deeds of young men who sacrificed themselves out of supreme loyalty and patriotism," and compared the White Tiger Brigade with "the young fighters of Curtatone, Giuseppe Garibaldi's 'Red Shirts,' and the boys who fought at Piave River."[84] Once again, onetime rebels were retroactively bestowed the honor of patriotism.

German admirers followed suit in 1935. In June of that year, the German military attache Hasso von Etzdor presented a stone monolith to honor the White Tiger Brigade. The monolith was dedicated "to the young samurai of Aizu, from the samurai of Germany" and placed at Mount Iimori.[85] These official acknowledgments from abroad lent further prestige to the White Tiger Brigade and the land of their birth. Aizu's glorious past had now become Japan's as well.

This ironic union between Aizu and Japan, brokered by the White Tiger Brigade, found perhaps its most overt expressions in theatrical scripts and screenplays. Novelist and playwright Okamoto Kidō wrote the play *Byakkotai* first in 1908 to be performed at the Meijiza in Tokyo, then revised it eight years later for the Kabukiza. Okamoto's retellings featured several departures from convention, the most significant being an enemy commander who

---

84. Hiraishi, *Aizu Boshin sensō,* p. 523. Curtatone was the site of a battle in 1848. Piave River presumably refers to the Italian triumph in 1918 against the Austro-Hungarians during World War I.

85. When the U.S. occupation forces arrived in Wakamatsu in 1945, they did not take kindly to these icons of Axis alliance. They ordered the removal of the German monolith, but it is said that a teashop keeper at Mount Iimori kept the monolith hidden until the Americans left and later returned it to Mount Iimori, where it still stands today. Miyasaki, *Aizu chimei jinmei sanpo.* The Americans were relatively forgiving of the Roman gift. The pillar itself was allowed to remain, though the rear inscription with the *bushidō* reference was scrubbed for its militaristic tone. Originally, the pillar was capped by a battle-ax, a lion, an eagle, and a sheath of arrows, but all of those decorations were removed, with the fitting exception of the eagle, which was spared and remains to this day. According to William Woodard, between late 1946 and May 1948, the U.S. occupation removed some 5,613 monuments and 354 statues nationwide, moved 890 monuments and 17 statues to less conspicuous locations, and altered the appearance or changed the inscriptions on 908 monuments and 29 statues so as to minimize their militaristic and ultranationalistic connotations. Woodard, *The Allied Occupation of Japan,* p. 153.

discovers the boys' bodies on Mount Iimori and praises them as "the flowers of Japan" in a fabricated ending that transcends historical partisanship.[86] Okamoto's theatrical rendition seems to have inspired the screenwriter Yahiro Fuji, who wrote the script for the 1954 film *Hana no Byakkotai*. In a bizarre blend of reality and fiction, this film also ends with the enemy commander—here in the person of Kirino Toshiaki of Satsuma, who would later die in the Seinan War—discovering the boys' remains and lamenting their deaths as a "loss to Japan" in an utterly fictive final scene.[87] All these were modern additions that once again asked the audience to forget historical differences in the name of unity under the nation.

The White Tiger Brigade thus helped reconcile the onetime rebel domain with imperial Japan, marrying the two through emotional empathy and shared virtues. The boys of the White Tiger Brigade became a collective trophy; Japan and Aizu alike could bask in its glow. People both in and out of Aizu worked the boys' image to a brilliant shine until its blemishes could no longer be seen. The apotheosis of the White Tiger Brigade was a collaborative effort that further helped to return Aizu to the nation, if only in idealized imagery, as a prize for all to claim.

Redeem the Past, Reclaim the Present

Aizu's war of historical reckoning, waged over memories of the past, tells us much about the role of remembrance in the making of modern Japan. It shows, first of all, that a good measure of negotiability could be found even in unexpected times and places. For all the talk about a vaunted "imperial restoration historiographical viewpoint" and a "master narrative" in Meiji Japan, the memory-keepers of Aizu were able to find their place in national memory, and an increasingly dignified place at that. What history took away from Aizu was restored to it through historiography. In truth, political and military failures had relegated Aizu to the margins of history for all to see. Its foes had the imperial banner, Aizu had not; they had won the day, Aizu had not. No amount of authorial finagling could alter those facts. Yet, revisionist historians could implore readers to consider, in retrospect, content over form, intent rather than result. Aizu could not beat the self-claimed loyalists in 1868, but it could certainly join them in due time and make the same claim for itself.

---

86. Okamoto, *Kidō gikyokushū*, p. 296; Kamijō, ed., *Kabukiza*, microfiche YD5-H-*toku* 117–58.

87. Yahiro, *Yahiro Fuji shinarioshū*. The film was directed by Tazaka Katsuhiko and featured the debut of two up-and-coming stars, Katsu Shintarō and Ichikawa Raizō.

The struggle over how to remember Aizu also speaks volumes about the nation's allure. Rather than demonstrate the limits of imperial nationhood, tussles over Aizu's past gave proof instead to the attractive powers of imperial nationhood, especially after the turn of the twentieth century. For all its rhetorical bravado and saber-rattling, Aizu's protest respected the boundaries of imperial nationhood. Indeed it may have confirmed them. Rehabilitative efforts eagerly appropriated nationalist idioms and assumptions to achieve their goal. They were quick to ingratiate themselves to the imperial cause; they longed for national inclusion above all. To escape the burden of the past, Aizu's memory-makers managed to redact the "rebel" half of the imperial–rebel dichotomy, leaving only the imperial, now incontestably nonpartisan, transcendent, and glorious. Aizu's rehabilitative historiography effectively erased rebels from Japan's recent history and, in so doing, reaffirmed the grandeur of imperial nationhood. Thus the once vanquished people of Aizu, too, could participate in forgetting—"a crucial factor in the creation of a nation"—and weave themselves into the tales of that creation.[88] Those forgetful, merciful narratives trumped past regional difference, bitter domainal partisanship, and even bloody conflicts to everyone's satisfaction. Old battlefields were carefully landscaped into a common ground where all imperial subjects could celebrate their loyalism together.

Ultimately, Aizu veterans and their descendants refused to claim "rebel" as their identity and attached little iconoclastic romanticism to their past struggle. They were mostly content to interpret and transmit their *bakumatsu* plight as national service, frustrated and unfruitful, but dutifully patriotic all the same. Such complicity might disappoint those who might expect a proud tradition of irreverence and resistance to emerge in a place like Aizu, but complicity was what worked for Aizu in imperial Japan. A strong local memory was created in Aizu after the war, but it could hardly be called "counter-history" or "counter-memory" vis-à-vis the nation. What allowed Aizu's historiographical challenge to achieve a good measure of success was its fundamentally unchallenging approach. Aizu's example reminds us just how difficult it is, for historians and our subjects alike, to divorce regional history from nationalist impulses.[89] Those concerned about Aizu's past wished only to assume their rightful role in national history, for imperial nationhood was what granted them the dignity and self-worth that their defunct homeland initially could not.[90]

---

88. Renan, "Qu'est-ce qu'une nation?" p. 11.

89. Roberts, "Cultivating Non-National Historical Understandings."

90. The emotional appeal of a nation and its capacity to supply a sense of worth is discussed in Greenfeld, "Transcending a Nation's Worth."

Whether it was through commemorations, historiography, or identity discourse, Aizu rediscovered itself in the glow of imperial nationhood, proving that nationhood could be an accommodating, multivalent attraction that invites unlikely elements to come and share its prestige. For a people who had tasted defeat and alienation, this proved to be an especially appealing proposition. When Arakawa Katsushige, a former domainal retainer and Boshin War veteran, retired from twenty-seven years of service as a schoolteacher in 1902, he prepared a vita. This record of his turbulent life concluded with the single line: "I have never been punished for a crime."[91] In his mind, the fifteen months of house arrest that he endured as a prisoner of war after the fall of Aizu were no punishment for a crime. Such a remembrance of the past allowed this aged samurai to look back proudly on the seventy years of his life and, in so doing, reserve some dignity for his old native land, too.

91. Arakawa, *Meiji nisshi,* p. 119.

Conclusion:
The Deliverance of a Princess

He wore a most regal imperial ensemble, with a courtly cap atop his head and an aristocratic baton in hand. She followed just behind him in a splendid purple twelve-layer garb. Facing the altar, the groom made his vows and the couple sipped the ceremonial sake. A single cannon shot was fired, then another, twenty-one salutes in all. And so a prince and a princess were wedded on a clear September morning in 1928. As the court's master of ceremonies later recorded, "It was like a picture scroll of the old imperial court, as if all the antiquity of the Heian period were recreated in the present."[1] Never mind that every detail of the seemingly ancient ceremony had only been codified thirty-nine years earlier.[2] This was a day of celebration, a most auspicious occasion in which Prince Chichibu, the reigning Shōwa emperor's younger brother and second in line to the imperial throne, was wedded to a princess who looked "as precious as a child, as beautiful as a Girls' Day doll."

Before this imperial union could take place, however, a few roadblocks had to be cleared. First, as is often the case, there was the matter of a father reluctant to part with his eldest daughter. Imperial household officials had worked hard to produce a list of suitable candidates for Prince Chichibu, a list that was headed by the teenaged daughter of Japan's ambassador to the United States. First, the imperial household minister sent a letter of request for marriage to the ambassador, but the father politely begged off. Then, in July 1927, Yamakawa Kenjirō was dispatched by the imperial household to personally negotiate the marriage, but again to no avail.[3] In October, Count Kabayama Aisuke, a personal friend of the ambassador, was sent to Washington, DC, to

1. Chichibunomiya kinenkai, ed., *Yasuhito shinnō gojiseki shiryō*, 2:182.
2. Kobayashi and Shima, eds., *Nihon rippō shiryō zenshū*, 16:152.
3. Tsūzokukyōiku fukyūkai, *Chichibunomiya-denka to Setsuko-hime*, p. 233.

persuade the still unwilling father. When Kabayama also returned to Tokyo empty-handed, he was sternly ordered by the prince's mother, the Empress Dowager Teimei, to return immediately to Washington and make the imperial will known in no uncertain terms. This time, the ambassador, who had been deprecating his high-school daughter as unsuitable and unqualified, allowed Count Kabayama to speak directly with the girl, who finally acceded.[4]

There was, too, the problem of appropriate status. Imperial household rules stipulated that imperial princes marry a member of the peerage at the least, but the ambassador's daughter was a commoner. As such, the girl, whom her mother humbly discounted as "ordinary, bland, and hardly personable," had received no special preparation or training befitting a future princess.[5] The technicality of status was resolved just a few days before the wedding by having the girl be temporarily adopted by her uncle Yamada Hideo, who was a count. Aristocratic decorum she would have to learn on the job.

Now only one issue remained. The girl's given name was Setsuko (節子) and happened to be written with the same characters as the Empress Dowager Teimei's given name, Sadako. This chance overlap was deemed inappropriate, and after some deliberation, the Empress Dowager chose new characters for the princess-to-be: "se" (勢) from Ise, where the official imperial shrine is located, and "tsu" (津) from Aizu, the land that the girl's old family, the Matsudaira, used to rule.[6] Thus, Princess Setsuko (勢津子) was born, personifying a remarkable union between the imperial family and the domainal family, between nation and region.

It was an occasion that would have been unfathomable to the princess's paternal grandfather Matsudaira Katamori, who had once been punished as an "enemy of the court." Yet, not only was the marriage realized, it happened to come in another Boshin year, exactly sixty years after the last fateful Boshin year of 1868. This poetic symmetry was not lost upon the people of Aizu, one of whom welcomed the news of the royal engagement with this poem:

> Now upon the glorious Shōwa
> the cycle of time has come full circle;
> Is it a dream or is it a vision;
> The skies of Boshin are clear again.[7]

Excited locals eagerly claimed Setsuko as their own. In truth, the princess was not, strictly speaking, from Aizu. Setsuko was born in London while her

---

4. Chichibunomiya, *Gin no bonboniēru*, pp. 141–44.
5. Ibid., p. 144.
6. *Fukushima minpō*, September 19, 1928, p. 1.
7. Ibid., July 27, 1928, p. 3.

father Matsudaira Tsuneo was stationed there as ambassador, lived for a time in Tokyo, and attended the Friends School in Washington, DC. She had never lived in Aizu and had only visited once, as a thirteen-year-old. Her father was born in 1877, nearly nine years after his father Katamori left Aizu in disgrace. None of this deterred the local daily, *Yūkan Aizu nippō,* from greeting Setsuko's arrival as a "homecoming" on its front page when the princess-to-be and her father visited Aizu two months before the wedding.[8] Exuberance caused others to exaggerate Setsuko's linkage to Aizu: "Princess Setsuko is a descendant of the proper Aizu bloodline," sang one celebratory report, "In her flows the Aizu blood that goes back as far as Lord Hoshina Masayuki."[9] It hardly mattered that Masayuki's direct line of descent ended in 1822 with the seventh lord Katahiro; Katamori and his descendants, including Setsuko, were not related to Masayuki by blood.

But this was no time to nitpick. From the moment the engagement was announced in January 1928, the news was received with unbridled cheer and jubilation. When Setsuko and her father arrived in Aizu in July 1928, elated residents offered numerous gifts, ranging from handkerchiefs to a bottle of Calpis, the sum of which had to be carried off in two large trucks. On the morning of July 29, thirty thousand area residents gathered at the old castle grounds in Wakamatsu for the official welcoming ceremony, with ten thousand more spilling out of the main arena. As one local daily breathlessly reported, "It is difficult for this paper to properly convey the 'Setsuko fever' that has gripped Wakamatsu and the five counties of Aizu."[10] Their joy carried over into the day of the wedding itself. At seven in the morning on September 8, cannons were fired in Wakamatsu as Setsuko was wedded in Tokyo. About ten thousand schoolchildren gathered at the Tsuruga Castle grounds, where they waved the Rising Sun flag and thrice shouted "Banzai!" in the direction of the imperial capital. More flags, lanterns, street vendors, and performers crowded the streets of Wakamatsu, and *bon odori* festivities—delayed for two weeks to coincide with the nuptials—delighted fifty thousand giddy city residents for two straight days.[11]

Having one of their own marry into the imperial household was reason enough to celebrate. But emotions in Aizu were all the more layered and complex because the occasion also evoked a deep sense of redemption. Setsuko's wedding relieved more than a few people of Aizu from the weight

8. *Yūkan Aizu nippō,* July 28, 1928, p. 1.
9. Takagi, *Shōnen kagayaku Byakkotai,* p. 528.
10. *Yūkan Aizu nippō,* July 28, 1928, p. 1.
11. Ibid., September 28, 1928, p. 2.

of history. For them, the fact that Lord Katamori's granddaughter was welcomed into the imperial family finally brought Aizu back into the national fold, out of the margins of history and into the very heart of empire. It was this satisfaction and gratitude that caused the now-elderly Yamakawa Kenjirō to call Setsuko's marriage "nothing short of divine intervention by the Emperors Kōmei and Meiji." As he wrote, "One Privy Council member said to me that the one thing that he wants erased from Restoration history has now been all but erased by this wedding. . . . Only a divine act could bring such pleasure to an old patriot like me."[12] He would die three years later.

This being Aizu, ghosts were never far away, even in a time of jubilation; only now, they were thought to be just as contented as the living. Certainly, the father of the bride was aware of the restorative effect that his daughter would have upon local remembrance. "The purpose of this visit," Matsudaira Tsuneo explained during their July homecoming to Aizu, "Is none other than to bring this auspicious news to the spirits of our ancestors and pay respect to the spirits of the Boshin war dead."[13] What might have been lip service still struck its intended chord because the yearning for redemption was so powerful and widely shared. Katamori's son was not the only one who saw Setsuko's wedding from the perspective of the dead. That Katamori's granddaughter would return to Wakamatsu as an imperial princess moved one man to compose this poem:

> The day of divine blessing has come at last;
> Our ancestors who excelled in loyalty,
> your innocence is hereby proven;
> Now in the time of Shōwa Boshin
> the rivers and mountains of Aizu live again;
> The pleasure of greeting
> the princess at Tsuruga Castle;
> To the departed White Tigers,
> lying at Mount Iimori
> Let us wish for you eternally
> the greatest joy
> enough to make your tombs quiver.[14]

Also in attendance at the castle grounds was Miyasaki Nagahachi, who was then a vocational school student in Wakamatsu and later a prominent local

12. Yamakawa, "Gokeiji wa kamiwaza," p. 1.
13. Ueno, *Chichibunomiya Setsuko hidenka to Takajo,* p. 96.
14. *Fukushima minpō,* July 27, 1928, p. 3.

historian. "'Reinstated'— this was the word carved into the hearts of everyone," he recalled of seeing the would-be princess. "The granddaughter of the old domainal lord had been invited into the imperial household. Aizu was back."[15] The outpouring of emotion was all the more remarkable considering that only a handful who witnessed Setsuko's wedding in the Shōwa Boshin were old enough to have experienced the humiliation of the Meiji Boshin personally. The joy and relief that were expressed nonetheless testified to the persistence of Aizu's local memory. In one fell swoop, Princess Setsuko managed to bestow upon the people of Aizu an entire generation's worth of redemption that not a few historians, educators, and other mythmakers had been working to bring for sixty years.

No wonder, then, that the people of Aizu embraced the princess for everything she represented. And the princess in turn was willing to embrace Aizu. In her remembrances, Setsuko fit herself squarely into the Aizu imagery and quite explicitly considered herself an inheritor of an Aizu spiritual essence. In one recollection of her childhood, Setsuko recalled the time she happened to walk into the family living room, where she found her father sitting alone in the formal position and staring intensely at a gleaming, naked blade in his hands. The young girl reflexively yelped, "My, how scary!" To this, her father rebuked, "How could a girl born into a samurai family be scared by a sword? When the castle in Aizu fell, even young girls like you died honorably along with their mothers and siblings for your grandfather's sake. Never forget your grandfather's suffering."[16] Matsudaira Tsuneo, as the sixth son of Katamori, was born much too late to know war and defeat personally, yet father and daughter alike considered themselves connected to that heavy past. As Setsuko wrote in her autobiography, "I still remember clearly how directly I touched my father's Aizu spirit, which he usually kept in the deep recess of his heart. . . . When I was scolded by my father and saw the bright, beautiful blade in his hands that night, I could not help but feel that Aizu blood flows in my veins."[17]

How could a girl who was born in London, raised in Tokyo, and attended high school in America imagine herself to be a part of this mental property called Aizu? Setsuko had spent only a handful of days in Aizu her entire life but she grew up in a household that continually impressed this heritage upon her, physically distant though she was from it. She had, for one, a governess named Taka who came from an Aizu samurai family. From this "simple and

---

15. Sakata, "Chichibunomiya Setsuko," p. 102.
16. Tokyo PR Tsūshinsha, ed., *Matsudaira Tsuneo tsuisōroku*, p. 3.
17. Chichibunomiya, *Gin no bonboniēru*, pp. 87–88.

rough *obasan* type," Setsuko and her brothers grew up hearing stories of Aizu domain's plight, which Setsuko said helped her "understand the Aizu people's heart and mind." "My brother and I often heard about the Aizu spirit from Taka," she recalled of her governess of sixteen years.[18] Indeed, Setsuko credited this spirit and her Aizu governess for helping her make the greatest decision of her life. Back in 1927, when Count Kabayama was unable to convince the eighteen-year-old Setsuko to marry the prince, he turned to Taka to persuade her. The governess and the girl shared a tearful conversation on the matter. When the girl worried about the troubles that her marriage would impose upon her family, Taka assured her, "They all carry the Aizu spirit within." Setsuko then recounted what happened next in the most melodramatic terms:

> The moment I heard the word "Aizu" from Taka's mouth, I for some reason recalled the time I was scolded by my father for being afraid of the blade he was holding in that house in Aoyama that night. I then felt a mysterious strength welling up from my heart, and this grew into a conviction that I should accept the Empress's will. It is true; just then the two characters "Aizu" lit the way along the path that I should now follow, like a ray of light shining through dark clouds. I confirmed the conviction in my heart and asked Taka to pass the word. It was Taka who started crying; I for my part remained calm.[19]

Setsuko's ability and willingness to incorporate herself into the emotive space of Aizu—if only in retrospect—is a remarkable example of how powerful claims to an Aizu self were, even for a girl then living in America. This was not lost upon those around her. Two nights before the wedding, Setsuko spent her last evening with her family in their Tokyo home where a banquet was held. Taka's diary captured the deep, complex satisfaction that was finally theirs.

> Fine sake was brought in from Aizu. The former domainal retainers' joy could not be any greater. Even the eighty-year-old Ikegami Haru, who has been a lady-in-waiting since Lord Katamori's days, stood up to join the other Aizu people. They started dancing along to some pipe music, singing, 'Mount Bandai in Aizu is a treasure of a mountain. . . .' No one could stop the joy felt by the people who carry the sadness of fallen Aizu in their hearts. . . . This is one day that I can never forget for the rest of my life.[20]

When the people of Aizu saw their princess, they recognized that she had finally delivered, if unwittingly, what they had sought for so long. She was,

18. Ibid., pp. 60, 88–89. Taka's real name was Takahashi Mutsu, but because Mutsu happened to be a part of the Meiji emperor's personal name Mutsuhito, the Matsudaira family refrained from calling her Mutsu.

19. Ibid., pp. 122–23.

20. Ueno, *Chichibunomiya Setsuko hidenka to Takajo*, pp. 109–10.

after all, their princess, just as Japan had become their country and Aizu their homeland.

Setsuko personified just how far Aizu had come since the Restoration. A princess named after both Japan and Aizu was a far cry from another "princess" who, some sixty years earlier, felt compelled to abandon Aizu through her name. In 1871, Yamakawa Sakiko, the eleven-year-old sister of Yamakawa Hiroshi and Kenjirō, was chosen to accompany the Iwakura Mission to the United States. She and four other girls were to remain in the United States and become the first Japanese females to receive an American education.

Upon receiving this news, her mother En gave her daughter a curious new name: Sutematsu (捨松). This unusual name has been explained as her mother's decision to "let go" (捨てて) and "wait" (待つ=松) for her daughter to return from America.[21] This is perfectly plausible, but perhaps the girl's new name had another meaning. Could the name have expressed hope that the young girl would "let go" of "Aizu" (松=若松=会津) as she embarked on a most extraordinary journey? The mother might well have been imploring her daughter not to feel burdened by her Aizu baggage and to start her new life in America free of her past.

In 1871, when the wounds of war and defeat were still fresh, such a concern was more than warranted. Sutematsu had experienced the siege of Wakamatsu as an eight-year-old girl huddled in Tsuruga Castle.[22] It was as if "Princess Stematz"—as she was often called in America—had to first separate herself from her heavy Aizu past before she could look forward to a brighter future. After she attended Hillhouse High School in New Haven, Connecticut, graduated from Vassar College, and returned to Japan in 1882 as its first female college graduate, she sought to devote herself to public education for "the good of Japan."[23] But she would always do so as Sutematsu, as someone who had left Aizu behind. In 1883 she lost her last nominal link to the old domain—her proud family name, Yamakawa—when she married, as fate would have it, the army minister General Ōyama Iwao, a cousin of Saigō Takamori. As a young Satsuma artillery captain in 1868, Ōyama had led the bombardment of Tsuruga Castle where little Sutematsu kept refuge.

Sutematsu was compelled to let go of Aizu when she became a state-sponsored student in 1871 and, as her friend Tsuda Umeko later put it, "in part

---

21. Kuno, *Rokumeikan no kifujin Ōyama Sutematsu*, pp. 56–57.

22. She later narrated this childhood experience to an American journalist, John Dwight ("The Marchioness Oyama," reproduced in McIvor, *Unexpected Destinations*, pp. 28–32).

23. Yamakawa Sutematsu's letter to Alice Bacon, dated August 2, 1882.

government property."[24] An entire generation later, Setsuko, too, became a government property of sorts but, unlike Sutematsu, Setsuko was allowed to affirm her Aizu heritage in the process. Somewhere between "Princess Stematz" and Princess Setsuko, the people of Aizu managed to find a comfortable convergence between locality and nationhood. By the same token, it is this convergence that has made regionalism in Japan seem weak and benign to some observers. Reconciliation did not always come easily; two generations' worth of both personal agency and historical vicissitudes were needed to bring it about. Still, this process managed to produce a regionalism that has endured because it rarely offended nationalist sensibilities. Indeed, innocuous regionalism became a necessary accessory to the new imperial polity and could find currency in Meiji Japan precisely for that reason. "Region," then, became Japan writ small, a politically useful spatial category that helped stabilize a nascent nationhood, which was itself still a new and unproven spatial concept.

Such complacent regionalism in turn yielded a sense of local self that was packed in so tightly with being national as to make them seem one and the same. Aizu's sense of difference—articulated through decades of identity rhetoric and captured by the idea of a so-called Aizu spirit—emerged out of an ultimately synthetic project whereby those who had once been deemed different sought to, and largely did, overcome that difference. In doing so, they could discover a homeland that satisfied local claims to legitimacy while ultimately confirming the nation's supremacy. Thus an *Aizuppo* could be undeniably and unapologetically Japanese; in fact, there could hardly be an *Aizuppo* without a Japanese.

The search for a meaningful regional identity was a mostly modern phenomenon. In Tokugawa times, Aizu's administrative structure and political culture were solidly provincial and self-contained. There was no sustained identity discourse in Aizu domain because there was no pressing need for one. The domain, in and of itself, was a bona fide, if rather limited, object of one's spatial affiliation, and it hardly needed defense. In Meiji times, the administrative structure in Aizu—insofar as there was such a discrete place after the domain's demise—became a subset of a national apparatus and part of an ever-burgeoning empire. To complicate matters further, Aizu was deemed to have fallen afoul of the newly prevailing ethos of imperial loyalism.

---

24. Tsuda Umeko—another member of the 1871 cohort, a Bryn Mawr graduate, and the founder of Tsuda College in Tokyo—called Sutematsu's marriage "a queer arrangement." Unlike Sutematsu, Umeko never married and went on to accomplish what Sutematsu ultimately could not. Tsuda, *The Attic Letters*, p. 114.

It was precisely then that Aizu's identity discourse began in full earnest, as a dislocated people felt compelled to find their homeland in a national landscape and stake out their proper place in a new world that was not always kind to them.

By the time Princess Setsuko wedded in 1928, Yamakawa Hiroshi, the onetime domainal elder who had once served her grandfather, was long dead. But the history he had written to redeem his old compatriots was still around, and still is. Gone, too, was the crusty war veteran Machino Mondo. But the memorials he had built to soothe the dead were still around, and still are. This is to say nothing of countless others, mostly ordinary and anonymous, who, fitfully but collectively, pondered the meaning of being local in a nationalizing world. What they helped to leave behind was the idea of a decent homeland, one that assured for posterity that their past was noble and themselves worthy. That way, even when their country would fail them, they could still come home again.

Bibliography

Aizu chōreigikai 会津弔霊議会, ed. *Boshin junnan tsuitōroku*「戊辰殉難追悼録」. Aizu Wakamatsu: Aizu chōreigikai, 1979.

———, ed. *Boshin junnansha no saishi to sono funbo*「戊辰殉難者の祭祀とその墳墓」. Aizu Wakamatsu: Aizu chōreigikai, 1967.

Aizu shiryō hozonkai 会津資料保存会, ed. *Aizu shiryō sōsho*「会津資料叢書」. Tokyo: Rekishi toshokan, 1974.

Aizu shikon fūunroku kankōkai 会津士魂風雲録刊行会. *Aizu shikon fūunroku*「会津士魂風雲録」. Aizu Wakamatsu: Aizu shikon fūunroku kankōkai, 1961.

Aizu Wakamatsu-shi 会津若松市, ed. *Aizu Wakamatsushi shiryō mokuroku* 「会津若松史史料目録」. Aizu Wakamatsu: Aizu Wamakatsu-shi, 1996.

———, ed. *Aizuhan daihachi hanshu Matsudaira Katataka* "Masaosama gonenpu"「会津藩第八藩主松平容敬 忠恭様御年譜」. Aizu Wakamatsu: Aizu Wakamatsu-shi, 2001.

———, ed. *Bakumatsu Aizuhan ōfuku monjo*「幕末会津藩往復文書」. 2 vols. Aizu Wakamatsu: Aizu Wakamatsu-shi, 2000.

Aizu Wakamatsushi shuppan iinkai 会津若松史出版委員会, ed. *Aizu Wakamatsushi*「会津若松史」. 12 vols. Aizu Wakamatsu: Aizu Wakamatsu-shi, 1965.

Aizu Wakamatsu shiyakusho 会津若松市役所. *Boshin sen'eki kyūjūnensai* 「戊辰戦役９０祭」. Aizu Wakamatsu: Aizu Wakamatsu-shi, 1959.

"Aizudamashii"「会津魂」. *Aizukaikaihō* 9 (December 1916): 20–22.

"Aizuhan zokumei setsujoku to Ugawa sensei"「会津藩賊名雪辱ト宇川先生」. *Aizukai zasshi* 59 (December 1941): 26.

"Aizujin no tokushoku"「会津人の特色」. *Aizukaikaihō* 13 (December 1918): 6.

"Aizujin shōbu kishō no suichō"「会津人尚武気象の衰兆」. *Aizukaikaihō* 9 (December 1916): 13–14.

"Aizukaikaihō hakkan no shishu"「会津会報発刊の旨趣」. *Aizukaikaihō* 1 (November 1916): 2–3.

"Aizuppo"「会津っぽ」. *Asahi shinbun* 朝日新聞. Fukushima edition. January 5, 1976.

Akitsuki Mashiko 秋月まし子. "Byakkotai Aizuhan fujin no junnan ni tsuite"「白虎隊会津藩婦人の殉難に就いて」. Transcript of a radio program aired by Sendai chūōkyoku, 1936. Aizu Wakamatsu: Aizu Wakamatsu City Library.

Akizuki Kazue 秋月一江, ed. *Aizuhan gohattogaki kaidokusho* 「会津藩御法度書解読書」. Aizu Wakamatsu: Rekishi shunjū, 1995.

Akizuki Kazuhiro 秋月胤造. Untitled. *Aizukaikaihō* 2 (December 1917): 17.

Akizuki Kazuhisa 秋月胤永. *Akizuki teiken shibunshū* 「秋月偉軒詩文集」. Aizu Wakamatsu: Aizu Wakamatsu City Library, date unknown.

Anderson, Benedict. *Imagined Communities*. Rev. ed. London: Verso, 1991.

Anzai Kunio 安在邦夫 and Tasaki Kimitsukasa 田崎公司, eds. *Aizu shokaidō to Ōshū dōchū* 「会津諸街道と奥州道中」. Tokyo: Yoshikawa kōbunkan, 2002.

Aomori-ken 青森県, ed. *Aomori kenshi* 「青森県史」. 8 vols. Aomori-shi: Aomori-ken, 1926.

Arakawa Katsushige 荒川勝茂. *Meiji nisshi* 「明治日誌」, ed. Hoshi Ryōichi. Tokyo: Shinjinbutsu ōraisha, 1992.

Araki Takeyuki 荒木武行. "Aizujin no seishin ni kaere" 「会津人の精神に還れ」. *Aizukaikaihō* 32 (June 1928): 5.

Baden-Powell, Robert. *Boy Scouts beyond the Seas*. London: C. Arthur Pearson, 1913.

Ban Hyakuetsu 伴百悦. *Senshi no bosho soezu* 「戦死之墓所麁絵図」. Aizu Wakamatsu: Aizu Wakamatsu City Library, seventh month, 1869.

Bannai Sōzan 阪内素山. *Shinsei Byakkotaishi* 「真正白虎隊詩」. Fukagawa: Shinsei Byakkotaishi hozon fukyūkai, 1979.

Berry, Mary Elizabeth. *Japan in Print: Information and Nation in the Early Modern Period*. Berkeley: University of California Press, 2006.

Bhabha, Homi. "DissemiNation: Time, Narrative, and the Margins of the Modern Nation." In *Nation and Narration*, edited by Homi Bhabha, pp. 291–322. London, New York: Routledge, 1990.

Biwa no ie 琵琶の家, ed. *Kokin biwa kashū* 「古今琵琶歌集」. Tokyo: National Diet Library Digital Archives, 1906.

Bolitho, Harold. "Aizu, 1853–1868." *Proceedings of the British Association for Japanese Studies* 2, no. 1 (1977): 1–17.

———. "Travelers' Tales: Three Eighteenth-Century Travel Journals." *Harvard Journal of Asiatic Studies* 50, no. 2 (December 1990): 485–504.

———. *Treasures among Men*. New Haven: Yale University Press, 1974.

Boshin senshisha chōreigikai 戊辰戦死者吊霊義会. *Boshin senshisha chōreigikai shuisho* 「戊辰戦死者吊霊義会趣意書」. Aizu Wakamatsu: Aizu Wakamatsu City Library, 1913.

"Bōto keibuhosa nado o sasshō su" 「暴徒警部補佐等を殺傷す」. *Yubin hōchi shinbun* 郵便報知新聞. October 31, 1876.

Brown, Sidney D., and Hirota Akiko, trans. *The Diary of Kido Takayoshi*. Tokyo: University of Tokyo, 1983.

Buck, James H. "The Satsuma Rebellion of 1877: From Kagoshima through the Siege of Kumamoto Castle." *Monumenta Nipponica* 28, no. 4 (Winter 1973): 427–46.

"Byakkotai" 白虎隊. *Shin Tōhoku* 17 (1926): 30–31.

Byakkotai eiyū kagami 「白虎隊英勇鑑」. Aizu Wakamatsu: Aizu Wakamatsu City Library, date unknown.

Chichibunomiya kinenkai 秩父宮記念会, ed. *Yasuhito shinnō gojiseki shiryō* 「雍仁 親王御事績資料」. Tokyo: Chichibunomiya kinenkai, 1972.

Chichibunomiya Setsuko 秩父宮妃勢津子. *Gin no bonboniēru* 「銀のボンボニエール」. Tokyo: Kōdansha, 1994.

Colley, Linda. *Britons: Forging the Nation, 1707–1837*. New Haven, CT: Yale University Press, 1992.

Confino, Alon. *The Nation as a Local Metaphor*. Chapel Hill: University of North Carolina Press, 1997.

Craig, Albert. *Chōshū in the Meiji Restoration*. Cambridge, MA: Harvard University Press, 1967.

Craig, Teruko, trans. *Remembering Aizu*. Honolulu: University of Hawaii Press, 1999.

Dajōkan 太政官. *Dajōkan nisshi*「太政官日誌」, ed. by Ishii Ryōsuke. 12 vols. Tokyo: Tokyodō, 1980–85.

———, ed. *Dajōruiten*「太政類典」217. Tokyo: National Archives of Japan microfilm.

———, ed. *Fukkoki*「復古記」. 15 vols. Tokyo: Naigai shoseki, 1929–31.

———, ed. *Fukkogaiki*「復古外記」. 9 vols. Tokyo: Naigai shoseki, 1929–31.

Dajōkan shūshikan 太政官修史館. *Meiji shiyō*「明治史要」. Tokyo: Hakubunsha, 1876.

Endō Heita 遠藤平太. *Aizu Boshin sensō jūgunki*「会津戊辰戦争従軍記」. Aizu Wakamatsu: Endō Susumu, 1987.

Endō Kōson 遠藤香村. *Aizuhan Karafuto shutsujin emaki*「会津藩唐太出陣絵巻」. Aizu Wakamatsu City Library, 1808.

Fujimoto Senzan 藤本箭山. *Shōgaku kokushiryaku*「小学国史略」. Tokyo: Maruya Zenshichi, 1877.

Fujitani, Tak. *Splendid Monarchy*. Berkeley: University of California Press, 1996.

Fukushima-ken 福島県, ed. *Fukushima kenshi*「福島県史」. 5 vols. Fukushima: Fukushima-ken, 1964–72.

———. *Fukushima kenze shiryō*「福島縣是資料」. 2 vols. Tokyo: Kokusho kankōkai, 1981.

Fukushima-ken keisatsushi hensan iinkai 福島県警察史編さん委員会, ed. *Fukushima-ken keisatsushi*「福島県警察史」. 2 vols. Fukushima: Fukushima-ken keisatsu honbu, 1980–82.

Fukushima-ken kyōiku iinkai 福島県教育委員会. *Fukushima kyōikushi hensan shiryō*「福島県教育史編さん史料」. Fukushima: Fukushima-ken kyōiku iinkai, 1971.

Fukushima-ken kyōikukai 福島県教育会, ed. *Nisshinkan dōjikun*「日新館童子訓」. Fukushima: Fukushima-ken kyōikukai, 1944.

Fukushima-ken shiryō kankōkai 福島県史料刊行会. *Fukushima-ken shiryō*「福島県史料」. 5 vols. Fukushima: Fukushima-ken shiryō kankōkai, 1953.

Fukuzawa Yukichi 福澤諭吉. *An Encouragement of Learning*. Translated by David Dilworth and Umeyo Hirano. Tokyo: Sophia University, 1969.

Furukawa Koshōken 古川古松軒. *Tōyū zakki*「東遊雑記」. Tokyo: Heibonsha, 1964.

Gluck, Carol. *Japan's Modern Myths*. Princeton, NJ: Princeton University Press, 1985.

Gotō Katsuya 後藤勝弥. "Byakkotai no meibo"「白虎隊の名簿」. *Aizu shidankaishi* 41: 1–5.

Greenfeld, Liah. "Transcending a Nation's Worth." *Daedalus* 122, no. 3 (Summer 1993): 47–62.

Hall, Stuart. "The Question of Cultural Identity." In *Modernity and its Futures*, edited by Stuart Hall, David Held, and Tony McGrew, pp. 273–316. Cambridge: Polity Press, 1992.

Hara Yoshiki 原由己, ed. *Nihonshiyō*「日本史要」. Tokyo: Yoshikawa Hanshichi, 1887.

Harootunian, Harry. "The Economic Rehabilitation of the Samurai in the Early Meiji Period." *Journal of Asian Studies* 19, no. 4 (August 1960): 433–44.

Hasegawa Yoshitsugu 長谷川吉次, ed. *Aizu uta nōsho / Makunouchi nōgyōki*「会津歌農書・幕内農業記」, vol. 20. *Nihon nōsho zenshū*. 72 vols. Tokyo: Nōson gyoson bunka kyōkai, 1982.

Hashimoto Sei 橋本晴. "Fukushima kenjin to sono shisō" 「福島県人とその思想」 *Fukushima-ken kyoiku* 29, no. 2 (February 1917): 3–6.

Hashizume Akira 橋爪陽. "Aizudamashii no kan'yō" 「会津魂の涵養」. *Aizukaikaihō* 9 (December 1916): 25.

Hayakawa Kiyoji 早川喜代次. *Fūgetsutei kaisō* 「風月亭回想」. Aizu Wakamatsu: Byakkotai kinenkan, 1982.

Heise, Richard. *Uber Loyalitat in Japan*. Translated by Yūki Shirō 結城司郎, as *Doitsujin no mitaru Aizu Byakkotai*. N.p.: Elle Heise, 1941.

Hiraishi Benzō 平石弁蔵. *Aizu Boshin sensō* 「会津戊辰戦争」. Wakamatsu: Maruhachi shōten shuppanbu, 1917.

Hirosawa Yasutake 広澤安宅 and Sōda Sanpei 荘田三平, eds. *Bakumatsu Aizu shishiden kōhon* 「幕末会津志士傳稿本」. Hachinohe: Hirosawa Yasutake, 1923.

Hoshi Ryōichi 星亮一. *Tonami ni ikita Aizuhan no hitobito* 「斗南に生きた会津藩の人々」. Aizu Wakamatsu: Rekishi shunjū, 1983.

Howell, David. *Capitalism from Within*. Berkeley: University of California Press, 1995.

Iimori Masanichi 飯盛正日, ed. *Byakkotai seishin hiwa* 「白虎隊精神秘話」. Aizu Wakamatsu: Rekishi shunjū, 2003.

Iinuma Sekiya 飯沼關彌, ed. *Aizu Matsudaira kafu* 「会津松平家譜」. Tokyo: Iinuma Sekiya, 1938.

Irokawa Daikichi 色川大吉 et al., eds. *Meiji kenpakusho shūsei* 「明治建白書集成」. 9 vols. Tokyo: Chikuma shobō, 1990.

Ishii Maki 石井牧. "Shianbashi jiken no kaiko" 「思案橋事件の回顧」. *Aizukaikaihō* 10 (June 1917): 33–36.

Ishimura Sadaichi 石村貞一. *Naikoku shiryaku* 「内国史略」. 2 vols. Tokyo: Tō'in'ya, 1874.

Kamijō Katsutarō 上条勝太郎, ed. *Kabukiza* 「歌舞伎座」. Tokyo: Kabukiza, 1912–26.

Kangun funbo meisaichō 「官軍墳墓明細帳」. Aizu Wakamatsu: Aizu Wakamatsu City Library, 1879.

Kasai Tomio 葛西富夫. *Aizu Tonami hanshi* 「会津・斗南藩史」. Tokyo: Tōyō, 1992.

Katō Chōshirō 加藤長四郎. *Senshi junnan jinmeiroku* 「戦死殉難人名録」. Wakamatsu: Katō Mutsu, 1911.

Kawahara Katsuharu 河原勝治. "Omoide" 「思い出」. *Aizushidan* 16 (1912): 39–40.

Kawaji Toshiyoshi 川路利良. *Ryūsen ikō* 「龍泉遺稿」. Tokyo: Higashinari Kamjirō, 1881.

Kawanishi Hidemichi 河西英通. *Tōhoku: tsukurareta ikyō* 「東北 つくられた異境」. Tokyo: Chūō kōron shinsha, 2001.

———. *Tōhoku zoku* 「東北.続」. Tokyo: Chūō kōron shinsha, 2007.

———. "Tōhokushi no imi to shatei" 「東北史の意味と射程」. *Rekishigaku kenkyū* 742 (October 2000): 90–98.

"Kengensho sono ta" 「建言書其の他」 Document F288. Fukushima: Fukushima-ken bunka sentā rekishishiryōkan.

"Kenminsei o kangaeru zadankai" 「県民性を考える座談会」. *Asahi shinbun*. Fukushima edition. January 18, 1976.

Kimotsuki Kanetake 肝付兼武. *Tōhoku fūdan* 「東北風談」. *Aomori kenritsu toshokan sōsho*, vol. 3, edited by Satō Katsuo. 4 vols. Aomori: Aomori kenritsu toshokan, 1932.

Kinseki Yoshinori 金関義則. "Yamakawa Kenjirō no hataraki" 「山川健次郎の働き」. *Misuzu* 200 (November 1976): 21–22.

Kitahara Masanaga 北原雅長. *Shichinenshi*「七年史」. 4 vols. Tokyo: Tokyo Daigaku shuppankai, (1904) 1978.

Kitakata shishi hensan iinkai 喜多方市史編纂委員会, ed. *Kitakata shishi*「喜多方市史」. 10 vols. Kitakata: Kitakata-shi, 2000.

Kitakawa Shunji 北川舜治, ed. *Meiji shinshi*「明治新史」. Shiga: Seichidō, 1876.

Kobayashi Hiroshi 小林宏 and Shima Yoshitaka 島善高, eds. *Nihon rippō shiryō zenshū*「日本立法資料全集」, vol. 16. 922 vols. Tokyo: Shinzansha, 1996.

Kobayashi Kenzō 小林健三 and Terunuma Yoshibumi 照沼好文. *Shōkonsha seiritsushi no kenkyū*「招魂社成立史の研究」. Tokyo: Kinseisha, 1969.

Kobayashi Yūshichirō 小林雄七郎. "Aizuron"「会津論」. *Aizukaikaihō* 25 (December 1923): 66.

Kōbunroku「公文録」. 18 vols. Tokyo: National Archives of Japan, 1868–1885.

Kodanshaku Yakamawa sensei kinenkai 故男爵山川先生記念会, ed. *Danshaku Yamakawa sensei ikō*「男爵山川先生遺稿」. Tokyo: Kodanshaku Yamakawa sensei kinenkai, 1937.

"Kohankō no gokijō ni kansuru ryōnai minshū no seigansho"「故藩侯の御帰城に関する領内民衆の請願書」. *Aizushidankaishi* 21: 1–4.

Kōjida Yasunao 小路田泰直. "Nihonshi no tanjō: *Dai Nihon hennenshi* no hensan ni tsuite"「日本史の誕生「大日本編年史」の編纂について」. In *Seiki tenkaiki no kokusai chitsujo to kokumin bunka no keisei,* edited by Nishikawa Nagao and Watanabe Kōzō, pp. 127–46. Tokyo: Shin'yōsha, 1995.

Kōtei Boshin junnansha meibo「校訂戊辰殉難者名簿」. Tokyo: Iinuma Kanji, 1927.

Kubo Tenzui 久保天随. *Kokin bushidōdan*「古今武士道譚」. Tokyo: National Diet Library Digital Archives, 1905.

Kuno Akiko 久野明子. *Rokumeikan no kifujin Ōyama Sutematsu*「鹿鳴館の貴婦人大山捨松」. Tokyo: Chūō kōronsha, 1988.

Kurokouchi Ryō 黒河内良. "Aikyō"「愛郷」. *Aizukaikaihō* 9 (December 1916): 5–6.

———. "Aizujinshi ni tsugu"「会津人士に告ぐ」. *Aizukaikaihō* 1 (November 1916): 11–14.

Kyū Aizuhan Boshin senshisha meiseki「舊会津藩戊辰戦死者名籍」. Aizu Wakamatsu: Aizu Wakamatsu City Library, 1891.

Lewis, Michael. *Becoming Apart.* Cambridge, MA: Harvard University Asia Center, 2000.

Lloyd, Arthur. "The White Tigers." *Aizushidankaishi* 18 (December 1938): 20–34.

Machino Mondo 町野主水. "Meiji Boshin sen'eki junnan no rei hōshi no yurai"「戊辰戦役殉難之霊奉祀の由来」. In *Boshin junnan tsuitōroku,* edited by Aizu chōreigikai, pp. 22–24. Aizu Wakamatsu: Aizu chōreigikai, 1978.

Maeda Tsuneharu 前田恒治. "Aizuhan no sonnō seishin"「会津藩の尊皇精神」. *Ganban shidan* 2, no. 11 (September 1937): 10.

Makabe Jin 真壁仁 and Nozoe Kenji 野添憲治, eds. *Minshūshi toshite no Tōhoku*「民衆史としての東北」. Tokyo: Nihonhōsō shuppan kyōkai, 1976.

Makihara Norio 槙原憲夫. *Kyakubun to kokumin no aida*「客分と国民のあいだ」. Tokyo: Yoshikawa kōbunka, 1998.

———. *Meiji shichi nen no daironsō*「明治七年の大論争」. Tokyo: Nihon keizai hyōronsha, 1990.

Matsumoto Jun 松本順. *Ranchū jiden*「蘭疇自伝」. Tokyo: Heibonsha, 1980.

Matsuo Masahito 松尾正人. "Meiji shinseifu no chihōshihai" 「明治新政府の地方支配」. *Chiikishi kenkyū* 146 (1977): 12–24.

———. "Meiji shonen no gan'akukahei mondai to shinseiken" 「明治初年の贋悪貨幣問題と新政権」. *Chūō Daigaku Daigakuin kenkyū nenpō* 6 (1976): 189–206.

Mishima chōshi hensan iinkai 三島町史編纂委員会, ed. *Mishima chōshi* 「三島町史」. 2 vols. Mishima: Mishima chōshi shuppan iinkai, 1968.

Miyachi Masato 宮地正人. "Bakumatsu Meiji zenki ni okeru rekishi ninshiki no kōzō" 「幕末・明治前期における歴史認識の構造」. *Nihon kindai shisō taikei*, vol. 13, edited by Miyachi and Tanaka Akira, pp. 510–547. 24 vols. Tokyo: Iwanami, 1991.

Miyamoto Yuriko 宮本百合子. *Mazushiki hitobito no mure* 「貧しき人々の群」. Tokyo: Shinkō, 1916.

Miyanouchi Takao 宮内隆夫. "Wakamatsujō nyūsatsu ni tsuite" 「若松城入札に就いて」. *Gandai shidan* 3, no. 1 (November 1937): 3–4.

Miyasaki Tomihachi 宮崎十三八, ed. *Aizu Boshin sensō shiryōshū* 「会津戊辰戦争史料集」. Tokyo: Shinjinbutsu ōraisha, 1991.

———. *Aizu chimei jinmei sanpo* 「会津地名人名散歩」. Aizu Wakamatsu: Rekishi shunjū, 1989.

Monbushō 文部省. *Kōtōshōgaku dokuhon* 「高等小學読本」. 4 vols. Tokyo: Monbushō, 1903.

———. *Shōgakkōyō rekishi hensan shuisho* 「小学校用歴史編纂趣意書」. Tokyo: Monbushō, 1887.

———. *Shōgaku kokushi* 「小学国史」. 2 vols. Tokyo: Monbushō, 1941.

Moriya Hidesuke 森谷秀亮. *Yasukuni Jinja hyakunenshi* 「靖國神社百年史」. Tokyo: Yasukuni Jinja, 1987.

Morris-Suzuki, Tessa. *Reinventing Japan: Time, Space, Nation*. Armonk, NY: M. E. Sharpe, 1998.

Motoyasu Hiroshi 本康宏史. *Gunto no irei kūkan: kokumin tōgō to senshishatachi* 「軍都の慰霊空間 国民統合と戦死者たち」. Tokyo: Yoshikawa kōbunkan, 2002.

Murakami Shigeyoshi 村上重良. *Kokka Shintō* 「国家神道」. Tokyo: Iwanami, 1970.

Nakagawa Yoshikazu 中川克一, ed. *Kinsei eijin hyakuwa* 「近世偉人百話」. Tokyo: National Diet Library Digital Archives, 1909.

Nakai, Kate. *Shogunal Politics*. Cambridge, MA: Harvard University Press, 1988.

Nakamura Ken 中村謙. *Byakkotai jiseki* 「白虎隊事績」. Tokyo: Kawai Genzō, 1894.

Nakamura Masamichi 中村昌道, ed. *Seigun funboshi* 「西軍墳墓志」. Aizu Wakamatsu: Aizu Wakamatsu City Library, 1882.

Nakamura Toshi 中村とし. *Aizu no kindaika o kangaeru* 「会津の近代化を考える」. Aizu Wakamatsu: Aizu kindai rekishi kenkyūjo, 1993.

Nanma Tsunanori 南摩綱紀. *Wakamatsuki* 「若松記」. Aizu Wakamatsu: Aizu Wakamatsu City Library, 1879.

Narita Ryūichi 成田龍一. "Teito Tokyo" 「帝都東京」. In *Iwanami kōza Nihon tsūshi*, vol. 16, edited by Asao Naohiro et al., pp. 175–214. 21 vols. Tokyo: Iwanami, 1994.

NHK Hōsō seron chōsajo NHK放送世論調査所. *Nihonjin no kenminsei* 「日本人の県民性」. Tokyo: Nihon hōsō shuppan kyōkai, 1979.

Nihei Yoshitami 二瓶由民. *Aizu retsujo no kagami* 「会津烈女の鑑」. Tokyo: National Diet Library Digital Archives, 1891.

———. *Byakkotai yūshi retsuden* 「白虎隊勇士列傳」. Wakamatsu: Saitō Hachishirō, 1895.

Nihon shiseki kyōkai 日本史籍協会, ed. *Kido Takayoshi monjo* 「木戸孝允文書」. 8 vols. Tokyo: Nihon shiseki kyōkai, 1929–31.

———, ed. *Ōkubo Toshimichi monjo* 「大久保利通文書」. 10 vols. Tokyo: Nihon shiseki kyōkai, 1927–29.

———, ed. *Ōkubo Toshimichi nikki* 「大久保利通日記」. 2 vols. Tokyo: Nihon shiseki kyōkai, 1927.

———, ed. *Ōkuma Shigenobu kankei monjo* 「大隈重信関係文書」. 6 vols. Tokyo: Nihon shiseki kyōkai, 1970.

Nihon shoseki 日本書籍, ed. *Kokugo dokuhō kyōjuhō oyobi kyōjuan* 「國語読方教授法及教授案」. Tokyo: Nihon shoseki, 1904.

Niigata-ken 新潟県, ed. *Niigata kenshi* 「新潟県史」. 5 vols. Niigata: Niigata-ken, 1980–88.

Nishi Aizuchōshi hensan iinkai 西会津町史編さん委員会, ed. *Nishi Aizuchōshi* 「西会津町史」. 2 vols. Nishi Aizu-chō: Nishi Aizuchōshi kankō iinkai, 1997.

Nishikawa Nagao 西川長夫 and Matsumiya Hideharu 松宮秀治, eds. *Bakumatsu Meijiki no kokumin kokka keisei to bunka hen'yō* 「幕末・明治期の国民国家形成と文化変容」. Tokyo: Shin'yōsha, 1995.

——— and Watanabe Kōzō 渡辺公三, eds. *Seiki tenkanki no kokusai chitsujo to kokumin-bunka no keisei* 「世紀転換期の国際秩序と国民文化の形成」. Tokyo: Kashiwa, 1999.

Nora, Pierre. "Between Memory and History: *Les Lieux de Memoire.*" *Representations* 26 (1989): 7–24.

Nōrinshō nōmukyoku 農林省農務局. *Fukushima-ken Asaka kokuei kaitakujigyō ni kansuru chōsa gaiyō* 「福島県安積国営開拓事業ニ関スル調査概要」. Tokyo: Nōrinshō nōmukyoku, 1927.

Obinata Sumio 大日方純夫. "Seinan sensō ni okeru 'junsa' no rinji bibo" 「西南戦争における「巡査」の臨時徴募」. *Nihon rekishi* 362 (July 1978): 50–66.

Oda Kanshi 織田完之. *Wakamatsu-ken hōshokuchū junsatsu nikki* 「若松県奉職中巡察日記」. Aizu Wakamatsu: Aizu Wakamatsu City Library, 1869.

Ōe Shinobu 大江志乃夫. "Ōkubo Toshimichi seikenka no shokusankōgyō seisaku seiritsu no seiji katei" 「大久保政権下の殖産興業政策成立の政治過程」. In *Keiseiki no Meiji kokka bakumatsu ishin ronshū*, edited by Tamura Sadao, pp. 213–62. Tokyo: Yoshikawa kōbunkan, 2001.

Ogasawara Katsunaga 小笠原勝修, et al., eds. *Zoku kokushiryaku zenhen* 「續國史畧前編」. 5 vols. Tokyo: Hakuetsudō, 1873.

———, ed. *Zoku kokushiryaku kōhen* 「續國史略後編」. 5 vols. Tokyo: Hakuetsudō, 1875.

Ogawa Chiyomatsu 小川千代松. "Aizu fujin ni tsuite" 「会津婦人に就て」. *Aizukaikaihō* 9 (December 1916): 23–24.

———. *Shigure zōshi* 「志ぐれ草紙」. Tokyo: Iinuma, 1935.

Okabe Seiichi 岡部精一. *Boshin sen'eki ni tsuite* 「戊辰戦役に就いて」. Tokyo: Historiographical Institute, University of Tokyo, 1917.

Okamoto Kansuke 岡本監輔, ed. *Kokushikiyō* 「國史紀要」. Tokyo: Hōkokudō, 1887.

Okamoto Kidō 岡本綺堂. *Kidō gikyokushū* 「綺堂戯曲集」. Tokyo: Shun'yōdō, 1925.

Okatani Shigetomi 岡谷繁実. "Aizu rakujōgo shochi ni kansuru jijitsu fujūrokuwa" 「会津落城後処置に関する事実附十六話」. *Shidankai sokkiroku*. vol. 19, pp. 85–102. 390 vols. Tokyo: Shidankai, 1884.

Ōkubo Toshiaki 大久保利謙. *Nihon kindai shigaku no seiritsu* 「日本近代史学の成立」. Tokyo: Yoshikawa kōbun, 1988.

Ōkurashō 大蔵省, ed. *Meiji zenki zaiseikeizai shiryōshūsei* 「明治前期財政経済史料集成」. 10 vols. Tokyo: Meiji bunken shiryō kankōkai, 1962.

O'Leary, Elizabeth. *To Die For: The Paradox of American Patriotism*. Princeton, NJ: Princeton University Press, 1999.

Ōtsuka Makoto 大塚実. "Kanshū funbo to Meiji seifu" 「官修墳墓と明治政府」. *Rekishi shunjū* 38 (January 1993): 30–38.

Ravina, Mark. *Land and Lordship in Early Modern Japan*. Stanford, CA: Stanford University Press, 1998.

Renan, Ernest. "Qu'est-ce qu'une nation?" In *Nation and Narration,* edited by Homi Bhabha, pp. 8–22. London and New York: Routledge, 1990.

Rinsetsuō 森雪翁. *Aizu kōshiden* 「会津孝子伝」. Aizu Wakamatsu: Aizu Wakamatsu City Library, 1742.

Roberts, Luke. "Cultivating Non-National Historical Understandings in Local History." In *Teleology of the Modern Nation-State: Japan and China,* edited by Joshua Fogel, pp. 161–73. Philadelphia: University of Pennsylvania Press, 2005.

———. *Mercantilism in a Japanese Domain*. Cambridge: Cambridge University Press, 1998.

———. *Performing the Great Peace: Political Space and Open Secrets in Tokugawa Japan*. Honolulu: University of Hawaii Press, 2012.

Saga Shōsaku 嵯峨正作, ed. *Nihonshikō* 「日本史綱」. Tokyo: Kobayashi Shinbei, 1888.

Saigō Tanomo 西郷頼母. *Aizu hanrō Saigō Tanomo jijoden* Seiunki 「会津藩老西郷頼母自叙伝「栖雲記」」, edited by Hotta Setsuo. Tokyo: Tokyo shoseki, 1993.

Saitō Mitsuo 斉藤光男. "Aizudamashii" 「会津魂」. *Aizu shidan* 64 (1990): 141.

Sakai Jun 酒井淳. "Kinsei nōmin no tabi" 「近世農民の旅」. *Rekishi shunjū* 17 (Spring 1983): 141–43.

Sakata Ikuko 佐方郁子. "Chichibunomiya Setsuko" 「秩父宮勢津子」. *Rekishi dokuhon* 33, no. 5 (1988): 102–102.

Sakuragi Jingo 桜木甚吾 et al. *Aizu chōreigikai dokuhon* 「会津弔霊義会読本」. Aizu Wakamatsu: Aizu chōreigikai, 1993.

Sakurai Tokutarō 桜井徳太郎. *Reikonkan no keifu* 「霊魂観の系譜」. Tokyo: Kōdansha, 1989.

Sasazawa Royō 笹沢魯羊. *Shimokita hantōshi* 「下北半嶋史」. Ōhata: Shimokita kyōdokai, 1952.

Sase Yojiemon 佐瀬与次右衛門. *Aizu nōsho / Aizu nōsho furoku* 「会津農書・会津農書付録」. In *Nihon nōsho zenshū,* vol. 19, edited by Shōji Kichinosuke. 72 vols. Tokyo: Nōson gyoson bunka kyōkai, 1982.

Sasuhara Yasuzō 指原安三. *Meiji seishi* 「明治政史」. Tokyo: Toyamabō, 1892.

Satō Kimihiko 佐藤公彦. "Meiji shonen no seifu chokkakuryō no keisei Aizu chihō no baai" 「明治初年の政府直轄領の形成 会津地方の場合」. *Fukushima shigaku kenkyū* 27–28 (1979): 107–19.

Satō Nitten 佐藤日天. "Aizu kishitsu o ushinau nakare" 「会津気質を失ふ勿れ」. *Aizukaikaihō* (December 1915): 13.

Sawa Zen'yū 澤全雄. "Gisei no seishin" 「犠牲の精神」. *Aizukaikaihō* (December 1919): 2.

Sekiba Tadatake 関場忠武. "Byakkotai jūrokushi den" 「白虎隊十六士傳」. *Yashidai ishin shiryō sōsho*, vol. 31, pp. 316–318. 34 vols. Tokyo: Tokyo Daigaku shuppankai, 1973.

Shiba Gosaburō 柴五三郎. "Senshisha sōin maisō no koto" 「戦死者総員埋葬之事」. Aizu Wakamatsu: Aizu Wakamatsu City Library, date unknown.

Shibusawa Eiichi 渋沢栄一. *Tokugawa Yoshinobukō den*「徳川慶喜公伝」. 8 vols. Tokyo: Ryūmonsha, 1918.

Shiotani Shichijūrō 塩谷七重郎. "Aizu hanshi no Seinan sensō sansen"「会津藩士の西南戦争参戦」. *Aizukaikaihō* 104 (1998): 91–93.

———. "Aizujin to Seinan sensō"「会津人と西南戦争」. *Aizushidan* 70 (1996): 139–41.

Shōji Kichinosuke 庄治吉之助, ed. *Aizu fudoki/fūzokuchō*「会津風土記・風俗帳」. Tokyo: Yoshikawa kōbunkan, 1979.

———. *Kindai chihō minshū undōshi*「近代地方民衆運動史」. Tokyo: Azakura, 1978.

Shōnen ongakukai 少年音楽會, ed. *Shintei gakkō gunka*「新訂學校軍歌」. Tokyo: National Diet Library Digital Archives, 1910.

Sōda Sanpei 荘田三平. "Boshin no eki Aizu junsetsu fujin no jiseki"「戊辰の役会津殉節婦人の事績」. *Aizushikaihō* 11 (June 1917): 8–9.

Sōda Shūson 荘田秋村. "Aizu damashii"「会津魂」. *Aizukaikaihō* 35 (December 1929): 35.

———. "Aizushi hensen no gi" 「会津史編撰の議」. *Aizukaikaihō* 6 (July 1915): 12.

———. "Meiyo no kaifuku o kisu"「名誉の回復を期す」. *Aizukaikaihō* 15 (December 1919): 3–4.

Sugimoto Hajime 杉本一. Untitled. *Aizukaikaihō* 17 (December 1920): 18.

Sugiura nisshi「杉浦日誌」. In *Aizu Takada chōshi,* edited by Aizu Takada chōshi hensan iinkai. Vol. 4. 7 vols. Aizu Takada: Aizu Takada-chō, 1995–2002.

Sugiura Yuzuru zenshū kankōkai 杉浦譲全集刊行会, ed. *Sugiura Yuzuru zenshū* 「杉浦譲全集」. 5 vols. Tokyo: Sugiura Yuzuru zenshū kankōkai, 1979.

Suzuki Zenzō 鈴木善三. "Aizu kifū no han'yō"「会津気風の繁養」. *Aizukaikaihō* 24 (June 1924): 6–8.

———. "Byakkotai no eiga to kokuminsei"「白虎隊の映画と国民性」. *Aizukai zasshi* 31 (December 1927): 17.

Tadami chōshi hensan iinkai 只見町史編さん委員会, ed. *Tadami chōshi shiryōshū*「只見町史資料集」. Tadami: Tadami-chō, 2002.

Tajima chōshi hensan iinkai 田島町史編纂委員会, ed. *Tajima chōshi*「田島町史」. 10 vols. Tajima: Tajima-chō, 1985–92.

Takagi Eiichirō 高木英一郎. *Shōnen kagayaku Byakkotai*「少年輝く白虎隊」. Tokyo: Daidōkan shoten, 1931.

Takahashi Tansui 高橋淡水. *Sōzetsu hizetsu Byakkotai*「壮絶悲絶白虎隊」. Tokyo: Isobe kōyōdō, 1909.

Takahashi Tetsuo 高橋哲夫. *Asaka kaitakushi*「安積開拓史」. Tokyo: Rironsha, 1963.

Takamine Keichū 高嶺慶忠, ed. *Aizu kagami*「会津鑑」. 5 vols. Tokyo: Yoshikawa kōbun, 1981–82.

Tasaki Kimitsukasa 田崎公司. "Aizu senso to chiiki hensei" 「会津戦争と地域編 成」. In *Meiji ishin no chiiki to minshū,* edited by Meiji ishin gakkai, pp. 3–26. Tokyo: Yoshikawa kōbunkan, 1996.

———. "Meiji shonen no chokkatsuchishihai saikō"「明治初年の直轄地支配再考」. *Osaka Shōgyō Daigaku ronshū* 126 (July 2003): 106–119.

Tatsuno Jirō 辰野次郎. *Aizu Byakkotai jūyūkyūshi jitsuden*「会津白虎隊十有九士實傳」. Aizu Wakamatsu: Tatsuno Jirō, 1907.

"TBS ga Aizu ni shazai: rekishi kuizu bangumi mondai de" TBS が会津に謝罪歴史クイズ番組問題で」. www.asahi.com (March 31, 2008).

Toby, Ronald. *State and Diplomacy in Early Modern Japan*. Princeton, NJ: Princeton University Press, 1984.

Tokutomi Sohō 徳富蘇峰. *Ishinshi ni okeru Aizu*「維新史に於ける会津」. Aizu Wakamatsu: Aizu Sohō kai, 1937.

———. *Kinsei Nihon kokuminshi*「近世日本国民史」. 100 vols. Tokyo: Kinsei Nihon kokuminshi kankōkai, 1962.

Tokyo PR tsūshinsha 東京PR通信社, ed. *Matsudaira Tsuneo tsuisōroku*「松平恒雄追想録」. Tokyo: Ko Matsudaira Tsuneoshi tsuiokukai, 1961.

Totman, Conrad. *Politics in the Tokugawa Bakufu, 1600–1843*. Cambridge, MA: Harvard University Press, 1967.

———, trans. and ed. *Tokugawa Japan*. Tokyo: University of Tokyo Press, 1990.

Toyoda Takeshi 豊田武, ed. *Aizu han kasei jikki*「会津藩家世実記」. 15 vols. Tokyo: Yoshikawa kōbunkan, 1975–89.

Tsubaki Jichū 椿時中. *Shōgaku kokushi kiji honmatsu*「小学國史紀事本末」. Tokyo: Maeda En, 1883.

Tsuda Umeko 津田梅子. *The Attic Letters: Ume Tsuda's Correspondence to Her American Mother,* edited by Yoshiko Furuki. New York: Weatherhill, 1991.

Tsukamoto Manabu 塚本学. "Chiikishikenkyū no kadai"「地域史研究の課題」. *Iwanami kōza Nihon rekishi,* vol. 25, edited by Asao Naohiro et al., pp. 333–68. 26 vols. Tokyo: Iwanami, 1976.

———. *Tokai to ianaka*「都会と田舎」. Tokyo: Heibonsha, 1991.

Tsūzoku kyōiku fukyūkai 通俗教育普及会. *Chichibunomiyadenka to Setsukohime* 「秩父宮殿下と節子姫」. Tokyo: Tsūzoku kyōiku fukyūkai, 1928.

Tsūzoku kyōiku kenkyūkai 通俗教育研究會, ed. *Tsūzoku kyōiku kōen shiryō* 「通俗教育講演資料」. Tokyo: Meiseikan, 1911.

Uda Tomoi 宇田友猪 and Wada Saburō 和田三郎, eds. *Jiyūtōshi*「自由党史」. Tokyo: Gosharō, 1910.

Ueda Kazutoshi 上田万年, ed. *Nihon rekishi gadan*「日本歴史畫譚」. Tokyo: National Diet Library Digital Archives, 1910.

Uehira Yasuhiro 上平泰博, Tanaka Haruhiko, and Nakajima Jun. *Shōnendan no rekishi*「少年団の歴史」. Tokyo: Hōbunsha, 1996.

Ueno Chizuko 上野千鶴子. *Nashonarizumu to jendā* 「ナショナリズムとジェンダー」. Tokyo: Seidosha, 1998.

Ueno Jirō 上野寿郎. *Chichibunomiya Setsuko hidenka to Takajo*「秩父宮勢津子妃殿下とたか女」. Kōriyama: Ueno Jirō, 1987.

Ugawa Hisae 宇川久衛. "*Shōgaku kokushi* ni tsukite"「小學國史ニ就キテ」. *Aizukai zasshi* 58 (June 1941): 10–14.

Vincent, E. R., trans. *I Miei Ricordi*. Oxford: Oxford University Press, 1966.

Vlastos, Stephen, ed. *Mirror of Modernity*. Berkeley: University of California Press, 1998.

———. *Peasant Protests and Uprisings in Tokugawa Japan*. Berkeley: University of California Press, 1986,

Wakamatsu shiyakusho 若松市役所. *Wakamatsushishi*「若松市史」. 2 vols. Wakamatsu: Wakamatsu shiyakusho, 1941–42.

Wakamatsu Tarō 若松太郎. "Aizujinshi"「会津人士」. *Ajia* (August 24, 1891): 2–3.

Watanabe Tadashi 渡辺正. "Aete Aizu no senpai ni uttau"「敢えて会津の先輩に訴ふ」. *Aizukaikaihō* 24 (June 1924): 9.

———. "Aizu kishitsu no yōsei"「会津気質の養成」. *Aizukaikaihō* 12 (June 1918): 9–10.

Weber, Eugen. *Peasants into Frenchmen: The Modernization of Rural France, 1870–1914*. Stanford, CA: Stanford University Press, 1976.

Wigen, Kären. "Constructing Shinano: The Invention of a Neo-Traditional Region." In *Mirror of Modernity*, edited by Stephen Vlastos, pp. 229–42. Berkeley: University of California Press, 1998.

———. *The Making of a Japanese Periphery, 1750–1920*. Berkeley: University of California Press, 1995.

———. *A Malleable Map*. Berkeley: University of California Press, 2010.

Willis, William. "Report to Sir Harry S. Parkes." January 23, 1869. Document FO 881/1673. Public Record Office, London.

Woodard, William. *The Allied Occupation of Japan 1945–1952 and Japanese Religions*. Leiden: Brill, 1972.

Yabe Yōzō 矢部洋三. *Asaka kaikon seisakushi*「安積開墾政策史」. Tokyo: Nihonkeizai hyōronsha, 1997.

Yahiro Fuji 八尋不二. *Yahiro Fuji shinarioshū*「八尋不二シナリオ集」. Tokyo: Eiga jidaisha, 1961.

Yamaguchi Kōhei 山口孝平. *Kinsei Aizushi no kenkyū*「近世会津史の研究」. 2 vols. Aizu Wakamatsu: Rekishi shunjū, 1978.

Yamakawa Hiroshi 山川浩. *Kyotoshugoshoku shimatsu*「京都守護職始末」. 2 vols. Tokyo: Heibonsha, 1930.

———. *Sakurayamashū*「桜山集」. Tochigi: Hasegawa Chōshichi, 1902.

——— et al. *Senshisha meiseki*「戦死者名籍」. Aizu Wakamatsu: Aizu Wakamatsu City Library, 1891.

Yamakawa Kenjirō 山川健次郎, ed. *Aizu Boshin senshi*「会津戊辰戦史」. Wakamatsu: Aizu Boshin senshi hensankai, 1938.

———. "Aizu rōjō yodan"「会津籠城余談」. In *Mandai Meiji shonen*, edited by Dōkōshidankai, pp. 275–76. Tokyo: Shin jinbutsu ōraisha, 1970.

———. "Gokeiji wa kamiwaza"「御慶事は神業」. *Aizukai zasshi* 33 (December 1928): 1.

Yamanouchi, Tamenosuke. *The White Tiger Band*. Tokyo: Taiseidō, 1937.

Yanada monjo goyō nikki「梁田文書御用日記」. Aizu Wakamatsu: Aizu Wakamatsu City Library, 1583.

Yanada monjo kōyōsekibo 簗田文書「公用籍簿」. Aizu Wakamatsu: Aizu Wakamatsu City Library, 1738, 1856.

Yashiro Kuniji 八代国治 et al., eds. *Kokushi daijiten*「國史大辞典」. Tokyo: Yoshikawa kōbunkan, 1908.

Yonemoto, Marcia. *Mapping Early Modern Japan*. Berkeley: University of California Press, 2003.

Yoshimizu Nishiki-ō 吉水錦翁. *Seishin kyōiku teikoku biwa renmashū*「精神教育帝国琵琶練磨集」. Tokyo: National Diet Library Digital Archives, 1904.

Yoshimura Gorō 吉村五郎. *Bykkotaishi jijinsha ni kansuru chōsa keika*「白虎隊士自刃者ニ関スル調査経過」. Wakamatsu: Yoshimura Gorō, 1936.

———. "Byakkotai jijinsha ni tsuki"「白虎隊自刃者につき」. *Kyōdo ganban shidan* 6 (1936): 235–36.

Yui Masaomi 由井正臣 et al., eds. *Nihon kindai shisō taikei*「日本近代思想大系」. 24 vols. Tokyo: Iwanami, 1989.

Index

Harvard East Asian Monographs
(titles now in print)

7. Chao Kuo-chün, *Economic Planning and Organization in Mainland China: A Documentary Study, 1949–1957*
13. S. M. Meng, *The Tsungli Yamen: Its Organization and Functions*
31. Madeleine Chi, *China Diplomacy, 1914–1918*
36. Peter Frost, *The Bakumatsu Currency Crisis*
38. Robert R. Campbell, *James Duncan Campbell: A Memoir by His Son*
39. Jerome Alan Cohen, ed., *The Dynamics of China's Foreign Relations*
40. V. V. Vishnyakova-Akimova, *Two Years in Revolutionary China, 1925–1927*, trans. Steven L. Levine
41. Meron Medzini, *French Policy in Japan during the Closing Years of the Tokugawa Regime*
46. W. P. J. Hall, *A Bibliographical Guide to Japanese Research on the Chinese Economy, 1958–1970*
47. Jack J. Gerson, *Horatio Nelson Lay and Sino-British Relations, 1854–1864*
48. Paul Richard Bohr, *Famine and the Missionary: Timothy Richard as Relief Administrator and Advocate of National Reform*
50. Britten Dean, *China and Great Britain: The Diplomacy of Commercial Relations, 1860–1864*
51. Ellsworth C. Carlson, *The Foochow Missionaries, 1847–1880*
53. Richard M. Pfeffer, *Understanding Business Contracts in China, 1949–1963*
55. Ranbir Vohra, *Lao She and the Chinese Revolution*
60. Noriko Kamachi, John K. Fairbank, and Chūzō Ichiko, *Japanese Studies of Modern China Since 1953: A Bibliographical Guide to Historical and Social-Science Research on the Nineteenth and Twentieth Centuries, Supplementary Volume for 1953–1969*
61. Donald A. Gibbs and Yun-chen Li, *A Bibliography of Studies and Translations of Modern Chinese Literature, 1918–1942*
62. Robert H. Silin, *Leadership and Values: The Organization of Large-Scale Taiwanese Enterprises*
63. David Pong, *A Critical Guide to the Kwangtung Provincial Archives Deposited at the Public Record Office of London*

69. Eric Widmer, *The Russian Ecclesiastical Mission in Peking during the Eighteenth Century*
73. Jon Sigurdson, *Rural Industrialism in China*
74. Kang Chao, *The Development of Cotton Textile Production in China*
75. Valentin Rabe, *The Home Base of American China Missions, 1880–1920*
78. Meishi Tsai, *Contemporary Chinese Novels and Short Stories, 1949–1974: An Annotated Bibliography*
80. Endymion Wilkinson, *Landlord and Labor in Late Imperial China: Case Studies from Shandong by Jing Su and Luo Lun*
84. J. W. Dower, *Empire and Aftermath: Yoshida Shigeru and the Japanese Experience, 1878–1954*
85. Martin Collcutt, *Five Mountains: The Rinzai Zen Monastic Institution in Medieval Japan*
86. Kwang Suk Kim and Michael Roemer, *Growth and Structural Transformation*
89. Sung Hwan Ban, Pal Yong Moon, and Dwight H. Perkins, *Rural Development*
92. Edward S. Mason, Dwight H. Perkins, Kwang Suk Kim, David C. Cole, Mahn Je Kim et al., *The Economic and Social Modernization of the Republic of Korea*
93. Robert Repetto, Tai Hwan Kwon, Son-Ung Kim, Dae Young Kim, John E. Sloboda, and Peter J. Donaldson, *Economic Development, Population Policy, and Demographic Transition in the Republic of Korea*
94. Parks M. Coble, Jr., *The Shanghai Capitalists and the Nationalist Government, 1927–1937*
96. Richard Wich, *Sino-Soviet Crisis Politics: A Study of Political Change and Communication*
97. Lillian M. Li, *China's Silk Trade: Traditional Industry in the Modern World, 1842–1937*
98. R. David Arkush, *Fei Xiaotong and Sociology in Revolutionary China*
100. James Reeve Pusey, *China and Charles Darwin*
101. Hoyt Cleveland Tillman, *Utilitarian Confucianism: Chen Liang's Challenge to Chu Hsi*
102. Thomas A. Stanley, *Ōsugi Sakae, Anarchist in Taishō Japan: The Creativity of the Ego*
103. Jonathan K. Ocko, *Bureaucratic Reform in Provincial China: Ting Jih-ch'ang in Restoration Kiangsu, 1867–1870*
104. James Reed, *The Missionary Mind and American East Asia Policy, 1911–1915*
105. Neil L. Waters, *Japan's Local Pragmatists: The Transition from Bakumatsu to Meiji in the Kawasaki Region*
106. David C. Cole and Yung Chul Park, *Financial Development in Korea, 1945–1978*
107. Roy Bahl, Chuk Kyo Kim, and Chong Kee Park, *Public Finances during the Korean Modernization Process*
108. William D. Wray, *Mitsubishi and the N.Y.K, 1870–1914: Business Strategy in the Japanese Shipping Industry*
109. Ralph William Huenemann, *The Dragon and the Iron Horse: The Economics of Railroads in China, 1876–1937*
111. Jane Kate Leonard, *Wei Yüan and China's Rediscovery of the Maritime World*

117. Andrew Gordon, *The Evolution of Labor Relations in Japan: Heavy Industry, 1853–1955*
119. Christine Guth Kanda, *Shinzō: Hachiman Imagery and Its Development*
121. Chang-tai Hung, *Going to the People: Chinese Intellectual and Folk Literature, 1918–1937*
123. Richard von Glahn, *The Country of Streams and Grottoes: Expansion, Settlement, and the Civilizing of the Sichuan Frontier in Song Times*
124. Steven D. Carter, *The Road to Komatsubara: A Classical Reading of the Renga Hyakuin*
126. Bob Tadashi Wakabayashi, *Anti-Foreignism and Western Learning in Early-Modern Japan: The "New Theses" of 1825*
127. Atsuko Hirai, *Individualism and Socialism: The Life and Thought of Kawai Eijirō (1891–1944)*
129. R. Kent Guy, *The Emperor's Four Treasuries: Scholars and the State in the Late Chien-lung Era*
130. Peter C. Perdue, *Exhausting the Earth: State and Peasant in Hunan, 1500–1850*
131. Susan Chan Egan, *A Latterday Confucian: Reminiscences of William Hung (1893–1980)*
132. James T. C. Liu, *China Turning Inward: Intellectual-Political Changes in the Early Twelfth Century*
134. Kate Wildman Nakai, *Shogunal Politics: Arai Hakuseki and the Premises of Tokugawa Rule*
137. Susan Downing Videen, *Tales of Heichū*
138. Heinz Morioka and Miyoko Sasaki, *Rakugo: The Popular Narrative Art of Japan*
139. Joshua A. Fogel, *Nakae Ushikichi in China: The Mourning of Spirit*
140. Alexander Barton Woodside, *Vietnam and the Chinese Model: A Comparative Study of Vietnamese and Chinese Government in the First Half of the Nineteenth Century*
141. George Elison, *Deus Destroyed: The Image of Christianity in Early Modern Japan*
144. Marie Anchordoguy, *Computers, Inc.: Japan's Challenge to IBM*
146. Mary Elizabeth Berry, *Hideyoshi*
147. Laura E. Hein, *Fueling Growth: The Energy Revolution and Economic Policy in Postwar Japan*
148. Wen-hsin Yeh, *The Alienated Academy: Culture and Politics in Republican China, 1919–1937*
149. Dru C. Gladney, *Muslim Chinese: Ethnic Nationalism in the People's Republic*
150. Merle Goldman and Paul A. Cohen, eds., *Ideas Across Cultures: Essays on Chinese Thought in Honor of Benjamin L Schwartz*
151. James M. Polachek, *The Inner Opium War*
152. Gail Lee Bernstein, *Japanese Marxist: A Portrait of Kawakami Hajime, 1879–1946*
154. Mark Mason, *American Multinationals and Japan: The Political Economy of Japanese Capital Controls, 1899–1980*
155. Richard J. Smith, John K. Fairbank, and Katherine F. Bruner, *Robert Hart and China's Early Modernization: His Journals, 1863–1866*
157. William Wayne Farris, *Heavenly Warriors: The Evolution of Japan's Military, 500–1300*

159. James B. Palais, *Politics and Policy in Traditional Korea*
161. Roger R. Thompson, *China's Local Councils in the Age of Constitutional Reform, 1898–1911*
162. William Johnston, *The Modern Epidemic: History of Tuberculosis in Japan*
163. Constantine Nomikos Vaporis, *Breaking Barriers: Travel and the State in Early Modern Japan*
164. Irmela Hijiya-Kirschnereit, *Rituals of Self-Revelation: Shishōsetsu as Literary Genre and Socio-Cultural Phenomenon*
165. James C. Baxter, *The Meiji Unification through the Lens of Ishikawa Prefecture*
166. Thomas R. H. Havens, *Architects of Affluence: The Tsutsumi Family and the Seibu-Saison Enterprises in Twentieth-Century Japan*
167. Anthony Hood Chambers, *The Secret Window: Ideal Worlds in Tanizaki's Fiction*
168. Steven J. Ericson, *The Sound of the Whistle: Railroads and the State in Meiji Japan*
169. Andrew Edmund Goble, *Kenmu: Go-Daigo's Revolution*
170. Denise Potrzeba Lett, *In Pursuit of Status: The Making of South Korea's "New" Urban Middle Class*
171. Mimi Hall Yiengpruksawan, *Hiraizumi: Buddhist Art and Regional Politics in Twelfth-Century Japan*
173. Aviad E. Raz, *Riding the Black Ship: Japan and Tokyo Disneyland*
174. Deborah J. Milly, *Poverty, Equality, and Growth: The Politics of Economic Need in Postwar Japan*
175. See Heng Teow, *Japan's Cultural Policy toward China, 1918–1931: A Comparative Perspective*
176. Michael A. Fuller, *An Introduction to Literary Chinese*
177. Frederick R. Dickinson, *War and National Reinvention: Japan in the Great War, 1914–1919*
178. John Solt, *Shredding the Tapestry of Meaning: The Poetry and Poetics of Kitasono Katue (1902–1978)*
179. Edward Pratt, *Japan's Protoindustrial Elite: The Economic Foundations of the Gōnō*
180. Atsuko Sakaki, *Recontextualizing Texts: Narrative Performance in Modern Japanese Fiction*
181. Soon-Won Park, *Colonial Industrialization and Labor in Korea: The Onoda Cement Factory*
182. JaHyun Kim Haboush and Martina Deuchler, *Culture and the State in Late Chosŏn Korea*
183. John W. Chaffee, *Branches of Heaven: A History of the Imperial Clan of Sung China*
184. Gi-Wook Shin and Michael Robinson, eds., *Colonial Modernity in Korea*
185. Nam-lin Hur, *Prayer and Play in Late Tokugawa Japan: Asakusa Sensōji and Edo Society*
186. Kristin Stapleton, *Civilizing Chengdu: Chinese Urban Reform, 1895–1937*
187. Hyung Il Pai, *Constructing "Korean" Origins: A Critical Review of Archaeology, Historiography, and Racial Myth in Korean State-Formation Theories*
188. Brian D. Ruppert, *Jewel in the Ashes: Buddha Relics and Power in Early Medieval Japan*
189. Susan Daruvala, *Zhou Zuoren and an Alternative Chinese Response to Modernity*

191. Kerry Smith, *A Time of Crisis: Japan, the Great Depression, and Rural Revitalization*
192. Michael Lewis, *Becoming Apart: National Power and Local Politics in Toyama, 1868–1945*
193. William C. Kirby, Man-houng Lin, James Chin Shih, and David A. Pietz, eds., *State and Economy in Republican China: A Handbook for Scholars*
194. Timothy S. George, *Minamata: Pollution and the Struggle for Democracy in Postwar Japan*
195. Billy K. L. So, *Prosperity, Region, and Institutions in Maritime China: The South Fukien Pattern, 946–1368*
196. Yoshihisa Tak Matsusaka, *The Making of Japanese Manchuria, 1904–1932*
197. Maram Epstein, *Competing Discourses: Orthodoxy, Authenticity, and Engendered Meanings in Late Imperial Chinese Fiction*
199. Haruo Iguchi, *Unfinished Business: Ayukawa Yoshisuke and U.S.-Japan Relations, 1937–1952*
200. Scott Pearce, Audrey Spiro, and Patricia Ebrey, *Culture and Power in the Reconstitution of the Chinese Realm, 200–600*
201. Terry Kawashima, *Writing Margins: The Textual Construction of Gender in Heian and Kamakura Japan*
202. Martin W. Huang, *Desire and Fictional Narrative in Late Imperial China*
203. Robert S. Ross and Jiang Changbin, eds., *Re-examining the Cold War: U.S.-China Diplomacy, 1954–1973*
204. Guanhua Wang, *In Search of Justice: The 1905–1906 Chinese Anti-American Boycott*
205. David Schaberg, *A Patterned Past: Form and Thought in Early Chinese Historiography*
206. Christine Yano, *Tears of Longing: Nostalgia and the Nation in Japanese Popular Song*
207. Milena Doleželová-Velingerová and Oldřich Král, with Graham Sanders, eds., *The Appropriation of Cultural Capital: China's May Fourth Project*
208. Robert N. Huey, *The Making of 'Shinkokinshū'*
209. Lee Butler, *Emperor and Aristocracy in Japan, 1467–1680: Resilience and Renewal*
210. Suzanne Ogden, *Inklings of Democracy in China*
211. Kenneth J. Ruoff, *The People's Emperor: Democracy and the Japanese Monarchy, 1945–1995*
212. Haun Saussy, *Great Walls of Discourse and Other Adventures in Cultural China*
213. Aviad E. Raz, *Emotions at Work: Normative Control, Organizations, and Culture in Japan and America*
214. Rebecca E. Karl and Peter Zarrow, eds., *Rethinking the 1898 Reform Period: Political and Cultural Change in Late Qing China*
215. Kevin O'Rourke, *The Book of Korean Shijo*
216. Ezra F. Vogel, ed., *The Golden Age of the U.S.-China-Japan Triangle, 1972–1989*
217. Thomas A. Wilson, ed., *On Sacred Grounds: Culture, Society, Politics, and the Formation of the Cult of Confucius*
218. Donald S. Sutton, *Steps of Perfection: Exorcistic Performers and Chinese Religion in Twentieth-Century Taiwan*

219. Daqing Yang, *Technology of Empire: Telecommunications and Japanese Expansionism in Asia, 1883–1945*
220. Qianshen Bai, *Fu Shan's World: The Transformation of Chinese Calligraphy in the Seventeenth Century*
221. Paul Jakov Smith and Richard von Glahn, eds., *The Song-Yuan-Ming Transition in Chinese History*
222. Rania Huntington, *Alien Kind: Foxes and Late Imperial Chinese Narrative*
223. Jordan Sand, *House and Home in Modern Japan: Architecture, Domestic Space, and Bourgeois Culture, 1880–1930*
224. Karl Gerth, *China Made: Consumer Culture and the Creation of the Nation*
225. Xiaoshan Yang, *Metamorphosis of the Private Sphere: Gardens and Objects in Tang-Song Poetry*
226. Barbara Mittler, *A Newspaper for China? Power, Identity, and Change in Shanghai's News Media, 1872–1912*
227. Joyce A. Madancy, *The Troublesome Legacy of Commissioner Lin: The Opium Trade and Opium Suppression in Fujian Province, 1820s to 1920s*
228. John Makeham, *Transmitters and Creators: Chinese Commentators and Commentaries on the Analects*
229. Elisabeth Köll, *From Cotton Mill to Business Empire: The Emergence of Regional Enterprises in Modern China*
230. Emma Teng, *Taiwan's Imagined Geography: Chinese Colonial Travel Writing and Pictures, 1683–1895*
231. Wilt Idema and Beata Grant, *The Red Brush: Writing Women of Imperial China*
232. Eric C. Rath, *The Ethos of Noh: Actors and Their Art*
233. Elizabeth Remick, *Building Local States: China during the Republican and Post-Mao Eras*
234. Lynn Struve, ed., *The Qing Formation in World-Historical Time*
235. D. Max Moerman, *Localizing Paradise: Kumano Pilgrimage and the Religious Landscape of Premodern Japan*
236. Antonia Finnane, *Speaking of Yangzhou: A Chinese City, 1550–1850*
237. Brian Platt, *Burning and Building: Schooling and State Formation in Japan, 1750–1890*
238. Gail Bernstein, Andrew Gordon, and Kate Wildman Nakai, eds., *Public Spheres, Private Lives in Modern Japan, 1600–1950: Essays in Honor of Albert Craig*
239. Wu Hung and Katherine R. Tsiang, *Body and Face in Chinese Visual Culture*
240. Stephen Dodd, *Writing Home: Representations of the Native Place in Modern Japanese Literature*
241. David Anthony Bello, *Opium and the Limits of Empire: Drug Prohibition in the Chinese Interior, 1729–1850*
242. Hosea Hirata, *Discourses of Seduction: History, Evil, Desire, and Modern Japanese Literature*
243. Kyung Moon Hwang, *Beyond Birth: Social Status in the Emergence of Modern Korea*
244. Brian R. Dott, *Identity Reflections: Pilgrimages to Mount Tai in Late Imperial China*
245. Mark McNally, *Proving the Way: Conflict and Practice in the History of Japanese Nativism*

246. Yongping Wu, *A Political Explanation of Economic Growth: State Survival, Bureaucratic Politics, and Private Enterprises in the Making of Taiwan's Economy, 1950–1985*
247. Kyu Hyun Kim, *The Age of Visions and Arguments: Parliamentarianism and the National Public Sphere in Early Meiji Japan*
248. Zvi Ben-Dor Benite, *The Dao of Muhammad: A Cultural History of Muslims in Late Imperial China*
249. David Der-wei Wang and Shang Wei, eds., *Dynastic Crisis and Cultural Innovation: From the Late Ming to the Late Qing and Beyond*
250. Wilt L. Idema, Wai-yee Li, and Ellen Widmer, eds., *Trauma and Transcendence in Early Qing Literature*
251. Barbara Molony and Kathleen Uno, eds., *Gendering Modern Japanese History*
252. Hiroshi Aoyagi, *Islands of Eight Million Smiles: Idol Performance and Symbolic Production in Contemporary Japan*
253. Wai-yee Li, *The Readability of the Past in Early Chinese Historiography*
254. William C. Kirby, Robert S. Ross, and Gong Li, eds., *Normalization of U.S.-China Relations: An International History*
255. Ellen Gardner Nakamura, *Practical Pursuits: Takano Chōei, Takahashi Keisaku, and Western Medicine in Nineteenth-Century Japan*
256. Jonathan W. Best, *A History of the Early Korean Kingdom of Paekche, together with an annotated translation of* The Paekche Annals *of the* Samguk sagi
257. Liang Pan, *The United Nations in Japan's Foreign and Security Policymaking, 1945–1992: National Security, Party Politics, and International Status*
258. Richard Belsky, *Localities at the Center: Native Place, Space, and Power in Late Imperial Beijing*
259. Zwia Lipkin, *"Useless to the State": "Social Problems" and Social Engineering in Nationalist Nanjing, 1927–1937*
260. William O. Gardner, *Advertising Tower: Japanese Modernism and Modernity in the 1920s*
261. Stephen Owen, *The Making of Early Chinese Classical Poetry*
262. Martin J. Powers, *Pattern and Person: Ornament, Society, and Self in Classical China*
263. Anna M. Shields, *Crafting a Collection: The Cultural Contexts and Poetic Practice of the* Huajian ji 花間集 *(Collection from among the Flowers)*
264. Stephen Owen, *The Late Tang: Chinese Poetry of the Mid-Ninth Century (827–860)*
265. Sara L. Friedman, *Intimate Politics: Marriage, the Market, and State Power in Southeastern China*
266. Patricia Buckley Ebrey and Maggie Bickford, *Emperor Huizong and Late Northern Song China: The Politics of Culture and the Culture of Politics*
267. Sophie Volpp, *Worldly Stage: Theatricality in Seventeenth-Century China*
268. Ellen Widmer, *The Beauty and the Book: Women and Fiction in Nineteenth-Century China*
269. Steven B. Miles, *The Sea of Learning: Mobility and Identity in Nineteenth-Century Guangzhou*
270. Man-houng Lin, *China Upside Down: Currency, Society, and Ideologies, 1808–1856*

271. Ronald Egan, *The Problem of Beauty: Aesthetic Thought and Pursuits in Northern Song Dynasty China*
272. Mark Halperin, *Out of the Cloister: Literati Perspectives on Buddhism in Sung China, 960–1279*
273. Helen Dunstan, *State or Merchant? Political Economy and Political Process in 1740s China*
274. Sabina Knight, *The Heart of Time: Moral Agency in Twentieth-Century Chinese Fiction*
275. Timothy J. Van Compernolle, *The Uses of Memory: The Critique of Modernity in the Fiction of Higuchi Ichiyō*
276. Paul Rouzer, *A New Practical Primer of Literary Chinese*
277. Jonathan Zwicker, *Practices of the Sentimental Imagination: Melodrama, the Novel, and the Social Imaginary in Nineteenth-Century Japan*
278. Franziska Seraphim, *War Memory and Social Politics in Japan, 1945–2005*
280. Cynthia J. Brokaw, *Commerce in Culture: The Sibao Book Trade in the Qing and Republican Periods*
281. Eugene Y. Park, *Between Dreams and Reality: The Military Examination in Late Chosŏn Korea, 1600–1894*
282. Nam-lin Hur, *Death and Social Order in Tokugawa Japan: Buddhism, Anti-Christianity, and the* Danka *System*
283. Patricia M. Thornton, *Disciplining the State: Virtue, Violence, and State-Making in Modern China*
284. Vincent Goossaert, *The Taoists of Peking, 1800–1949: A Social History of Urban Clerics*
286. Charo B. D'Etcheverry, *Love after* The Tale of Genji*: Rewriting the World of the Shining Prince*
287. Michael G. Chang, *A Court on Horseback:Imperial Touring & the Construction of Qing Rule, 1680–1785*
288. Carol Richmond Tsang, *War and Faith:* Ikkō Ikki *in Late Muromachi Japan*
289. Hilde De Weerdt, *Competition over Content: Negotiating Standards for the Civil Service Examinations in Imperial China (1127–1279)*
290. Eve Zimmerman, *Out of the Alleyway: Nakagami Kenji and the Poetics of Outcaste Fiction*
291. Robert Culp, *Articulating Citizenship: Civic Education and Student Politics in Southeastern China, 1912–1940*
292. Richard J. Smethurst, *From Foot Soldier to Finance Minister: Takahashi Korekiyo, Japan's Keynes*
293. John E. Herman, *Amid the Clouds and Mist: China's Colonization of Guizhou, 1200–1700*
294. Tomoko Shiroyama, *China during the Great Depression: Market, State, and the World Economy, 1929–1937*
295. Kirk W. Larsen, *Tradition, Treaties and Trade: Qing Imperialism and Chosŏn Korea, 1850–1910*
296. Gregory Golley, *When Our Eyes No Longer See: Realism, Science, and Ecology in Japanese Literary Modernism*

297. Barbara Ambros, *Emplacing a Pilgrimage: The Ōyama Cult and Regional Religion in Early Modern Japan*
298. Rebecca Suter, *The Japanization of Modernity: Murakami Haruki between Japan and the United States*
299. Yuma Totani, *The Tokyo War Crimes Trial: The Pursuit of Justice in the Wake of World War II*
301. David M. Robinson, ed., *Culture, Courtiers, and Competition: The Ming Court (1368–1644)*
302. Calvin Chen, *Some Assembly Required: Work, Community, and Politics in China's Rural Enterprises*
303. Sem Vermeersch, *The Power of the Buddhas: The Politics of Buddhism During the Koryŏ Dynasty* (918–1392)
304. Tina Lu, *Accidental Incest, Filial Cannibalism, and Other Peculiar Encounters in Late Imperial Chinese Literature*
305. Chang Woei Ong, *Men of Letters Within the Passes: Guanzhong Literati in Chinese History, 907–1911*
306. Wendy Swartz, *Reading Tao Yuanming: Shifting Paradigms of Historical Reception (427–1900)*
307. Peter K. Bol, *Neo-Confucianism in History*
308. Carlos Rojas, *The Naked Gaze: Reflections on Chinese Modernity*
309. Kelly H. Chong, *Deliverance and Submission: Evangelical Women and the Negotiation of Patriarchy in South Korea*
310. Rachel DiNitto, *Uchida Hyakken: A Critique of Modernity and Militarism in Prewar Japan*
311. Jeffrey Snyder-Reinke, *Dry Spells: State Rainmaking and Local Governance in Late Imperial China*
312. Jay Dautcher, *Down a Narrow Road: Identity and Masculinity in a Uyghur Community in Xinjiang China*
313. Xun Liu, *Daoist Modern: Innovation, Lay Practice, and the Community of Inner Alchemy in Republican Shanghai*
314. Jacob Eyferth, *Eating Rice from Bamboo Roots: The Social History of a Community of Handicraft Papermakers in Rural Sichuan, 1920–2000*
315. David Johnson, *Spectacle and Sacrifice: The Ritual Foundations of Village Life in North China*
316. James Robson, *Power of Place: The Religious Landscape of the Southern Sacred Peak (Nanyue* 南嶽*) in Medieval China*
317. Lori Watt, *When Empire Comes Home: Repatriation and Reintegration in Postwar Japan*
318. James Dorsey, *Critical Aesthetics: Kobayashi Hideo, Modernity, and Wartime Japan*
319. Christopher Bolton, *Sublime Voices: The Fictional Science and Scientific Fiction of Abe Kōbō*
320. Si-yen Fei, *Negotiating Urban Space: Urbanization and Late Ming Nanjing*
321. Christopher Gerteis, *Gender Struggles: Wage-Earning Women and Male-Dominated Unions in Postwar Japan*
322. Rebecca Nedostup, *Superstitious Regimes: Religion and the Politics of Chinese Modernity*

323. Lucien Bianco, *Wretched Rebels: Rural Disturbances on the Eve of the Chinese Revolution*
324. Cathryn H. Clayton, *Sovereignty at the Edge: Macau and the Question of Chineseness*
325. Micah S. Muscolino, *Fishing Wars and Environmental Change in Late Imperial and Modern China*
326. Robert I. Hellyer, *Defining Engagement: Japan and Global Contexts, 1750–1868*
327. Robert Ashmore, *The Transport of Reading: Text and Understanding in the World of Tao Qian (365–427)*
328. Mark A. Jones, *Children as Treasures: Childhood and the Middle Class in Early Twentieth Century Japan*
329. Miryam Sas, *Experimental Arts in Postwar Japan: Moments of Encounter, Engagement, and Imagined Return*
330. H. Mack Horton, *Traversing the Frontier: The* Man'yōshū *Account of a Japanese Mission to Silla in 736–737*
331. Dennis J. Frost, *Seeing Stars: Sports Celebrity, Identity, and Body Culture in Modern Japan*
332. Marnie S. Anderson, *A Place in Public: Women's Rights in Meiji Japan*
333. Peter Mauch, *Sailor Diplomat: Nomura Kichisaburō and the Japanese-American War*
334. Ethan Isaac Segal, *Coins, Trade, and the State: Economic Growth in Early Medieval Japan*
335. David B. Lurie, *Realms of Literacy: Early Japan and the History of Writing*
336. Lillian Lan-ying Tseng, *Picturing Heaven in Early China*
337. Jun Uchida, *Brokers of Empire: Japanese Settler Colonialism in Korea, 1876–1945*
338. Patricia L. Maclachlan, *The People's Post Office: The History and Politics of the Japanese Postal System, 1871–2010*
339. Michael Schiltz, *The Money Doctors from Japan: Finance, Imperialism, and the Building of the Yen Bloc, 1895–1937*
340. Daqing Yang, Jie Liu, Hiroshi Mitani, and Andrew Gordon, eds., *Toward a History beyond Borders: Contentious Issues in Sino-Japanese Relations*
341. Sonia Ryang, *Reading North Korea: An Ethnological Inquiry*
342. Susan Huang, *Picturing the True Form: Daoist Visual Culture in Traditional China*
343. Barbara Mittler, *A Continuous Revolution: Making Sense of Cultural Revolution Culture*
344. Hwansoo Ilmee Kim, *Empire of the Dharma: Korean and Japanese Buddhism, 1877–1912*
345. Satoru Saito, *Detective Fiction and the Rise of the Japanese Novel, 1880–1930*
346. Jung-Sun N. Han, *An Imperial Path to Modernity: Yoshino Sakuzō and a New Liberal Order in East Asia, 1905–1937*
347. Atsuko Hirai, *Government by Mourning: Death and Political Integration in Japan, 1603–1912*
348. Darryl E. Flaherty, *Public Law, Private Practice: Politics, Profit, and the Legal Profession in Nineteenth-Century Japan*
349. Jeffrey Paul Bayliss, *On the Margins of Empire: Buraku and Korean Identity in Prewar and Wartime Japan*
350. Barry Eichengreen, Dwight H. Perkins, and Kwanho Shin, *From Miracle to Maturity: The Growth of the Korean Economy*

Harvard East Asian Monographs

351. Michel Mohr, *Buddhism, Unitarianism, and the Meiji Competition for Universality*
352. J. Keith Vincent, *Two-Timing Modernity: Homosocial Narrative in Modern Japanese Fiction*
353. Suzanne G. O'Brien, *Customizing Daily Life: Representing and Reforming Customs in Nineteenth-Century Japan*
354. Chong-Bum An and Barry Bosworth, *Income Inequality in Korea: An Analysis of Trends, Causes, and Answers*
355. Jamie L. Newhard, *Knowing the Amorous Man: A History of Scholarship on* Tales of Ise
356. Sho Konishi, *Anarchist Modernity: Cooperatism and Japanese-Russian Intellectual Relations in Modern Japan*
357. Christopher P. Hanscom, *The Real Modern: Literary Modernism and the Crisis of Representation in Colonial Korea*
358. Michael Wert, *Meiji Restoration Losers: Memory and Tokugawa Supporters in Modern Japan*
359. Garret P. S. Olberding, ed., *Facing the Monarch: Modes of Advice in the Early Chinese Court*
360. Xiaojue Wang, *Modernity with a Cold War Face: Reimagining the Nation in Chinese Literature Across the 1949 Divide*
361. David Spafford, *A Sense of Place: The Political Landscape in Late Medieval Japan*
362. Jongryn Mo and Barry Weingast, *Korean Political and Economic Development: Crisis, Security, and Economic Rebalancing*
363. Melek Ortabasi, *The Undiscovered Country: Text, Translation, and Modernity in the Work of Yanagita Kunio*
364. Hiraku Shimoda, *Lost and Found: Recovering Regional Identity in Imperial Japan*
365. Trent E. Maxey, *The "Greatest Problem": Religion and State Formation in Meiji Japan*
366. Gina Cogan, *The Princess Nun: Bunchi, Buddhist Reform, and Gender in Early Edo Japan*
367. Eric C. Han, *Rise of a Japanese Chinatown: Yokohama, 1894–1972*